Jesus in Kashmir

The Lost Tomb

सत्यमेव जयते

Suzanne Olsson

Jesus in Kashmir   The Lost Tomb

Credits

All pictures, maps, and photographs, unless otherwise noted, are from the author's private collection. The rest are widely available in the public domain. Attempts to locate many artists have been unsuccessful. Images are ineligible for copyright and deemed in the public domain when they consist entirely of information that is common property and contains no original authorship. The copyright protected appears here with permission, and are duly acknowledged. If you believe you are the copyright owner of anything that appears in this book, please submit the information in order that you can be properly credited in the next edition.

Who is buried in the tomb, a crucified prophet, or a crucified king?

'*Light of the World*' by William Holman Hunt (1827-1910) Tate Museum

Sue Olsson Murree Pakistan 2001-2002

'Do to me what is worthy of thee, not what is worthy of me.'

Jalahuddin

Acknowledgments

'Surely he who makes his companions laugh is worthy of Paradise." Qu'ran

~~~

Fida Hassnain, hero, guru.

Mary, sister, hopeless loveable critic since age 7

Michele Doucette, editor, cheerleader

Karen Lyster, Mary Leue, Abu, thanks for years of laughter and encouragement

Arif Khan and Tomb of Jesus website, dedicated seekers of truth

Church of the East, Canada

The Directors of Roza Bal tomb

And an assortment of personal heroes that include tuck-tuck drivers, sherpas, shepherds, chowkidars, Northern Alliance, ISI ,Taliban, Sunnis, Shias, Ahmaddiyas, Sikhs, Buddhists, Hindus, and a few Jawans…and thanks to all those who told the blond when to duck and when to run…..

A moment within each mind, each heart.. Where stillness, peace, and knowing start... A blend of universe and you... No boundaries, no limits of body or view... That is God.

FOREWORD

I have lived in ten countries in as many years during times when acts of war, violence, and cultural terrorism prevailed. The losses of both life and cultural heritage have always been alarming. Like human losses, truth also becomes a victim. I did not start this journey with the intent of writing a book, but this has become personal, intimate, and expressive for me, part political, part religious, and full of curiosity for the way things have been and could be.

Like golden apples strewn on the path, temptations lure one in many directions. I have tried to keep the focus on the presence of Jews in India beginning with claims that Adam was buried there. Some say that Jesus went to India to preach to "the Lost Tribes.' Why were they 'lost' in India? If they were there in such great numbers, they must have had an impact, a presence felt in India, and indeed they did! India's roots are as Jewish as Israel's. Jewish influence on culture and history of India is, at least in part, the entire history of India from its trade and mining to its rajas and emperors and kings, and even to its religions. This Jewish influence is found in the Mahabharata, the Puranas and the Bhagavad-Gita. No portion of Indian history and culture is without a strong Jewish presence as rabbis, rishis, Christians, Brahmins and Buddhists vie for supremacy of the Indian heart and mind. The unique people of India today are the culmination of this great diversity of ideas and influences.

We will follow the trail of Biblical figures and Jewish traditions that are well known in India from the days of Adam to the days of Jesus. We will examine why Jesus went to India at least twice in his lifetime, first when he was a youth, and again for years after the crucifixion. Yes, he did survive the crucifixion, and the proof has been strewn about for all to see. I have gathered together many references to the life of Jesus *after* the crucifixion from those who saw him and knew him best.

No, you wont find 'Jesus" in India because rarely was he known as 'Jesus' in India. You will find him as Parshva (Sanskrit for Yeshua-Joshua) or as Issa, as Iosha or Eosha (Greek) on coins from Taxila, and as Pravarasena at the Fourth Buddhist Council. This is a title inherited through his family's Egyptian ancestors, Ra Sena and Shepherd King Pharaohs. Did Jesus go to India to study Hinduism or Buddhism? The answers will surprise you, as they certainly surprised me.

You will find the importance of the Rod of Moses in the life of Jesus, how it had something to do with the magi arriving for his birth, and its importance with the events surrounding his crucifixion. You will discover Jesus as the King of Kashmir, and realize that the titulus on the cross was not a mockery, but a statement of fact. His second death was to simply lie down peacefully in a meadow and let his soul slip away with the rishis when he was over 100 years old. It was not a dramatic death, but it was a dignified and proper death that included some elements of the mysteries that surrounding his birth. It was a noble death in the tradition of Abraham, Solomon, and Moses.

You will journey with me to his tomb in India and understand the long, complex, and turbulent history surrounding it. What Jesus accomplished in 100 years, what the world has never seen and never given him credit for until now will amaze you. He was an extraordinary survivor from a long line of extraordinary men and women. Like others, I have had many unique experiences on the Old Silk Road. I never walked alone. Every experience was shared with another sentient being. However this is the story of the Jews in India, this is *not* my story, it is theirs, and so I have left the "I" out of this book for the most part. This book is a fact-finder, a historical roadmap of clues to examine later when you continue the journey of discovery, and I know that many of you will.

The best kept secret has been the realization that the great Indian epics and philosophers, their great gods, saints and heroes have been ours too. Sarah is Sarasvati and Brahma is Abraham, and Yudhisthira is David.

This book is *primarily* about cultural and archaeological terrorism, and those who hide behind their religion to perpetrate crimes against society. Destruction of the Bamiyan Buddha was the 9-11 with respect to cultural history, but it was neither the beginning nor the end for this kind of annihilation. For those of us who were very near to such devastation, deep and troubling questions are beginning to arise. How much more will we lose? How can we prevent people from hiding behind their religion in order to perpetrate cultural crimes? The scale of the heritage we are losing is far bigger than most realize. The time to stand up and say "NO" is now.

As this book goes to reprint in April 2007, it has been suggested that the Department of Tourism in India and Kashmir may begin managing Hari Parbat Fort and possibly the tomb of Jesus as a means of helping to promote tourism in Kashmir.

I see this as a major step toward the preservation of the history of Jesus in Kashmir. India deserves to be commended for standing up and taking action to save this rich world heritage.

However, the tomb relics and DNA still remain unavailable to scholars and researchers. It is anticipated that this situation will improve soon. It is my belief that all relics associated with the Roza Bal tomb must be recovered and placed in a proper museum setting to safeguard them for future generations. Although progress is slow, these monumental steps forward have already begun.

Edward Burke once said "Evil wins when good men do nothing". I can no longer stand quietly by. This book represents my effort to do something.

Suzanne Olsson   New York, March 2007

Special Note: On referencing and Bibliography: I have taken an unconventional approach to acknowledging source material. The Bibliography is numbered and I refer you to these numbers. I lived with just one suitcase for many years and often spent weeks at a time without access to cell phones or computers. I did not start this journey with the intention of writing a book. If I made notes and references at all while in libraries and universities abroad, it was to discuss with others, not to use as source material for a book. What books I acquired were quickly forwarded on to scholars in Kashmir who otherwise had no way to obtain them. Further, the direction and purpose of a book did not take shape until the very last moment. This has compromised my ability to quote exact page numbers and sources that are no longer available to me. My apologies to you, dear reader, who would desire better from your author. I hope this does not impede you as we share the knowledge I have gathered.

Chapter 1

Genesis to Jesus- Biblical Patriarchs- The Great Debate, Who was Adam?-
E=MC2- The Universe and You- A Matter of Life and Death- God is the Mind
of the Universe-The Races-Sarasvati and the Sumerians- Kosher in the
Garden of Eden- Nagas of Kashmir- Genetic Errors? Or Genetic Markers?-
Six Pointed Stars- Were Hebrews Hindus?- Indians in the New World

Chapter 2

Mount Meru- Shangri La on the Old Silk Road- Shangri La as the Garden of
Eden- History of the Old Silk Road- Ascensions and Miracles, Is Religion
Science or Science Fiction?

Chapter 3

Enoch to Noah- Noah in India- The Flood- Kurgan Graves and the Grave of
Noah

Chapter 4

Abraham and Sarah- Sarah as Sarasvati in India- Abraham's Many Names in
India- Understanding Hinduism-Vedas- Puranas- Mahabharata and Rama-
yana- Yudhisthira and Pandera- Krishna- Shiva and Shiva Lingams- Islam-
Graves of Abraham and Sarah- Cave of Machpelah

Chapter 5

Moses and Aaron- Birth of Moses- Genealogies and Legitimacy- Establishment of the High Priesthood- Thy Rod and Staff Shall Comfort Me- Sacred Almond Groves- First and Second Temples- Resurrections Revisited- Dome of the Rock- A Prophet Like Moses- Messiahs- Rebirths- Reincarnations- The Grave of Aaron- The Grave of Moses

Chapter 6

Solomon- How to say Rose in Sanskrit- Magadha and Magdalene- Jesus in Sanskrit- Arctic Home of the Vedas? Identifying Kings- Following the Trail of Jesus on the Old Silk Road- Guru Nanak and the Sikhs, The Indian Crusaders- Tahkt-i-Suleiman- Martand- The Sword in the Sun Temple- Winter Solstice, Let There Be Light- Throne of Solomon and Ark of the Covenant- Disappearing Evidence- Ethiopian Connections

Chapter 7

Buddha- The Jewish Family of Buddha-Jew in the Lotus- South-East Asian Hebrews- China- Buddhists Were not Brahmins-Buddha, Socrates, and Jesus- Royal Cities, Ivy League Colleges- Taxila University, Jesus Goes to School- The Graduates- Struggles of Buddhism in India- The Three Baskets-Caves

Chapter 8

Surviving Crucifixion

Surviving Crucifixion- The Clues- Survival- Pontius Pilate- Conspiracy Theories- Mention of Jesus' Survival in Other Sources- Josephus-The Bible-Temple Pillars- Ignatius-Bhavishya Mahapurana- Irenaeus- Clement of Alexander-Gospel of Phillip- Eusebius of Caesarea- Askew Codex- Panarion-Rajatarangini- Book of the Bee-Re-Evaluating Salvation

Chapter 9

Thomas in India

Thomas in India- History of Pakistan- Taxila- The Carpenters- The Church in India-Death of Thomas- Thomasian Christians- The Q Gospels

Chapter 10

Kings of Kashmir

Kings of Kashmir- Rajatarangini- Secrets of the Ark-,Tektons, Tertons, Sacred Geometry- Kings; Sandimatti,Megavahana, Pravarasena,The Mayas, Marys, and Queens- Unraveling the Story- Ethiopians, Magdhas- Hiranya- Toraman-The Grandchild, Pravarasena 2

Chapter 11

Mother Mary- History of Murree- Magi- Virgin Births- Death of Mary- Going Home- The Journey

Chapter 12

Tomb of Jesus- Jews in Kashmir- Aaron Revisited- Fourth Buddhist Council- Influence of Jesus in India and China- The Survivor- Rod of Moses-Waqfs- World Symposium on Cultural Terrorism in Asia-Visiting the Grave Today- Desposynoi, DNA of God-Descendants of Jesus Today-Final Death of Jesus- Journey Home-

Brief Table of Contents

You Are Here

(Where Are They?)

Are we alone? What did Jesus think
about this?

1. Adam

Go to the beginning to get to the end, learn what is real to find the pretend. (Pinocchio)

From Genesis to Jesus

Jesus is a study into the mind and its reasons for religion, any religion, to explain the unexplainable, the strange encounters men experienced centuries ago. This is as good a beginning as any into the Bible.

From Genesis to Jesus in India is another matter. It is a long and complicated journey of a different kind. Where should we begin? Should we begin with Genesis and Jehovah, or Gilgamesh and the Anunnaki? Is this going to be a search for God, or for alien encounters? Mythology or theology? Is this about the creationists verses the evolutionists? Is there a genetic marker in our genes or on our DNA that points to genetic engineering? Is this a search for a special bloodline? Was Jesus married? Or is this simply going to be about comparative philosophies and religious studies and whose religion is oldest, truest, 'right' or 'better?'

We live in times when a very real 'clash of civilizations' exists because these questions are not understood, and have, to this day, remained unanswered. Should we approach Jesus as the solution to these world problems? Do we turn to the wisdom of Buddha, Krishna or Mohammed for the answers? We have choices but it is never easy to decide.

All religions are not equal. If one is right, then the others cannot be because each religion is diametrically opposed to the teachings of the others. All but one of the world religions (Islam) contains identical 'commandments.' Thou shalt not.... So in some respects all religions are basically the same on the surface, or were influenced by the same religious teachers. Do not confuse 'spirituality' with religion. All people can be spiritual, regardless what religion they profess. The *spiritual* experience is the same for all mankind. The religious experience is not. A religion may prevent you from shaving, or insist you shave your head. One worships a cow but does not eat its meat. Another eats the meat but does not worship the cow. Getting circumcised or getting baptized is not what the true spiritual *experience* means. When we try to understand the experiences Jesus had, then we are on a quest to understand God. Is he real? What did Jesus see? Who did he speak with?

In our journey from the Ice Age to the Space Age, are we outgrowing the need for a God, casting him aside like an obsolete product with a 'use by' date on the scientific supermarket shelves? Or is the quest for God deeply programmed into every atom, cell, and gene within our bodies? Is this something that we inherently know and instinctively feel? Is God programmed into our genes like something we will always remember from our primordial beginnings, and instinctively be drawn back to again and again?

Perhaps this should be a search for the *race* of Jesus. Was he Egyptian? African? Hebrew? A dark man or a light man? Mediterranean, Basque, Roman? Could he have been a Brahmin, or perhaps even a Buddha? Was he Tocharian, Scythian, Celtic, or Asian? In what era should we begin looking for answers? In what country? What languages were used when speaking about him? When writing about him? Does it involve research into Conical texts, Gnostic, or Apocryphal? What about hidden gospels, parables, brotherhoods, secret societies, coded sacred texts, astronomy, astrology, sacred geometry, and kabala? Who were the magi, Druids, priest-kings, rishis, and rajas?

The oldest Biblical patriarch whose name is found in India is not Jesus, but Adam. By beginning with Adam in India we soon come to realize that there exists an entire trail of clues left in the ancient world, clues that lead us directly to the tomb of Jesus. By following those clues left since Adam, we will find the answers to most of the questions asked above. It is only against the backdrop of the ancient history of the family of Jesus in India that we can finally understand Jesus in India. We study his life and it become almost anti-climatic set against a huge panoramic historical background.

Biblical Patriarchs

Understanding the Bible is like having a half-filled glass of water, and then asking someone to describe it. To one it may appear half-empty, but to another it may appear half-full. We tend to fill in the missing portions with personal expectations of the heart and mind. This is because we lack the hard-core, irrefutable evidence for any absolute and singular interpretation. We carry in our minds very stereotypical images of great prophets and sages like Socrates. We have a tendency to visualize them clad, Hollywood style, in long white robes and sandals, but the facts are that these men and women traveled great distances in their lifetimes, through all kinds of terrain and weather. They had to dress adequately to survive, and often they dressed elegantly too.

Reading about their lives provides us with an important glimpse into how they supervised great assemblies of people, organized wars, built planned cities complete with irrigation, drainage and flood control systems, food storage, complex building projects, and even elaborate hidden tombs aligned with astronomical observations that we are still discovering today. Their lives were richer and fuller than what is available in many countries today.

They may have been the ancients of old, our great prophets and teachers, but they were definitely not simple peasants and shepherds just because they lacked modern technology. Their worlds were both complex and challenging. Through the stories of their lives we share with them their loves and marriages, their hopes and their disappointments. We are able to witness their losses and betrayals. We are with them when they bury their dead. We are at their side as they struggle to understand what morality and mortality are really all about. We are still asking the same questions they asked. Their struggle has become ours as we continue to seek out our ultimate faith, and our ultimate fate. Their gods were somewhat like benevolent big brothers looking down from some far-away place, always ready to give them a helpful lift up.

By the time we read the books of Enoch, we have come to realize that we are being told about highly organized, space-dwelling members of a great cosmic society far older than anything on earth. We learn about people and events far away. We learn about their rights and wrongs. We read about space and gravity, propulsion systems, geometry, and the continued help that they are providing to us so that we too can lay down a new world order 'on earth as it is in heaven.' **(70).**

These apparent space-dwelling societies played a most decisive role in the history of our planet, accomplishing all this through one family line, a line designated long ago as the 'reluctant messengers' between God and man. Our morality and our survival have been very important to these gods. They seemed most concerned with how we conduct ourselves within these carbon based bodies. God, however, seems most concerned with what comes *after* this. Our primary question, as we seek to understand the experiences of Mary and Jesus, could they have met the Elohim of Genesis? Would this explain the continued 'immaculate conceptions,' ascensions, and miracles? They spoke of gods, but they also defined God. They knew the difference. There was the realization that these were separate identities. They spoke with the gods. They worshipped God.

The Great Debate, Who Was Adam?

Adam is at the very heart of the creation vs. evolution debate. The questions about our origins are not confined to Christianity. The answers affect everyone on the planet. We want to know who we are, where we came from, and, if possible, where we are going.

1. Adam

Applying modern research to the fields of anthropology, biology, and DNA, we are able to trace the route of Adam in evolutionary terms. There is little doubt that evolution by means of *natural selection* is a valid premise. Why then is the appearance of Adam in *Genesis* made to seem so sudden? What is it that sets him apart from all men who existed before? Why is he described as a fully developed man with a sudden wealth of knowledge, including astronomy and higher mathematics? Where did this knowledge come from?

The Bible is neither the first nor the oldest surviving record of man: the Sumerian records predate the Bible. Although the sudden appearance of Adam may be quite literally true, the Bible is not a lazy man's book. Like a miner, we have to work hard and dig deep to get to the real jewels, for the sparkle of ultimate truth is often hidden behind the scantiest of words and clues.

> 'The Bible is everybody's concern. It contains our story of creation, our founding principles of monotheistic religion, and some of our western civilization's most powerful prophecy, poetry, and religious laws. In a word, it contains our spiritual legacy. And that legacy has a thousand shades of meaning and wealth of insight to give. But is it history? Is it an accurate chronicle, arranged in chronological order? Is that where its power lies? '
>
> (*The Bible Unearthed: Archaeology's New Vision of Ancient Israel and the Origin of Its Sacred Texts* by Israel Finkelstein and Neil Asher Silberman)

Somewhere between the Ice Age and the Space Age, we have found three possible ways to interpret the Bible. First, it can be about ultimate faith in a Supreme Being, one who directly inspired an accurate telling of events. The world was created in six days and angels could fly to earth. Every word of the Bible is literal and true.

Or we can believe that it is all myth. The Bible is a study of man's imaginary efforts to control the world around him. It is more about man's self-aggrandizement than about any possibility of a 'real' God interacting with mankind, and indeed the entire Universe, on such a personal, one on one relationship. Thus, there was no creation. The world evolved in a sequence of random happenings that are explained through science. There is nothing supernatural about the universe. There was no sudden appearance of an 'Adam.' There were no immaculate conceptions. There were no ascensions on heavenly clouds. There are no angels and no miracles. There is no God.

But now that we've entered the Space Age, it has changed the playing field. We have found hieroglyphs and petroglyphs and ancient art that give a whole new meaning to the possibilities of 'ascensions' and 'flying chariots.' We can perform the same miracles as the ancient priests. We can replicate unlimited 'immaculate conceptions.' We can fly!

Regardless what explanation we choose to embrace, it will have its flaws. There is no way forward but with an open mind and a willingness to embrace every conceivable explanation, even for the unexplained.

By allowing ourselves a broad range of freedom to research and explore all new possibilities, we can go forward, trying to stay as grounded in fact as possible, but with an occasional wink and a nod toward the mysterious, the magic, and the unexplained that will always trouble our minds. Was Adam a myth, a composite of many ancient traditions? What basis is there for the Biblical description of gods and of God? Is it possible Adam and his experiences were real? What do we know of the universe now that might support this view? Are we alone in the universe? Are there others like us? Or would they be vastly different? It certainly matters to understand the possibilities if we are to search for, and believe in the experiences of the Biblical Adam. Enter science to the help with the answers.

$$E = mc^2$$

The Universe

The author George Saunders gives us this unique perspective of the universe:

'When viewing the universe from our (apparently) fixed vantage point, it is sometimes hard to realize that we are undergoing several types of motion at once. We are on a spinning planet orbiting a star. That star is in turn part of a spiral arm of a spinning galaxy, orbiting around a vast source of energy at the galactic core. That galaxy is in turn rapidly hurtling away from all of its neighbors and toward the constellation of Vega. Said galaxy is also part of what may be a rotating universe (not an im-

6

possible notion, if it is in fact finite and unbounded, as Einstein suggested, rather than infinite) which may be part of a vaster multiverse.

While most of our units of time are based on simple cosmic motions, few of us are willing to go to the lengths of reckoning Galactic Years. Yet in ancient times the precession of the equinoxes established the crucially important Great Year of approximately 25,900 years. It may be that the Eons (Yugas) of the Hindus may have been based on accurate notions of cosmic time, with the idea that the movement of the Earth through space might change the influences on the planet - the idea of World or Zodiacal Ages.'

In 1961 American astronomers Frank Drake and Carl Sagan formulated *The Drake Equation.* This states that approximately one in 1 million stars might harbor creatures capable of communicating with each other. Approximately 1 million civilizations in the Milky Way could be using radio telescopes or other means to reach across immense interstellar distances to their neighbors. But there are millions of galaxies containing billions of stars, and trillions of light years between them. Even with the odds of 100 billion stars in our Milky Way containing one million advanced life forms, they are too far apart and too different to matter. The hopeless conclusion is that if we aren't alone, we are almost alone.

However, let us consider the Elohim who first appear in *Genesis* as visiting angels who married women from earth. Scientifically, this makes no sense at all. We know that evolution is true. We contain the same basic four-letter DNA strands as ancient pond scum. Nothing is different or unusual about us. All life on earth is represented by exactly the same four-letter DNA codes in endless different combinations. If all life on earth were to be wiped out, and had to begin all over again from nothing but a teaspoon of surviving pond scum, this DNA will remain unchanged. Even millions of years into the future, all new life on earth would include exactly the same four letter DNA molecules that we have now.

But would this apply to other places and on other planets? How could they replicate using exactly the same four letter codes that we have? There is an answer to some, if not all, planetary evolution. These genetic codes and programs may have been spread billions of years ago by civilizations that had a huge leap ahead of us. We hope to take our place among the great colonizers of space without considering that millions may have left the starting gate before us and colonized planets that have long since perished. We may only be the end product of a cycle that was begun by others billions of years ago. What they initially started with is what they carried with them for the next few million years, even down to their DNA. Thus, the original four-letter combination that proved successful billions of years ago in some faraway galaxy may even have dispersed by riding it out on meteors or abandoned space probes long after their home planets were gone.

The universe does not consist of a huge number of laws. The universe consists of a few basic laws that are repeated again and again in endless combinations, just like DNA sequencing. It may have been repeated in many kingdoms throughout the universe, dispersed in ways that we are not yet aware of.

> 'Out of the cradle onto dry land, here it is standing, these atoms with consciousness, this matter with curiosity.' (Richard Feynman)

However, in order for the universe to work as it's expected to work, one more element is necessary. It still needs a translator, a clockmaker, a thinker; someone who knows how to read and assemble the DNA codes, the atoms and molecules. It still needs God.

God is the Mind of the Universe

Now we are right back to asking how the existence of God as a creator is possible. Chris Michael Langan suggests this solution in *The Cognitive Theoretical Model of the Universe;*

> 'DNA is a macromolecule, a physical, material object. The information contained in a tiny string of DNA or protein can achieve everything, but there must be a cognitive force in place to read and interpret it correctly. Information is meaningless without a 'material transducer.' There has to be a relationship existing between physical and deep reality, or, put simply, mind over matter. Some level of cognizance is required to identify matter, and the information processes of understanding it. Language is a mathematical paradigm unto itself. Every formula or working theory of science and mathematics is a language.

Every sentient creature constantly affirms the linguistic structure of nature so it can perceive, conceptualize, and refer to it.'

A Matter of Life and Death

What was Jesus experiencing and speaking about to us? Who or
what was this God he knew of?   If God is *not* carbon-based like us, then
what could he be? *Light!* Scientists now predict that *light-based intelligence* will also be discovered in the universe. Light-based intelligence
would not be subjected to death in the same way that carbon-based life
forms are. And throughout the Bible we are constantly aware of two kinds
of heavenly encounters; those with the gods, and those with God. God is
different. God is imageless. God is light. Although Jesus seemed to
comprehend this concept, this is a highly profound concept for mankind,
especially when we can compare it favorably with science.

1st Epistle of John, the 1st chapter: "This is the message we have
received from him and proclaim to you, that God is light and in him there
is no darkness at all."

So where does this lead us as men and women? It is probable
that through highly developed consciousness, we are able to retain
thoughts *after* our carbon bodies cease to exist. In the tiny speck of
light retained within each of us lay all of our thought processes, our
memory, and our passions. This is our soul. In the space around you
right now, there could exist millions of 'specks of light' that were once
sentient beings just like you. Everything in the world is made up of
energy, even light, and our energy can be controlled by our thoughts
and feelings. This kind of 'thought' energy can travel long distances,
and yet still follow the laws of the universe. 'Prayer' is like a form of
ESP, mental telepathy, high speed inter-galactic communications
between minds, between us and the streams of light-consciousness.
We need only see ourselves as one small example of the potential for
the entire universe. God is a concept of the best of us, but on a bigger
scale. The universe becomes a playground for the mind, the mind of
God.

The Bible tells us about Elohim, about many gods who exist in
great societies in the universe. When we were described as 'made in
his image' this could not have meant in the image of our bodies, our
physical carbon forms that die, but the imageless within us, the spark
of light, the soul. Thus we comprehend the two kinds of life forms,

carbon and light, coexisting side by side. We are a small part of a much greater 'whole.' Otherwise communications with, and an awareness of God as a *different* form of intelligence would not be possible.

Returning to the Search for Jesus in India

The subject of race comes up frequently when discussing Jesus. Whether you consider him African, Middle Eastern, or a blue-eyed blond, you are going to face opponents. So can we ever really identify the race of Jesus? Absolutely yes. By tracing the story in India, we are tracing the migrations of the people from whom Adam and Noah were descended, and we can arrive at an understanding of what Jesus must have looked like. In the northern part of India it is known that a band of people who called themselves the Aryans were driven from their northern most homelands because of a mini-Ice Age. They settled the lower Himalayas and all the land in northern India. From these people sprang Jesus. They represent his tribe, his family. They returned again and again to their Himalayan origins, their ancient ancestral homes.

The first great civilizations on earth, the Sumerians and Sarasvati-Harappa cultures, were linked with these people, we came to know as the 'Indo-Europeans.' DNA evidence currently links the Sumerians with the Kurgans, Tocharians and Scythians of the Russian steppes. The word Kurgan is a Russian word for tumulus, the distinctive mound-graves of their culture, and indeed we will find graves for Noah and Moses that derive from this culture. As the Kurgans fanned out and mixed with local populations, each branch developed into unique local cultures that are still retained today. Celts and Indo-Europeans were Kurgans. So too were the Sumerians, Egyptian pharaohs and Ethiopians. And, so too was the family of Jesus. This is especially why we find them returning again and again through the generations to their homelands in the Himalayas and in Kashmir. Here there are graves for many of the old Patriarchs, a grave for Adam in Sri Lanka, and one for Noah, Aaron, and Moses in old Kashmir. Further the Iron Age grave for Noah bears a striking cultural resemblance, and dates to around the same era as Tara Hill in Ireland, the hill of Kings.

Shocking as it may first seem, names like Noah, Aaron, and Moses are considered very real people who lived and died in Kashmir. They are not allegories or myths. Myths don't have real burial sites that can be analyzed by archaeologists. The Bible only covered a portion of their lives, the time spent in the Holy Land. It was never intended to be the full and complete story of each of their lives. Where the trail leaves off in the west, we can pick it up again in the east.

Recent DNA analysis has been able to follow the migratory patterns of early mankind. It has been shown that the bulk of Haplogroup R is represented in lineages R1a and R1b. We have learned that R1a originated in the Eurasian steppes, north of the Black and Caspian Seas. It is this subgroup, R1a that has been linked to Kurgans and Proto-Indo-European expansion. Modern and ancient DNA indicates that Haplogroup **Q,** another component of Tocharian DNA, arose 15,000 to 20,000 years ago in Siberia. **(41,65)**

Reading the king lists from India, Egypt, and Sumer confirms this route of DNA. However, here is also where the Kashmir connections come in. The first king of Kashmir was Kashyap, whose name translates to the word for the Caspian Sea. The Caspian Sea was location of the tribe of Aryans known as the 'Lunar Aryans' **(107)** who shared the same language, culture, and DNA as the Himalayan Aryans of Kashmir and Tibet. We are searching for the origins of Jesus in this particular group because they once predominated in India and Tibet where Jesus spent a large portion of his life. We are looking for genetic connections that link Jesus with the Himalayas. This would also explain the physical appearance of Jesus that we should expect to find. Thus Jesus may have looked more like a Viking or a Russian than a Semitic Jew or Arab. We have been looking for the race of Jesus in all the wrong places.

(20, 25, 41, 51,54, 56, 60, 68, 88, 93, 104)

The Races

Tocharian mummies that are nearly 4,000 years old have been recovered in almost perfect condition near Kashmir. **(41)** One of the most famous of these has been the discovery of the undisturbed 4,000-year-old 'Beauty of Loulan.' There is theory among some in India, based on excerpts from the great wars of the *Mahabharata,* that India went through an 'Aryan invasion.' Aryans purportedly came down from the north in a vast horde, destroying dams, cities, and entire indigenous native populations all in one horrific advance. However, the wars of the *Mahabharata* occurred approximately 950 B.C., about the time of King David. This was thousands of years *after* Aryans had already arrived and built their great cities. The Tocharian mummies, Aryan mummies, are over 4,000 years old and were the first, original, and only settlers of northern India. **(41)** The remains of any other race or tribe of people has never been discovered there. The Tocharians, not the Mongolians, were there first.

The brilliant Indian scholar Dyanand declares that anyone who says there was ever an Aryan invasion is completely wrong. He points out that the Vedas themselves declare that the *first* inhabitants of India arrived from Russia and through the mountains of Tibet to colonize the country. Dyanand further states that the word naga was taken from the name of the first king who arrived in India from the north. He had a snake-like emblem on his scepter, and from this the nagas were associated with snake worship, which he believes was a complete misunderstanding of the symbol.

(Map of Aryan migrations provided by Kelley L. Ross (http://www.friesian.com)

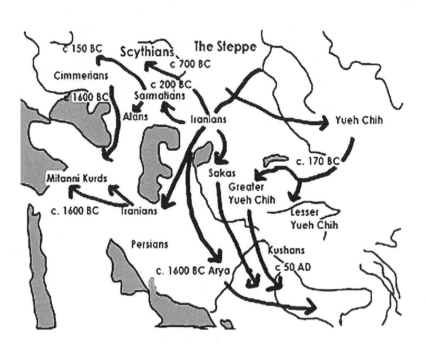

The Tocharian graves have yielded an amazing amount of information that has caused history to be rewritten not only about India, but about Mongolia, and, indeed, about all of China. It was because of natural barriers like the Gobi Desert, the Himalayas, the Great Rift Valley, the Sahara Desert, the Atlantic and Pacific Oceans, that races were cut off from each other and developed local unique characteristics. None are better or worse, just unique to a specific geographical location.

The most unexpected discovery about the Tocharians is that they were the *only* race inhabiting the Himalayan ranges long before the arrival of the Dravidians and Mongolians who eventually displaced them. The Tocharians represented the first race that seemed most adept at surviving cold, high mountain altitudes. The Tocharians gradually divided into 'groups within groups.' They became the Sumerians, Egyptians, Sogdians and Kurgans. In the broadest of terms, these people were lumped together as the 'Indo-Europeans.' The recovered mummy of Yuya (Joseph) pharaoh of Egypt, with his bright yellow hair is identical in features and even burial customs with many Tocharian mummies of the same era.

These people of the Himalayas will appear frequently in the history of India and Central Asia. *The Histories of Herodotus* refers to them as the Sakyas or Indo-Aryans.

Professor Oswald Szemerenyi (1913-1996) spent his life writing about the etymology of words that he explained as 'the four Old Iranian' ethnic names: Scythian-Skudra-Sogdian-Saka, and they all originated as Indo-European words.

Magi in traditional dress; breeches, cape, Phrygian hats; they were excellent horse-men, and usually wore riding attire. This is the same attire worn by the man painted at the Ajanta Caves.

Located at the Mosaic Basilica of St. Apollonarius, Ravenna, Italy.

Given that DNA studies on Egyptian mummies are still scanty, no definitive statements can yet be made about their bloodlines, although DNA testing has now begun and more will be known soon. For now we have to rely on the physical resemblances and applied sciences like language, textiles, and trade items found in their graves. The earliest Egyptian pharaohs often had yellow or red hair matching the Tocharian mummies.

Kurgans, Solutrians, and Tocharians shared many cultural distinctions with the Celts. One was their love for ephedra, a mild stimulant. Tocharian mummies carried it in little pouches in their pockets, practically bathing in it for their weddings and funerals. Celts carried it in pouches hung around their necks.

The features of several of these groups of Indo-Europeans are remarkable for hair that ranged in color from white (platinum blonde) to shades of red and yellow. Those Scythians who settled away from the main trade routes in more remote northerly reaches of Ireland, Scotland, Finland, Norway, Sweden, and Denmark are still clearly identifiable by these unique features. These colors of hair are the rarest on earth, and are the result of the most recessive gene for hair coloring. At least seventy-five percent of the world's people will always have black hair, brown eyes, and darker skin tones.

Tocharians wore clothing that was intricately sewn, woven in a complex manner used by both Celts and ancient Egyptians. The Egyptian mummy of Queen Tiye (see photo) who may also have been mother of Akhenaten/Moses (according to author Ahmed Osman) bears a striking resemblance to he 'Beauty of Loulan' from the Tarim Basin.

1. Adam

Tocharian Mummy found by Ariel Stein in 1910 in Himalayas above Kashmir; 3,000 years old, in perfect condition due to dry desert; They were often over 6 feet tall, blue eyes, curly red and blond braided hair, intricate sewn clothes; DNA has been recovered.

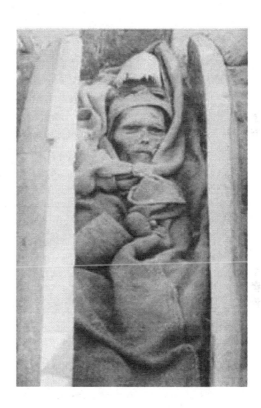

4,000 year old mummy, the 'Beauty of Loulan' found in the Tarim Basin and how she must have looked when alive.

Left, Egyptian mummy of Queen Tiye, her husband was Pharaoh Yuya (Joseph) right, reconstructed. DNA has been recovered.

Sarasvati and the Sumerians

The Sumerian civilization is where the Biblical stories and the Egyptian pharaohs and kings had their origins, thus Jesus had at least some of his lineage back there too. So who were these people? They *seemed* to have sprung up quite suddenly, with little historical precedence for their technology anywhere else on the planet. However, this is not correct because the rise of civilization in Sumer coincides with the rise of the Indus Valley and Sarasvati civilization. DNA proves they were the same family known as Indo-Europeans. Their vast backyard stretched not hundreds, but thousands of miles, yet they traveled the distances with ease as they traded goods and intermarried.

The races from Africa and China were developing their own great cultures that were quite distinct and independent from the Central Asians because of the isolation created by natural barriers like the oceans, the Gobi Desert, Himalayas, Sahara Desert and Great Rift Valley. These effectively isolated man and led to distinct little families or 'races,' each with its own unique features and talents.

Sumer is an area of the Fertile Crescent that was first inhabited about 6,000 B.C. One of the first major cities of Sumer was Lagash, which was founded about 3,000 B.C. At this time, the Harappan, or Sarasvati-Indus civilization was also in full swing. The Sumerians called them the 'Meluhha." Their civilizations paralleled each other like twin sisters. Today where aboriginal Sindhi tribes of fishermen and sailors live, they are called by the ancient name 'Mohana' referring to the original people who settled here and were known as builders of mounds for the dead. **(52)**

They shared the same development, growth, and knowledge at precisely the same time, even to their extensive knowledge of astronomy. They also shared the same king list. The first king of Kashmir was Kashyap (or Gyumart)**(16)**. This would be the Sumerian king, Enmebaragasi of Kish. His son was Enlil, or Nila **(16,24)**. Nila (Neela) represented the first god of the nagas of Kashmir. This indicates prolonged and extensive contact between these ancient people separated by thousands of miles.

Harappa was essentially a huge city of brick, a city sustained through the use of surplus agriculture and extensive commerce. This included trade with Sumerians and Egyptians. Harappa was part of the Sarasvati civilization. The word Sarasvati comes from Sarah, wife of Abraham, because, in fact, she actually lived there at one time as we shall see. Loosely translated, Sarasvati culture means 'the civilization of Sarah's India' which spans a period of several thousand years.

Like Sumer, Harappan cities also featured straight, organized, well-laid out streets, elaborate drainage systems, public baths, religious centers, schools, granaries, and public meeting spaces. In fact many villages and towns in present-day Pakistan and Afghanistan do not possess the level of development exhibited there 4,000 years ago. Weights and measures were standardized. Cotton was woven and dyed. Pottery was made on a wheel. Many children, and adults, attended schools as a necessity for business and trade. This empire, which covered an area the size of Western Europe, used variations of the same script. This is the civilization that India associates with Abraham and Sarah.

Historians are fond to point out that most Biblical stories have their origins in the written records of ancient Sumer. However, the Sumerians most probably acquired these legends from the Sarasvati civilization, because here, in fact, is where the Biblical patriarchs had their true origins.

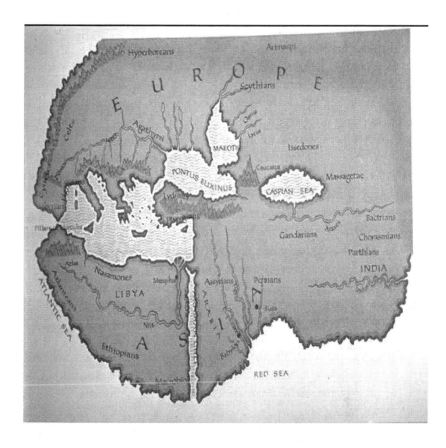

Atlantic Ocean to India-One big, local neighborhood.

Ancient Greek map courtesy Pakistan Historical Department

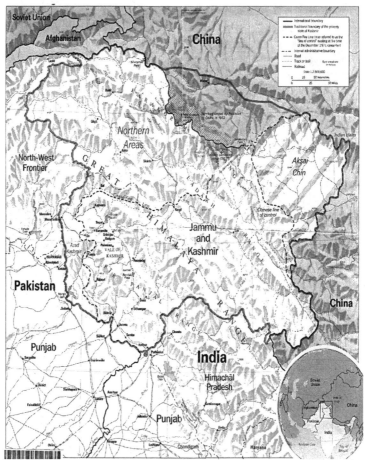

Map courtesy of Hindunet.org

The Himalayan Mountain range acted as a natural barrier between India and China.

1. Adam

Sumerian built ziggurats since circa 3,000 B.C. During rule of King Matagalpa (Magda-Migal) 2,445 B.C., ziggurats became established part of religious ceremonies and soon appeared around the world. Based on this concept, church steeples and minarets identify places used for religious services today. Is it possible the word Magdal, Magadha, and Magdalene had their origins with this king and his religion? This was the era of Shem, also a great religious leader and temple builder. Is there a connection?

The Sumerian root word Cush-Kush first appeared on the Sumerian king list as Kishar, ruler of the Grand Assembly of the Anunnaki. The first ruler of Kashmir was Kashyap. He was also known as Kai Vishtasp, Purushapa, and Prajapati. Kashyap is also the Sanskrit word for Caspian, referring to the 'Lunar Scythians,' who dwelled near the Caspian Sea. Their first god was the Sumerian god Enlil, who is Nila (Neela) on the Kashmir king list. A later ruler of Kashmir was Khashayarsha, known to the Greeks as Artaxerxes (c.425.BC). He was the same ruler as the Greco-Persian king, Ardehsier.

The Sumerian and Biblical king lists are still in a process of evolution. Broad assumptions are still being made, and timelines still vary somewhat. Adam may be identified with Alulim, the first king of Eridu. He may, as others suggest, have been the sage Adapa instead. Enoch has sometimes been equated with Enmenduranna's sage, Utuabzu, who was the seventh and last sage to ascend to heaven.

The modern Persian word 'Kush' has a different meaning from the older Sumerian word. In Old Persian it is derived from the verb 'kushtan'- meaning to defeat, subdue, or kill. Thus the Hindu-Kush mountains, entry into India, became known as the 'Hindu killers' (kill-kush) because so many Hindus fought and died here while protecting their motherland from wave after wave of invaders.

The word kasheer, a common root word in Sanskrit, is associated with 'shimmering mountains of water', a reference to the many rivers that flow down from the Himalayas to the agricultural valleys below. Great rivers like the Vitasta (known as the Jhelum River in Kashmir, and as the Hydaspes River to the Greeks) the Ganges and the Indus River, all have their source in the Himalayas.

Nagas

The Nagas of Nagaland, a state in eastern India, are a South-East Asian people with little to none Indo-European DNA traces. Their culture and people are distinctly part of South-East Asia, which means they arrived in this area later on the historical scene. However, the word naga occurs frequently in association with important events in India, and is often associated with the word magi, so we should try to establish who they were. The Nagas of northern India and Kashmir are quite different, tracing their origins to the Vedic/Aryan civilization whose roots in that area have been traced back to circa 6500 B.C. They possessed a rare knowledge of the inner working of nature and the universe. The Nagas were instructors to the Brahmins, who chose the naga hooded serpent as their totem. The city of Nagpur, located at the geographical centre of India, was considered the capital of their empire called Naga Dwipa, previously known as Bharata Varsha.

James Fergusson, author of *'Tree and Serpent Worship'* (1868) identifies the Nagas as originally a race of Turanian stock. Turania is an area of East Turkistan, one of the Central Provinces of Russia. It is situated between Afghanistan and the Caspian Sea, an area famous for its gifted stone masons. The Pallava dynasty, which held sway during the fourth to eighth centuries, traces its lineage to Naga ancestors, as did many Royal families in Kashmir. Taxila, the great centre of learning, existed as the chief city of the Nagas in the north. Originally called Takshasila, the city was named after the great Naga chief, Takshala, referred to as a 'carpenter' and a great healer in Vedic literature. He was also looked upon as a patron of the medical profession. Interestingly, Jesus is also associated with Taxila, which will be discussed again later.

The Caduceus, the emblem of the profession to this day, was first identified with Takshaka. The coiled serpent around a central rod was a Naga emblem. It was in Kashmir that Apollonius of Tyrana, a Pythagorean philosopher, became instructed by the Nagas and completed his initiation into the 'mysteries' which included healing, and we shall speak of him again later.

Ancient Central and South American Indian civilizations named their medicine men, magicians or initiates, Nargals, as did the Chaldeans. To this day Buddhist monk initiates are referred to as nagas in training.

In Uruguay, the word Nagal means 'chief', a teacher or a 'serpent'. The Nagals were known, it seems, to the ancient Aryans and the Sanskrit word for the South American Nagals is 'Uragas'. There are legends about the Indian Nagas being the ancestors of the Uragas whose homeland was Uruguay. In Mexico, the word becomes 'Nagaul'. Quetazcoatl, the Mexican 'Plumed Serpent God', instructor of the populace, came accompanied by builders, painters, and astronomers. He built roads, civilized the people and departed across the sea on a magic 'raft of serpents'.

Humboldt, the German naturalist and explorer, states: 'The Hieroglyphs, cosmological monuments and institutions of the peoples of Central and South America prove indisputably the existence of communication between America and India'.

It is that race of 'wise serpents' whose totem was the Hooded Cobra found inscribed on the soapstone seals of the Indus Valley Civilization who are the Nagas of Indian philosophy, and that is why the Cobra, known as Nag or Naga, has been raised throughout the country to the rank of a Divine Being. (www.indiaprofile.com)

The word naga is now associated with snakes and snake worship. According to author Philip Gardiner, 'Cush-Hiv-viah' is based upon the worship of serpents associated with dragons. This is connected with 'Ophia' and 'S'ophia,' which means 'wisdom.' Somehow through time, we have come to associate nagas with snakes, not wisdom. The symbol on the Naga rods of kingship resembled a Caduse, entwined snakes with wings over them. Some believe this could have been a symbol for a dragon, or even for the DNA molecule.

The word naga is also associated with trees, mountains, the sun, the number seven, and an initiate into wisdom. In Burma, nagas are called Nats, in Mexico they are Nagals (medicine men). In Kashmir, nagas were wise men who were 'visiting earth from another place.' Nagas were the ancestors of the magi.

The snake symbol associated with the nagas was known to Romans as 'The Caduceus of Mercury' (Hermes) or the 'Karykeion' of the Greeks. It may appear as a single snake entwined around a staff, or as a pair of entwined snakes with a winged symbol above them. It is also called 'The Healing Staff' on a Sumerian vase dating from 2,000 B.C. representing 'Ningi-shita,' a close approximation to the word naga. The 'Staff of Asclepius' is also considered the symbol for doctors and healers; the word caduceus now means all of these emblems.

In the Bible are numerous references to snakes, wisdom, and healing. "And the Lord said unto Moses, Make thee a fiery serpent, and set it upon a pole." Numbers 21:8

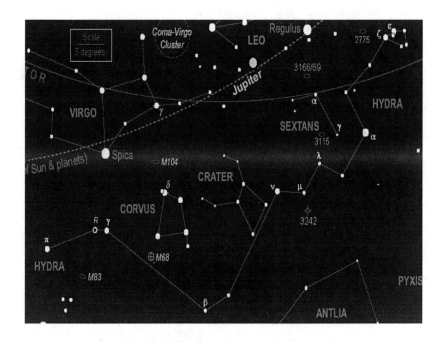

The constellation 'Hydra' largest visible in night sky contains over a hundred galaxies. Modern telescopes are rediscovering the stars and galaxies known to the ancients. Star map courtesy of angelfire.com

Motifs of Zoroastrian Astrology

The Snake.......Hydra   The Bull.........Taurus
Lion........Leo

The Dog.........Canus   The Scorpion....Scorpio

The Raven.......Corvus   Ears of Wheat....Virgo

In Latin the magi are magus, in Greek magoi. They represent the three families descended from Noah. The word Assaya is Aramaic (Greek Essenoi) and this means 'physician' or to heal. In Theravada Buddhism magi were also called nagas, and to this day candidates for monkhood are still addressed by the title naga as 'keepers of the faith' during their acceptance ceremony.

In *Genesis*, we are told that a snake dwelled in the Garden of Eden, and was associated with wisdom. In Kashmir the 'tree of knowledge or 'tree of life' was known as 'the wishing tree' and also associated with wisdom, but not necessarily with a snake. Nagas were regarded as the original 'keepers of the wisdom' passed down from Adam to Noah.

Genetic Errors, Or Genetic Markers?

There is a Persian history book called *The Akbar-Nama of Abu-il-Fazl*. In 1903 the Bengal Asiatic Society asked Sir William Beveridge, an Englishman and Persian scholar, to translate this book into English **(8)**. It is apparent that this book gave the history of a family directly descended from Adam. It was written in the same style as the Bible, listing prophets, kings, and memorable events about their lives.

Had it not been for his efforts over many years to record what he found in ancient manuscripts, we would have no other way of knowing about vanished manuscripts and historical traditions. It is the very specific physical description of Adam that is of the most interest to us here because it is specifically describing a typical Tocharian. Adam now has a race and a face. The following excerpts have been taken from a much larger portion of text:

> 'It is well-known that Adam came into existence 7,000 years ago (this date is based on a lunar calendar in use at the time) through the perfect power of God, without the intervention of a father's loins or a mother's womb... Adam was of lofty stature, with curling wheaten-colored hair and a handsome countenance... He grew tall in stature... He was the world's first great Uriah (teacher) and God gave him all the instructions needed for mankind... Some have said that Adam wrote about elixirs and other sciences...

When God cast Adam out of Paradise, he went to live in Ceylon for many years. It is believed that Adam died in India and was buried on a mountain in Ceylon now known by the name of Quadamgah-i-adam (Adam's footprint or Adam's Peak). Eve died one year later and was buried beside him. It is believed at the time of the flood that Noah recovered their graves for safety and brought them on the Ark with him, and his son Seth buried Adam and Eve side by side on the mountain.'

There are several key points in this. The first and obvious is that Adam was regarded as a living, flesh and blood man who required a grave and a burial. This is not the *hypothetical* or allegorical 'first man' we know from the Bible. We will turn to the specific mention of the hair color. In many instances when the ancient writings refer to another 'miraculous' birth, they take the time to mention an odd feature about the children of these conceptions, specifically their white or very light hair, in a way that makes it clear to us that they are not referring to albinos, or to a child with the *expected* physical features of that family. It does not matter whether the miraculous child was born in Ethiopia, Australia, Japan, or Ayodiya, or to what race his parents belonged, for these were not meant to be racial commentaries.

Was this white hair a genetic *error* or a genetic *marker*? Something made these children stand apart regardless the race they were born into. Something specific and unusual happened repeatedly across all cultures and races. Blond hair, especially the lightest shade of platinum, is linked to a recessive gene, one that is fast disappearing. According to a BBC commentary in September, 2004, this gene characteristic is now on the verge of extinction because of the accelerated rate of global travel and mixed marriages. Within a hundred years, this naturally pale blond hair will only appear in one percent of the human population, down from its peak of nearly one third in the past century. That is a very rapid extinc-tion. When such a unique characteristic as this unusual hair color is noted, is becomes of interest to ask why and look closer at the circum-stances. Was it introduced into the general population as result of the interference from Elohim? Genetic engineering? Obviously it was not the normal appearance expected of the parents.

Based on the above cited passage from the *Akbar Nama we* can positively connect Adam with India. Today, Adam's Peak is a place of pilgrimage, a steep climb of several hours to the temple at the summit of a huge mountain in order to see the rock that bears the symbol for the 'footprint' of Adam. Hindus believe it is the footprint of Shiva and Buddhists believe it is the footprint of Buddha. They may all be right. The summit may have been reached by each one of them.

Adam's Peak in Sri Lanka, altitude of 2245 meters (7242 feet). The steep, slippery climb takes several hours. Buddhists make the pilgrimage because they believe that Gautama Buddha left his footprint at the summit, while Hindus argue that it is the footprint of Lord Shiva. Buddhists believe that the real markings are hidden underneath the larger footprint. Were the remains of Adam and Eve moved here in ossuaries at time of Noah's flood?

Six Pointed Stars

An ancient black rock was found near Adam's Peak that was carved with a sign Kashmiris has always known as 'the star of Kashmir.' Brides still wear this 'star of Kashmir' at their weddings even if they are Muslims. In India and Tibet it is an ancient mandala symbol. To be more precise, it is the Magen-David or Shield of David, the six-pointed star identifying Jews. If, as we shall discuss soon, Jews had roots in Kashmir and India, then it would not be unusual that they carried this sacred symbol out of India. In magic papyri, it is frequently found on amulets bearing the Jewish names of God. This symbol was also used in Tibet, among Zoroastrians, and has been associated with the Druid Kabala.

Hebrew Star was found at Katagarama, near Adam's Peak; another, located in Kashmir, is known as the shrine of Chakreshvari, now dedicated to the goddess Sarasvati (Sarah) . Tamil word 'Om' (amen) appears in the center. These are vital links to Biblical Jewish traditions as part of Indian culture.

Another 'Star of David' that is similar to this and just as ancient is in Kashmir at the shrine of Chakreshvari. Did they all have roots in a common origin?

This symbol is also believed by some to have been the original symbol for the portal to the Garden of Eden. The six points represented a shield of protection around the Garden from all directions. To Hebrews it also represents, quite simply, a star, signifying God's place in Heaven. In yoga this chakra is the symbol for Anahata, the heart, center of love, compassion, higher emotions, and universal well-being.

1. Adam

At the southern most tip of India, leading to Adam's Peak is Adam's Bridge, clearly identifiable from space. It is now a sunken land bridge across the Palk Straights that has become an obstacle to the shipping lanes. The photos from space reveal a clearly defined sunken land-bridge from India to Sri Lanka that once had a city built on it. A similar fate was met by the lost city of Atlantis described by Plato. Something (global warming? Earthquakes?) caused these locations to sink into the water.

Some Hindus are uneasy about acknowledging these Hebrew relic words and symbols in their motherland, and they would much prefer to rename Adam's Bridge as Hanuman Bridge or The Bridge of Rama, referring to a story from the Mahabharata. Ceylon became Sri Lanka in 1972. The island was called Lanka in ancient history. According to local legend, the Sinhalese are descended from the exiled Prince Vijaya and his party of several hundred who arrived on the island between 543 to 483 BCE. The language prevailing in Lanka has strong Sumerian links. Prince Vijaya brought with him the 'Lions of Zion,' a Judaic emblem that would appear where ever Jewish royalty settled.

Flag of Sri Lanka with Lion of Judah symbol brought there by King Vijaya, also appears on symbol of India

The lion (sinha) on the flag of Ceylon represents the family of Vijaya. Archeological findings have indicated that the timing of the Vijaya legend coincides with the arrival of the 'Aryan' ancestors of the Sinhalese on Sri Lanka. They came from the Punjab, home of Indo-Aryans and their Jewish ancestors. Most of their language and DNA is traced to Sumer and northern India which indicates the flow of the migrations was from north to south. The Lankan DNA of today, however, indicates a very well mixed general population.

Gautama Buddha visited Ceylon when it was ruled by the Sakyas of the Mauryan dynasties, relatives of his family. Gautama visited Adam's Peak when the mountain was also known as Sri Pada (sri/holy-pada/father-Adam) and the patron god was Samanta. Lankans believe it is Gautama's footprint on the summit. It has always been a famous site of Buddhist pilgrimage.

Why would Buddha visit Adam's Peak? Perhaps it was to pay tribute to Adam as one of *his* direct Hebrew ancestors. The Sinhalese have always been proud of their ancestry and kept genealogical records that exist to this day. These records trace Siddhartha Buddha's Jewish roots through several of his ancestors. Yudhisthira, the names Tissa-Tessa from the Talmud, and the Ra-senas, Pharaohs who led to a branch of Jesus' family. **(77)**

Were Hebrews Hindus?

In his *History of the Jews* the Jewish scholar and theologian Flavius Josephus (37-100 CE) wrote that the Greek philosopher Aristotle had said:

> These Jews are derived from the Indian philosophers. They are named by the Indians 'Calani.'

Clearchus of Soll:

> The Jews descended from the philosophers of India. The philosophers are called in India 'Calanians.' In Syria the same people are called Jews. The name of their capital...is called 'Jerusalem.'

Godfrey Higgins, *The Anacalypsis:*

> All this seems to confirm the very close connection which there must have been in some former time, between Siam, Afghanistan, Western Syria, and Ireland. Indeed I cannot doubt that there has been really one grand empire, or one Universal, one Pandean, or one Catholic religion, with one language, which has extended over the whole of the world; uniting or governing at the same time.

1. Adam

The theory presented in *The Anacalypsis, by Jeffery Higgins,* is that a secret religious order, which he labeled Pandeism, had continued from ancient times to the present day, stretching at least from Greece to India, and possibly having once covered the entire world:

> "All this seems to confirm the very close connection which there must have been in some former time, between Siam, Afghanistan, Western Syria, and Ireland. Indeed I cannot doubt that there has been really one grand empire, or one Universal, one Pandæan, or one Catholic religion, with one language, which has extended over the whole of the world; uniting or governing at the same time..."

Among the many theories presented in this book is that the Celtic, Druids, and the Jews originated in India - and that the name of the Biblical Abraham is really a variation of the word Brahma, created by shifting the last letter to the beginning: Abrahma.

Martin Haug, PhD, *The Sacred Language, Writings, and Religions of the Parsis:*

The Magi... called their religion Kesh-i-Ibrahim. They traced their religious books to Abraham, who was believed to have brought them from Heaven.

Edward Pococke, *India in Greece:*

Rome's great deified heroes were the chiefs of Castwar and Balik-Castor & Polluk: the former son of Leda and brother of Pollox that is both the Kashmiris and the people of Balk sprang from Leda-or Ladakh (adjoins Tibet). Behold now the simple fact: The Cabeiri are Cuvera (Kubera), the Hindu god of wealth and the regent of the north- in simple language, the Khyber. Its region is wealthy and abounds with rubies; gold is found in its rivers, and it was the ruling northern power in those days. There is yet another important view in which the Khaiberi are to be considered. They are the Kebrew, or Hebrews. The tribe of Yudah (Judah) is in fact the Yadu (Yadevas). Hence, it is that among the Greek writers of antiquity such a stress is always laid on the piety of the Hyperboreans- that is the people of Khayber (Khyber) the Hebrews. I have no doubt whatever that the northern limits of Afghanistan (Kashmir) will be demonstrated to be the starting point of these two great families of language, and consequently of nations. The Afghans have claimed descent from the Jews, or Iudaioi (Yudai-oi) but the reverse is the case. The Hebrews or Khaibrews are descended from the Yadoos. In the lands of the Yadoos, among the Afghans still remain the feeble remnants of Jewish antiquity.

Tomas Doreste, *Moises y los Extraterrestres*, reprinted by author Gene Matlock:

Voltaire was of the opinion that Abraham descended from some of the numerous Brahmin priests who left India and spread their teachings throughout the world, and in support of his thesis he presented the following elements; the similarity of names and the fact that the city of Ur, land of the patriarchs, was near the border of Persia and the road to India and the place where Brahma (Abraham) had been born. This name of Brahma was highly respected in India and his influence spread throughout Persia and as far as the lands bathed by the rivers Euphrates and Tigres. The Persians adopted Brahma as their own. Later they would say that God arrived from Bactria. Bactria was a region of ancient Afghanistan, the locality of the prototypical Jewish nation called Judah or Jaguda, also called Ur-Jaguda.This was the entry route from Russia and from between the Caspian and Aral Seas. Ur means 'place or town,' Therefore, the Bible was correct in stating that Abraham came from 'Ur of the Chaldeans (Kaul-Deva or Holy Kauls). It was not the name of a specific ethnicity but the title of an ancient Hindu-Brahmanical priestly caste that lived in what are now Afghanistan, Pakistan, and the Indian state of Kashmir.

The tribe of Ioud, the Brahma-Abrahams, were expelled from or left Maturea and settled in Goshen, the House of the Sun in Heliopolis in Egypt, and gave it the same name as the place they left in India, Maturea.

The Persians also claim Ibrahim, i.e. Abraham, for their founder, as well as the Jews. Thus we see that according to all ancient history the Persians and Jews are descendants of Abraham...We are told that Terah, the father of Abraham, originally came from an Eastern country called Ur of the Chaldees or Culdees, to dwell in a district called Mesopotamia. Some time after he had dwelt there, Abraham, or Abram, Brahma, and his wife Sara or Sarai, or Sara-isvati, left their father's family and came into Canaan. The identity of Abraham and Sara with Brahma and Sarasvati was first pointed out by the Jesuit missionaries.

Gene Matlock continues:

Establishing the fact of the ancient Greek connection with India so often alluded to by so many writers, so perniciously denied by some, suspected by others: there to the north dwelt the singularly ingenious and enterprising people of Phoenicia. Their first home was Afghanistan, the land of the Ophi-enses, the 'Serpent Tribe' whose symbol was the serpent. This people were styled Bhainikoi (Phainikol) or the 'Hyas.' Their Sanskrit names meant Pani (Trader) and Yuddhi (Warrior or conqueror*) (44)*

The exodus out of ancient India did not occur all at once, but over a period of several thousand years. Why has history not mentioned these great migrations of people? If one is paying attention, history does; they are mentioned as Kassites, Hittites, Syrians, Assyrians, Hurrians, Armaneans, Hyksos, Mittanians, Amalekites, Aethiops, Chaldeans and Phoenicians.

The word Phoenicia comes from 'Pancika.' Pani means trader and sikha means 'a priest to the foreigners.' **(44)** Our history books usually lump them all together as 'Indo-Europeans.' In the ancient world, especially in India, people were not thought of in terms of races and tribes, but in terms of their social functions and castes.

The World Hindu Council believes that India was once an empire of over 75 countries stretching from Cambodia to Iran and into the Holy Land. India was not then and never was a 'nation.' It was known as Bharata ('brotherhood' based upon the name of a descendent of Kashyap). It represents a collection of nations, just like Europe is a collection of nations. The Sumerians however, would disagree and say it happened in reverse; the Sumerian culture extended from Sumer into India. Either way, it is all the same people and culture who shared the same traditions, gods, and genealogies.

Indians in the New World

The historian A.D. Pusalker believes that Ram was alive in 1950 B.C. This would be about the time that Abraham, the Indo-European Hebrews, and the Aryans made the greatest India to Middle East migration since the great flood of Noah. They continued colonizing into the New World. From studies of specific flint and bead-making techniques, we know that Solutreans were in America as far back as 25, 000 years ago, and continued arriving in small groups even before the Asians began arriving across the Bering Straights.

At first, these early North American inhabitants were called Indians (of India) because the fifteenth century Spanish and Portuguese explorers initially thought America *was* India. The name stuck and Native Americans have been called Indians ever since. In an odd twist of fate, the original Indians of eastern North America may, in fact, have been from India after all (Indo-Europeans). Although DNA studies are far from complete, there have been several examples that strongly support this view.

The oldest language that can be traced with certainty in the world is the Proto-Uralic-Finno-Ugric group. Many Native Americans today still use a language of this group. Gene Matlock tells us through his research that the Apache original name was Him-day or In-de, from the river named 'Sind-he' or 'Sind-hu' from which we derive the word India. The Pima name for medicine man is Javet-Makai, or Jayapeti. This comes from Javet, meaning 'of Japheth.' The word makai is for magi. The tribe called Yutes got their name from Yude-Yahood (Jewish Warriors). The Mayans called themselves Kishay-Quiche, which in Sanskrit is Kashtryia and refers to the caste of Siddhartha Buddha. The word Kishay or Quishe translates to Isvaras or Messiahs (teachers). **(44)**

As our search for Jesus in India continues, it becomes even more apparent that, since the appearance of Adam in India, and the importance of Abraham and Sarah, that Hebrews have an ancient presence there, and this becomes important to understanding later why Jesus himself would return there. It is also clear that the great Jewish teachers had indeed gone global and transatlantic

Phoenician ship found depicted in Texas. A long inscription was found in Brazil a century ago, which, when... translated, told the story of a voyage from the Red Sea to the Brazilian coast in the tenth century B.C.E. Similar inscriptions have turned up on the east coast of North America, as well as inland. Two such inscriptions have been found in the drainage of the Rio Grande, one in New Mexico, the other in the Big Bend area of Texas. The New Mexico stone is inscribed in what appears to be early Hebrew in a Phoenician alphabet of a form used about 1000 B.C.E. in the eastern Mediterranean. (University-of-Texas-at-San-Antonio) This would indicate that by the era of Jesus, America was a well-known place. This theory is still in its infancy and is being examined by several researchers.

2. Shangri-La

Shangri-La in Kashmir

The question that looms large still remains unanswered. Why were the Biblical patriarchs returning to India? Why does India have historical accounts of many of their graves and 'ascensions'? There has to have been a compelling reason for them to return again and again. One of those reasons may be associated with the Himalayan legend of Shangri-La. Shangri-La is to the east what the Garden of Eden is to the west. By looking at some legends of Shangri-La we may reach clues to the identity, location, and even the historical influence of Eden on western man.

To the Sumerians it was known as Mount Meru. It is Valhalla to the Vikings, Shambhalla to the Tibetans, and Shangri-La in its western form. Its location is on the edge of the Himalayas near Kashmir. It is a sacred mountain to four religions; Buddhists, Hindus, Jains and Tibetan Bons.

The author Ralph Ellis is best noted for his studies of the Pyramids. It seems strange then that he made a trip to Pakistan, risking the perils of a dangerous mountain like K-12 just to write his book, *K-12, Quest of the Gods* **(19).** Even more interesting is the fact that he used Egyptian star maps and Egyptian hieroglyphs to find his way to K-12. It is his belief that the Great Pyramid of Giza is based upon a hidden chamber inside a specific Himalayan mountain. He believes that inside the mountain is where ancient secret knowledge is hidden, knowledge about the star people who visited here and left this wisdom for mankind.

Alexander the Great made the same journey after being secretly anointed in Siwa by the Egyptian priests. They told him of a place called 'The Great Hall of Records' hidden in Shangri-La. Alexander believed that the Hebrew kings who once came here held the secrets to ancient wisdom from the stars, and how to contact the gods directly. Having been on the brink of completely defeating the Persians, he chose instead to turn his back on them and trek in a different direction through the Hindu-Kush Mountains in search of that ancient legend. Why? Neither Alexander the Great nor Ralph Ellis was seeking power or great riches in this direction.

Instead, each went in search of knowledge both believed was brought to us directly from the gods. There has been a host of historical others who went in search of Shangri-La. Marco Polo, Nicholas Roerich (who was instrumental in getting the Great Seal of the United States placed on the American dollar) Nicholas Notovich (who returned with legends of Jesus from the Hemis Monastery) , Adolph Hitler (who sent Sven Hedin) the great archaeologist Ariel Stein, all went in search of Shangri-La.

Is Shangri-La a mountain? Yes and no. Mountains help us to identify specific places in the world. Mount Meru, Mount Kailasa, Mount Katagarama, and Adam's Peak are mountains associated with specific dwelling places for the gods. However, the oldest form of the word Shangri-La actually means 'a gathering on the plains' or 'the plains of gathering.'

Charles Allen, *The Search for Shangri-La*:

> Shangri-La was a place of great learning, where men and women came from all over the earth to meet and learn. They exchanged trading goods and knowledge in astronomy, medicine, and surgery. It was said that the gods of Egypt, Babylon, Celtic and Nordic nations, Greeks, Asians, and the Chinese all made a pact of unity and peace here. It was a place of pilgrimage where young initiates came for their ceremonies to become magi and kings before setting out in the world.

Buddha and Christ both came here. It was a place still visited several centuries after Christ, and then no more was said of it, nor was it ever seen again.

The historian Theopompus wrote that the people who inhabited Atlantis were from Meru. Dionysus, Hermes (Thoth), and Hercules, brother of Dionysus, ventured there. Hindus believe that Shiva's abode was Mount Kailasa. Abraham dwelled near this same mountain. It is where he went in search of the legendary 'pillars of fire.' To Hindus this represents Brahma, whose legends parallel those of Abraham. Brahma also went there to search for the pillars of fire.

The 'pillars of fire' are mentioned several times in the Bible. Abraham saw it, and so did Moses on at lest two occasions. It was not a burning fire, but a light source that moved in a fixed direction or could remain stationary, as when it led the Exodus out of Egypt. Why did they believe the source of this light could be found in the Himalayas?

Edward Polocke, *India in Greece:*

> Kubera-Kuvera was the brilliant Phoenician mountain king who first learned how to smelt copper, gold, and other metals in the kingdom named after him, Khyber. The area has nothing but craggy mountains and according to Hindu legend, Kuvera and Shiva (Brahma-Abraham) once lived at a pyramidal mountain peak called Kailasa.

Mount Kailasa, a sacred mountain similar to Shangri-La, has proportions that almost match the Egyptian pyramids. Mount Kailasa was also the site of Kubera's city, Alakha-Elokhim. Elokhim is Hebrew for 'land of the teachers.' Is it possible that the Sumerians and Egyptians were accessing knowledge hidden in the Himalayas? Pyramids were constructed to serve two purposes: as a repository for valuable knowledge, and as a repository for dead kings. Time and again history tells us about efforts to save knowledge for the future of mankind. Some of this knowledge was basic and simple, like knowledge of metals, animal husbandry, farming and irrigation, textile weaving and pottery making. But ancient knowledge also included geometry, higher mathematics, astronomy, astrology, and the great philosophical ideals that mankind built his civilizations with.

In *The Search for Shangri-La* **(2)** Charles Allen continues:

> Beyul (a Tibetan word) refers to one of 21 earthly hiding places for the faithful and the secret treasures in times of danger. To Hindus, 'Tsi-lu-pa' has the same meaning as Beyul, but the meaning changes slightly to indicate a place of happiness associated with the Kalacakra Tantra, the 'Wheel of Time Thread.' La-Lo is the name of the predicted anti-god who conquers half the world before he will be defeated.

Shangri-La has been designated as one of the six places on earth specifically set aside as a meeting place for gods and men. Shangri-La also means heaven or moksha, 'a place of liberation.' Hindus say it was the first home of Lord Shiva (Abraham-Ram-Brahma) and Sarasvati (Sarah).

Kashmir was also known as Sharadapeeth, the place of great learning associated with the abode of the goddess Sarasvati-Sarah. For Jesus, these secret places were part of his cultural heritage. In keeping with a deep family reverence and tradition for these places, he would follow their trail back to the legendary sources of their knowledge and wisdom. The trail of his ancestors led him directly to these mountains, and to Shambhalla.

N.K. Singh, *Buddhism in Kashmir* **(62)**

'The Tibetans refer to the 'Great Mountain Lord' and his home in the Himalayas as the terma, a place of hidden treasures that could only be found by tertons, those with special knowledge and gifts.'

The Tibetan cave paintings show the Great Mountain Lords to be typical Kurgans, even in their dress, their pale hair and eyes. *The Saga of the Aryans* is a Tibetan classic, a historical novel on the origins of the Aryan people. The Saga deals with the lives of the ancient Indo-Europeans about

20,000 years ago who were proudly calling themselves Aryans, which means 'the noble ones.' Volume 1 of this Saga vividly describes the 'Great Migration' of the Aryans from their homeland called Airyanam Viejo (our noble homeland) near the North Pole. They were forced to find new homes because the climate change became too severe.

In the sacred scriptures of the Aryan Zoroastrians this journey is again authenticated, speaking of the trials and tribulations that befell them during this great journey. In these stories the Aryans display great heroism against bitter cold and blizzards, wild animals, and savage barbarians. Romance blooms among the young and all pause to mourn their dead. They carried with them great knowledge about the *secrets of the interior parts of the earth,* more than likely a reference to secret chambers where knowledge and artifacts could be safely hidden.

The Buddhists speak of designated meeting places between men and gods. They also speak of *Jin ten Chagtsu,* which is the belief that there is a time limit placed on both gods and men for each visit. If one were to stay too long outside an accustomed environment, one would lose the ability to return to their natural environment safely. Our physical bodies begin to change and adapt permanently to new environments, especially to space environments, as any astronaut can tell you. Serious and permanent medical problems develop because the body is under great stress to make these kinds of permanent changes. In the Tibetan view of the world, if we were visiting the gods, or the gods were visiting us, this 'time limitation' makes perfect sense.

The recurring number forty in the Bible may be a direct reference to this; forty days Noah spent in the Ark, forty days Moses spent on the mountain, forty days Solomon spent gaining wisdom from God, and forty days Jesus spent in the wilderness (meaning 'far away' and out of sight), these may all have a much deeper significance, a cosmological significance that we can only imagine. Were these limited visits with the Elohim? Perhaps the encounters in Genesis were still happening.

Recall the writings of Enoch. Here was a man who didn't just have visions of angels; he actually took several extended trips with them. He returned with highly accurate descriptions of the galaxies and the universe, accounts that are kept in the "Books of Enoch' available for us to read to this day. **(63)** Even in the Space Age, his descriptions appear accurate to us. He was not having 'visions' of 'messenger' angels but actual physical encounters with an entire culture. **(70)** In India flying vehicles are called vimanas, and Indian history is rich with descriptions of them, even how to build them and flight instructions. **(108)** Such encounters cannot be classed the same as most messengers and angels mentioned in the Bible. How are we to interpret such information? What logic can we apply to dismiss these as mythology?

Kashmir-Shangri-La as the Garden of Eden

Ezekiel 28:13-14:

> 'You (Lucifer) were in Eden, the Garden of God…You were the anointed cherub who covers…and I (God) placed you there…You were on the holy mountain of God. '

The location of the Garden of Eden has never truly been identified. The Bible says it was near the source of four easterly flowing rivers. The only four rivers that now come close to meeting this description are the Tigris, Euphrates, Pishon and Gihon, yet there is still endless speculation about the exact location. There have been other possible locations in the Middle East near Mesopotamia, as well as in Ethiopia, Java, Sri Lanka (Adam's Peak) and, according to the Latter Day Saints, even in America. Some New Age theorists have even tried to link the lost city of Atlantis with the Garden of Eden. Yet in all this speculation, Kashmir has never once been considered, as it should.

Kashmir has been linked to Eden through more historical clues than any other place on earth. In *Genesis*, it clearly stated that there was a holy mountain at one end of the Garden. There are several ancient holy mountains in the Himalayas that could easily fit this description. In addition, this area has been the source of ever-changing rivers that constantly flowed from the Himalayas. Today there are still four mighty rivers that flow from the basin of Mount Kailash.

The word Punjab is a combination of the Persian word 'pani' or panj (penta) for five, and 'ab' for water, which quite literally translates to 'the land of five rivers.' It is but one of the many great river basins that flow down from the Himalayas. Today, however, the Punjab has been reduced to a small state in northern India. Previous to this, the Punjab extended across the entire Indus Valley Civilization.

North of the Punjab are Kashmir and Tibet, and just a little further north are the Tarim Basin and the Taklamakan Desert, where the Tocharian mummies were discovered. There is a modest hotel in the North Frontier of Pakistan, in Skardu, named 'Shangri-La' that, although charming and set against a very dramatic backdrop, is not the location we are seeking here.

Due to plate tectonics, this area experiences some of the fastest geological changes and most dramatic earthquakes in the world. Over 85,000 Pakistan men, women, and children were killed in October, 2005 as the result of just one such violent earthquake. Why does this happen with such severity and frequency here?

Approximately 20 million years ago India was connected to the south-east tip of Africa. The earth's crust split and India began drifting northerly. Several million years later, it rammed into the Eurasian Plate and has been pushing against it and sliding under it ever since. What had previously been deep under the sea was now being thrust upward, creating the Himalayan Mountains of today. Ancient sea fossils are now found on its craggiest summits, not because of a global flood, but because these were once much lower, at the very bottom of the ocean floor. Finding ancient sea shells on mountaintops may have led some to think the entire world must have been inundated by God during Noah's flood (these very same shells prove the whole world was not flooded because the exposed shells are not uniform but are separated by hundreds and thousands of geological years in different parts of the world). These mountains continue to rise violently at about the same rate every year that your hair and fingernails grow. This rapidly alters the geology, landscape, and weather patterns on the entire continent. Where once lush and fertile plains formed dozens of little Camelots and Kashmir valleys, deserts like the Gobi now exist.

It is clear that these mountains have been a natural barrier to the movement of people for tens of thousands of years. They have prevented the intermingling of people from Southern Russia and the Indian subcontinent with those people from China and Mongolia. It is for this very reason that these people developed languages, histories, and customs independently of each other. Even though the Himalayas span thousands of miles, they are impenetrable. The only possible crossings are known as the northern and southern Old Silk Roads.

Between Peshawar and Islamabad, one can start a journey on the Karakoram Highway (KKH) which goes all the way to Kashgar, China and Tibet. China first gained control of this region in the first century. Kashgar is a sprawling and chaotic city, somewhat similar to Katmandu, which reminds one instantly of the word 'Babylon,' a place for mingling of hugely diverse cultures. This has always been a critical area in world history, an area where the silk routes and diverse cultures from north-south and east-west all meet.

Flag of Tibet with lions of Judah

The completion of the KKH, which paved directly over one of the ancient Silk routes, was a joint effort between Pakistan and China. Now that the roads are somewhat level and paved, they have begun to attract more mountain climbers and tourists to the area. In the lower reaches of the mountains a few lush green valleys like Kashmir still remain intact. Each valley is a surprisingly beautiful paradise in miniature, made all the more dramatic because of the sheer granite rock walls that rise straight up a thousand feet or more all around them. Many are covered in snow that is thousands of years old. Any one of these hidden valleys could have been the fabled lost Garden of Eden, but none more so than Kashmir.

Over 20,000 petroglyphs have thus far been discovered carved along this KKH stretch of Silk Road. Nestorian Christians left the rocks carved with crosses and Celtic symbols. The lands along the road are wild, somewhat dangerous, and sparsely populated. Strangers are regarded curiously, but suspiciously, while the wars and conflicts over disputed territories like Kashmir keep much of the outside world out.

Up to 10,000 people in a single day attend the outdoor markets of Kashgar. The archaeologists and scientists who are working on documenting the Tocharian mummies congregate here each season. There is the possibility, if enough interest is shown, that DNA samples can be extracted from another very interesting grave found here. It's called the grave of Bibi Anjeela, 'the lady from the Bible.' She may prove to be one of the most vital clues to the family of Jesus. Professor Fida Hassnain has been investigating this grave for many years, and he believes it to be the original grave of Mary Magdalene, especially because it lies within such close proximity to other Biblical graves.

Shangri-La and the Garden of Eden could well have existed here long ago. The memory of the place would have been known in Sumer and Samaria by the Aryans. Samaria, now in present day Israel (the West Bank) is actually a geographic term that means 'a mountainous region.' The word in Tibet for a mountainous region is 'Somaron.' The slightly different word Sumer (as in Sumerian) refers to a people who dwelled *between the land of two rivers.*

They were Sakyas, or Scythians, described in ancient history by the Hebrew word Ashkenaz (in *Genesis* 3;1 and *Chronicles* 6, and *The Book of Jeremiah*, 27-28, they were descended from Noah's third son, Japheth), the Ashkenazie were also identified as the European Jews, most of whom were wiped out by Hitler during the Holocaust.

Theirs is the trail we are following. We know their route by the barrow graves they left along the way, and their gold artifacts, weapons, horsemanship, weaving, clothing, and most especially their DNA trails. It leads through Europe, down the Russian Steppes, into the Himalayas, and across Central Asia in one vast looping highway of connected civilizations.

Aziz Kashmiri wrote *Christ in Kashmir* **(36)** He identified literally hundreds of Hebrew names and places that were identical to both Kashmir and Israel. Ayodiya (Iodia) is Judea, Magdha is Magadha, Kashir is Kosher, Bethpeor (*Deut.*34.6) is Bethpeor (Bandipore) Harwan (11*Kings*, 19:12) is Haran, Tibhath (1 *Chron.*18:8) is Tibet, Laadah (1 *Chron.* 4:21) is Ladak and Heshbon (*Deut:* 4:46) is Hasbal. These are but a few of the many hundreds of names that can both confuse and mislead us. There are many duplicate names like these. What are we left to think? We thought all Biblical references were places we knew in Judea. We never considered that they may have been hundreds or even thousands of miles away in another place. Take as an example the name Magadha associated with Mary Magdalene. This could not have Magadha in Judea because it did not exist there in her lifetime. However Magadha *is* the location of a vast and important empire located in India, a place where traditions from the Eastern Thomasine churches place both Magdalene and Jesus. There is also a temple of Magdha located in the lands of Ethiopia, near the old palace of Bilque, Queen of Sheba and consort of Solomon. **(100)** So it becomes apparent that reading the Bible is only half the story. It is left to us to determine the actual geographical locations.

The Garden of Eden we have been searching for may be lost to us forever somewhere in the mountains of the Himalayas, crushed to its death by plate tectonics, and now a dim collective memory of something unique from mankind's past.

Aristobolus the historian said that he once sent scouts into the area around the foothills of the Sarasvati Valley. They discovered that well over a thousand cities had simply been abandoned. Floods? Earthquakes? What happened that made these people abandon the great and vibrant cities they had built over the centuries? Even when Alexander the Great passed through, if he left the main trails he could easily have traveled for days or weeks before encountering another human settlement.

The enormous Sarasvati River as seen from satellite photos was once nearly five miles across, and it had dramatically changed its course four times in history before emptying into the Arabian Sea. This great Sarasvati River and the civilization named after it was once home to Abraham and Sarah. Today there are over 2,000 archaeology sites from this area. Many of the recovered treasures are exquisite in their complexity and are now on view in museums around the world. This was the rich cultural heritage of Adam and Noah in India, and of Abraham and Sarah. Theirs was the path that Jesus followed to India.

History of the Old Silk Road

The Silk Road represents an ancient and vast network of trade routes covering between 5,000 and 6,000 miles, or ¼ of the earth. Most all of the Biblical patriarchs and apostles would have known about these routes, and traveled portions of it themselves, probably several times in their lives. These roads played an integral part of determining who they were and shaping their destiny. The trails wound from Venice to Beijing and from Korea to Kyoto (Japan) following natural geographical definitions such as oceans, rivers, and mountains. The Great Rift Valley, the Sahara Desert, the Himalayan Mountains, the Gobi Desert, jungles, and wild rivers all served to determine the direction of trade, civilizations, and, ultimately, of gene pools.

Khyber Pass bombed out and lifeless, it has carried too many armies and conquerors into India; connecting Afghanistan and Pakistan, it is an important part of the Old Silk Road and the history of the entire world.

The Old Silk Road was a long journey made dangerous by the constant threats from pirates, opportunists, and marauders. By the second century B.C. it was finally fortified by a string of army garrisons, and only then did it become a safer journey.

50

According to the research of Dr. Victor H. Mair, the changes in the prevailing gene pools are clearly marked by this one historical event, the building of forts every ten miles or so along the most traveled and most dangerous parts of Old Silk Road.

Dr. David Frawley, a scholar of Ayurveda and Vedic Science, stated that from Persia to India, the Aryans were known as a culture of rich spiritual knowledge. Trade items like tin and metals from the Caucasus, lapis lazuli from Afghanistan, gold, peacocks, and jewels from India, silk from China, pearls from Japan, exquisite shells from South East Asia, all flowed through the Old Silk Road and could eventually be found in Rome, Egypt, and as far north as Ireland, Wales, and Scotland. Mummies wrapped in Ethiopia and Egypt contained strands of silk from China a thousand years before the knowledge of silk-making was believed to have arrived there.

Ancient jacket from the Old Silk Road trade: assembled from Chinese silks, and then sewn and exquisitely embroidered in Tibet as a trade item. *'When Silk Was Gold"* exhibit at Cleveland Museum with permission

The Romans complained of the vast cost incurred in buying these trade items that served primarily as status symbols. Silk was the famous commodity that gave the Silk route its name in the first place. Oddly pointed hats found on Tocharian mummies bore a strong resemblance to specific weaves also found in Celtic graves. In fact they were linked because they were Scythian families willing to travel vast distances to trade in brides and visit family members. Such great journeys seemed almost routine for them.

It might take upwards of three years for a silk merchant starting from Chang'an to guide a fully loaded donkey to Venice or Rome, but the profit margins were so high that it paid to risk the perils and make the journey at least once or twice in one's lifetime. We know that these roads closely followed rivers and streams. The oxen and donkeys had to have access to food and water in the evenings. The Old Silk Road was not used solely for the purpose of trade. It was also used by armies, families, prophets, kings, philosophers, and missionaries of all faiths. It was such an important main thoroughfare that Abraham, Solomon, Moses, Aaron, and Jesus would have traveled portions of it several times in the course of their lives.

It was on these very roads that people became aware of Zoroastrians, Buddhists, Christians, Hindus, Nestorians, Manicheans, Platonists, Socrates, Cleopatra, and Alexander the Great. From the China Sea to the Mediterranean, information traveled at surprisingly rapid speeds. The Old Silk Road was a veritable high-speed super conduit for information Merchants, kings, princes, rishis, monks, magi, members of the Great Secret Brotherhoods and the Kabbalah, Druids, philosophers and wandering prophets all traveled these routes.

There was a commonality in the themes they discussed, a knowledge that embraced all mankind. It was called 'The Way.' It became known as the Yoga Dharma of India, the Tao of China, Ma'at of Egypt, Asha of Persia and the Liga Natura (Natural Law) of Rome. The oldest surviving mention of all these great philosophical teachings comes to us not from Egypt, but from Tibet, India, and the Himalayas.

When we think of Zoroastrians, we think of the Persians and the magi, especially those magi who visited Jesus at his birth. We think of magi as priests or kings who lived in Persia, without realizing that they may have been Greeks, Ethiopians, Egyptians, Afghans, or even Brits. *The Oxford Bible Commentary* regards the magi as spiritual Hebrew leaders, not as 'India' astrologers and mystics. Furthermore, as we shall see soon, these magi may have been uncles and cousins of Jesus.

Don't underestimate the speed news travels on the camel
wireless.   Painting by Tom Dubois

Magi

It is impossible to discuss Jesus without mention of the
magi, and it is impossible to discuss the magi without understanding Zoroastrians and the history of the Persian Empire. It
is through these connections that we will come to understand
why the magi visited Jesus at his birth, and just who these
magi really were. The clues to their identity begin here, in the
Persian Empire. The first Zoroastrian was *not* Zarathustra the
Persian prophet of 600 B.C. That was a title, not his actual
name. Long before this Noah was known by the title Zarathustra (or Zia Sudra according to Laurence Gardner). This seems

to be a form of 'zaota,' an Old Persian word meaning 'priest.' Noah and Zoroaster had *direct* experiences with God, and it left a profound effect on both men.

In trying to explain their experiences, and to pass this experience on to others, they each founded a monotheistic religion that emphasized an imageless God of light. This seems to rule out 'God' as a great mortal king from earth, as some researchers have suggested. The present-day concepts of God began to take on their final development during the Persian Empire, especially during the reign of Cyrus the Great, one of the most brilliant leaders of all times who consolidated the largest and most successful empires the world had ever seen. It was during this period, while within the folds of the Persian Empire, that Judaism made its greatest changes and emerged in the form we know it today.

Cyrus the Great

Among his accomplishments, the first Charter of Human Rights ever written in the world, the first postal system, and recognition for the Jews because, he said, 'We are of the same blood.'

The magi were at their most active and best organized during the great freedoms in the Persian Empire. Magi were a 'fraternity,' a brotherhood represented by several religions, races, and stations in life. The order of magi might be comparable with the Freemasons of today. Freemasonry is not a religion, nor a substitute for religion. There is no separate Masonic God, although all members must believe in a Supreme God. They are a fraternity of like-minded individuals held together by a moral and metaphysical system of beliefs that includes public service and high moral standards. A magus could be a Zoroastrian King or a Hebrew priest, a Brahmin scholar, an astronomer, an administrator, a member of the White Brotherhood, the Silent Brotherhood, yet still be a 'magi.'

Historian William Drummond (1585-1649) refers to the main religions of the entire world as 'Tsabaism.' This covers a broad spectrum of star based religions represented by fire, light and celestial sun worshippers. This Tsabaism that Drummond refers to is also known as Saivism (not to be confused with the god Shiva, which is a separate path of Hinduism).To put it simply, the roots of all star-based religions, especially Judaism, lay within Zoroastrianism. It defines the moment when people abandoned the worship of physical earth-grounded symbols like cows, water, and trees, and started looking skyward for their gods and their inspiration. Thus the metaphysical aspect of man began.

Metaphysical is derived from the Greek *meta-ta-physika* ('after the things of nature') referring to an idea, doctrine, or posited reality outside of human sense perception. Metaphysics refers to the studies of what *cannot* be reached through objective studies of material reality. Metaphysical studies are concerned with explaining the features of reality that exist *beyond* the physical world and our immediate senses. Metaphysics might include the study of the nature of the human mind, the definition and meaning of existence, or the nature of space, time, and/or causality. Philosophy is a metaphysical concept. So is God. The experience of religion was much simpler when we could simply point to a cow and pray for milk. But *proving* the 'experience' of God has led us into some very complex concepts for which there is no 'one answer that satisfies all.' This represents a metaphysical topic.

Mary Boyce, author of *Zoroastrians* **(10)** said:

> Zoroastrianism is of enormous importance in the history of religions. It became the state religion of three great empires and influenced other world faiths, including northern Buddhism, Judaism, Christianity, and Islam.

Rituals that began in Sumeria were continued by the Egyptians, then the Hebrews and Hindus, and lastly, the Christians. The ritual best remembered in keeping with the Last Supper is the ritual of communion. Jesus used bread and wine as symbols of the corporal 'body' and 'blood' that are changed into spiritual elements representing our souls after death. This communion ritual has been practiced since the days of Noah's worshipping of the sun. The Egyptian temple priests practiced exactly the same rituals during the worship of Osiris, the Egyptian sun god (Dionysus to the Greeks). The coronation rituals followed by the Egyptians and King Solomon still exist today in British coronations. Baptism for Christians is the same as the Bar Mitzvah of the Hebrews and the 'twice-born' ritual of the Brahmins. This was the same for the initiate in ancient Greece standing before the god Dionysus. Lisa Ann Bargeman, *The Egyptian Origins of Christianity (7):*

> The anointing with oils, the rods of kingship made of olive and almond branches, the laying on of hands to heal, the use of cedar as incense, the beliefs in cher-ubs and angels, these concepts all traveled out of Egypt with the Hebrews. The seven sacraments of modern Catholicism also have their roots in ancient Egypt from this period. The gods and goddesses of many cultures have a common origin. Yahshua (Jesus) comes from the Greek healing god 'Ieso.' (This name also appears on coins found at Taxila and associated with Jesus) 'HIS' is the abbreviated form, the mystery surname of Bacchus, also known as Tammuz, and Ich-tus the Fish. But we never lose site of the fact that clearly Egyptian creation stories are on all levels paral-lel with those retained by modern Christianity.

There seems to be something overlooked here, and this is the fact that the Pharaohs of certain dynasties *were* also Hebrews. How, then, can we believe that the Jews *learned* these rights from the Egyptians? Would it not be just as practical to surmise that the Egyptians *learned* these rights from the Hebrew pharaohs and priests?

Egypt contributed much to world knowledge. However, by the time of King David in 1,000 B.C., the culture of the Dynastic Empire of the Egyptians would be significantly reduced to that of a minor world power that left behind a vast array of monuments and inscriptions. These still draw our attention and challenge our knowledge today. Sumer faded from glory during the period when Hammurabi of Babylon defeated Rim Sin of Larsa, becoming the sole ruler of Sumer and Akkad. Sumerian civilization was adopted almost in its entirety by Babylon. The three great epics of Sumerian civilization, the Creation epic, the Flood epic, and the Gilgamesh epic, had, by now, been carried around the world, becoming part of the lore of most cultures.

Ascensions, Miracles, Religion, Science or Science Fiction?

After Moses led the Hebrews out of Egypt (the Exodus) there was a sudden flurry of intellectual writings and new 'discoveries' in India. This of course was not the first or only Hebrew presence in India, but a new Hebrew presence not seen before, one invigorated and enriched with new knowledge. Now we can also begin to trace many Hindu customs back to these Egyptian Hebrews. For example, they still share religious holidays that began as celebrations of the winter solstice. The festival of lights marks both astronomical events and seasonal events. It has been handed down to us as Hanukah for the Hebrews, Deepavali (Diwali) in India among Hindus and Buddhists, the Druid festival of lights, and Christmas in Christianity.

One of the most striking experiences, however, shared simultaneously with the Hebrews and the Hindus that remain part of both their cultural heritage were their experiences with flight. The Bible is full of stories of flight, ascensions, and encounters with angels. We briefly discussed Enoch's experiences, but there were many others. We would not dedicate vast sums to research projects like SETI (Search for Extra-Terrestrial Intelligence) if we did not realize the probabilities for life like us in the universe. The experiences of the early prophets and kings strongly suggest that contact has already begun.

The author Paul Von Ward **(70)** details eons of non-human intervention in human history and determined that our very identity as a species hangs in the balance as we grapple to come to terms with the meaning of the Bible and of God himself.

The Egyptian temple pyramid wall in Abydos contains amazing depictions of flying craft. Sanskrit texts of this period are filled with references to gods who fought battles in the sky using vimanas equipped with weapons as deadly as any we can deploy today. A passage in the *Ramayana* talks in a matter of fact way about flight:

> 'The Pusaka car… that aerial car was excellent and would go anywhere at will; it resembled a bright cloud in the sky….and the king, Rama (Abraham) would get into this excellent car at the command of the Raghira, and rise up higher and higher into the atmosphere.'

Abydos, the Egyptian temple pyramid wall, circa
3200 B.C., contains stone relief of flying craft. In the
Sanskrit "*Samarangana Sutradhara*" it is written:
"Strong and durable must the body of the Vimana be
made, like a great flying bird of light material...The
movements of the Vimana are such that it can
vertically ascend, vertically descend, and move
slanting forwards and backwards. With the help of
the machines human beings can fly in the air and
heavenly beings can come down to earth."

There is no doubt that Indian scholars were familiar with
voyages in flight, as were the Egyptians. However, they were
writing about it in poetic terms, as opposed to scientific ones,
like Enoch's very scientific and accurate explanations about
the orbits of the galaxies. The Biblical writers, on the other
hand, were extremely vague and limited in the descriptions
they left us, almost too casual and matter-of-fact, as though
they presumed *everyone* could understand their experiences.
In many ways they were correct, because it was an experience
that was being shared across time and cultures. The beautiful
Lolladoff Plate , recovered from the Nepal Himalayas, estimated to be 7,000 years old, is interpreted by some to represent an exquisitely rendered flying disk with someone inside.
Clearly the world had very specific knowledge of flight more
than 2,000 years ago.

Enoch was probably the busiest inter-galactic traveler we have records of through the numerous *Books of Enoch*. In one encounter, he was trying to intercede between God and fallen angels. It was recorded how he made the journey of flight several times, and he left us with eloquent descriptions of the planets and their orbits, the universe, and the galactic societies beyond our solar system. We are then told that he chose to live with the gods among the stars; *Hebrews* 11:5.

'By faith Enoch was taken from this life so he did not experience death because God had taken him away. For before he was taken, he was commended as one who pleased God.'

The Chinese, rishis, Brahman priests, magi, and even Roman soldiers, all had been witnessing flights for centuries, and leaving us records of their experiences in both art and literature. From Adam to Jesus, the experiences have been consistent, compelling us to boldly ask, *'What if…?'* about every miracle and Immaculate Conception and 'ascension into the clouds' that we read about in the Bible. Could they have been real? Is that what the Hebrews and Hindus were talking about?

It is through their experiences that our hearts and minds have been opened to new possibilities for mankind. By sharing their experiences with us, they have passed down an incredible legacy, one that reflects our greatest source of inspiration and our most optimistic hope for the future. Their experiences have become the heart of all of our rituals and gods, our greatest and noblest beliefs. We have been given hope for a life beyond earth, a future in another place in the universe, where, if they understood the message from the gods correctly, if their experiences were valid, then mankind will one day join a vast galactic society already in place.

They have told us that we are not alone, not even nearly alone in the universe. We have made an incredibly rapid journey from the Ice Age to the Space Age, and we can only begin to imagine what lies ahead.

Magi History

The word Zarathustra, as previously mentioned, seems to be a form of 'zaota,' an Old Persian word meaning 'priest.' Zarathushtra preached that there was one God, whom he called Ahura Mazda. Ahura means 'Lord' and Mazda means 'Wise,' so Zoroastrians call God the 'Wise Lord.' Zarathushtra has been known in the West as Zoroaster, from the Greek transliteration of his name; in Persia and India he is known as Zarthosht. **(10, 28, 90,106)**

No one knows exactly when Zarathushtra lived. Zoroastrian tradition places him at around 600 B.C.E., but this date is thought by modern scholars to be far too late. The modern estimate of Zarathushtra's date is anywhere from 1500 to 1000 B.C.E. Zarathushtra received his prophetic calling in about his thirtieth year, in which he envisioned God through Vohu Manah, or 'Good Mind.' His prophecies were not foretelling of the future, but prophecy in the sense of the later Hebrew prophets: revolutionary messages of religious purity and social justice, speaking out against corrupt priests and potentates. Zarathushtra was never divine, not even in the most extravagant legends. He remained a man like all others, though divinely gifted with inspiration and closeness to Ahura Mazda.

Fire alter on coin of King Ardashir, Circa 240 C.E.

The Adar is the sacred fire of the Zoroastrians (Parsis). The fire symbolizes purity, the essence of life, and the presence of God. In a Zoroastrian creation story, fire is the last creation, but brings life to all that came before it. It is related to the concept of the Ruach ha Elohim, or Holy Spirit in the Hebrew Scriptures.

A sacred fire is kept burning continuously in Zoroastrian temples, and Zoroastrians must pray only in the presence of a fire. The Adar is the origin of the idea of an "eternal flame."

Zoroaster

The fraternity of magi was constantly evolving and took its final form during the Persian Empire. A king or a priest could also be a magi. Magi were a fraternity, a brotherhood represented by several religions and races and stations in life. The order of magi might be comparable with the Freemasons of today.

Freemasonry is neither a religion, nor a substitute for religion. There is no separate Masonic God, although all members must believe in a Supreme God. They are a fraternity of like-minded individuals held together by a moral and metaphysical system of beliefs that includes public service and high moral standards. A magi could also be a Zoroastrian king or an Essene priest, a Brahmin scholar, an astronomer, or administrator. There is a sacred Zoroastrian temple in Takab, West Azarbaijian, Iran that is on the World Heritage list. Dating back thousands of years, it was named after Solomon as Takht-i-Sulieman (Throne of Solomon). It is said in Parsi tradition that Solomon himself came here to be blessed by the sacred fire before assuming office as king.

Zoroastrians thrived until the arrival of Islam. Before Islam, the world had known only imperial conquests, where the conqueror, be he Alexander, Cyrus, Julius Caesar, Hannibal or any other, the war took place between opposing armies. The fate of the battle was decided on the battlefield alone. The common people, the unarmed civilians were not in danger of a victorious adversary imposing anything more than new taxes and new administrators. Life went on as usual.

However Islam often insisted upon total conversion and destruction of all traces of a country's history and culture. When the Persians resisted, they were killed in the hundreds and thousands, often accomplished by night raids on sleeping soldiers and civilians alike. This is attested to in the Quran itself where the actions of night killings was sanctioned with the deaths of al-Harith b. Suwayd b. Samit, Abu Afak, and Asma b. Marwan, a young mother of five who was killed in her own bed as her children watched in horror, and a poetess who criticized Mohammed. Another incident of night killing is discussed in the Hadith of Abu Dawud, Book 38, Number 4348, and yet another incident that involved Amr Umayya killing of a one-eyed shepherd. These were quickly followed by raids during times normally set aside for religious observances. Mohammed raised at least 65 military excursions in ten years and was still ordering war on his deathbed in 632 AD (source and information about each documented battle: howardbloom.net/militant_islam (and **80,82).** The accepted rules of warfare among all nations were useless against these unethical tactics. Thus began the view that Islam was forcefully spread by the sword. It raised the question 'what makes a man a messenger of God if not his deeds and good conduct?' These questions still divide and haunt the world today.

As Muslims advanced across Persia, Christians were wiped out in the hundreds of thousands and many Zoroastrians fled to India. So brutal and thorough was their eradication that barely 20,000 truly hereditary Zoroastrian families remain left in the world today. They do not believe that conversion makes one a Zoroastrian. These Persians believe they represent a unique bloodline and a unique religion.

Cyrus the Great consolidated the Persian Empire into a realm so vast that it encompassed all the lands where Hebrews, Zoroastrians, and Hindus could be found living. Cyrus' dominions comprised the largest empire the world had yet seen, stretching from Asia Minor and Judah in the west, to as far as the Indus Valley in the east.

Cyrus' conquests began a new era in the age of empire building where a vast superstate, comprising many dozens of countries, races, and languages, were ruled under a single administration headed by a central government in Persia. Centuries later, the administrative techniques created by Cyrus were adopted by the Greeks and Romans and by the British Empire in the modern era. **(6)**

Following an edict from Cyrus, the Jews returned from Babylon to rebuild their temple, and the Jews have honored him as a dignified and righteous king ever since. He is the only Gentile to be designated as a messiah, a divinely-appointed king, in the *Tanakh*. Koresh (Hebrew for Cyrus) is a common name for streets in Israel and is a relatively common Israeli family name.

The son of Cyrus was Cambyses, who was not liked by the magi. In retaliation for their rejection of him, Cambyses began repressing the magi until they revolted and tried to have him removed from office. They chose Gautama Artaxerges as their new king. He would serve under the title of 'Smerdis,' a Sanskrit word meaning 'a trained teacher.'

His election led to a split among the Tajiks. One of these Tajik groups of Scythians became the Kushan Empire. The other group drifted eastward, deep into Mongolia. Later we would see them return as a people completely altered by their contact with Mongolia and the Chinese. They returned as Mongolian warriors under Genghis Khan, founder of the Mongolian Empire (1206-1368) the next largest contiguous empire in world history.

By the time of Jesus' birth, the Roman Empire had replaced the Persian Empire in the Mediterranean, but the magi were still very active. Magi priests, rishis, and nagas were the individuals who managed the religious and judicial affairs of the world. They traveled the Old Silk routes and circumnavigated the world, appearing among all races. They were the administrators for entire kingdoms while princes and kings were off to wars, or on journeys that took them away for years at a time. It was the magi, who, upon hearing of the death of a king, would meet to elect a new king.

The word Sanhedrin comes from the Greek word 'sune-drion' or 'gerousia.' It means 'Council of Elders' because the original members had to be over the age of 60 and were elected for life. Josephus the Historian called them *boujeutal*, which in Tibetan is beyul or 'assembly of the ancients.'

Martin Haug, Ph.D. *The Sacred Language, Writings, and Religions of the Parsis* **(28)**

> The Magi are said to have called their religion Kesh-i-Ibrahim. They trace their religious books to Abraham, who is believed to have brought them from heaven. There are striking similarities between the Hindu god Brahma and his consort Sarasvati, and the Jewish Abraham and Sarah that are more than mere coinci-

dences. Although in all of India there remains just one temple dedicated to Brahma, this is the third largest Hindu sect.

As noted previously, in Latin the magi are magus (in Greek magoi) and they represent the three families descended from Noah. The word Asayya was used by a branch of the magi. It is Aramaic (in Greek it is Essenoi) and means 'physician' or to heal. From the word Essenoi we get the Essenes. Nazoreans were also known as Essenes. This was the small sect in which Jesus was born. Another branch of magi were skilled in astronomy, and said their wisdom had been passed down to them from Enoch, who, in turn, received it from Noah.

In Buddhism, the magi were called nagas, and to this day candidates for monkhood are referred to as nagas (not to be confused with the kingdom of Nagaland in India). Nagas were the 'keepers of the secret books of wisdom.' In Kashmir two shrines were built at Lake Wular for the Sushravas and Padma nagas who lived there. The main pass that leads to the grave of Moses follows the contour of this lake in the mountains, and passes by these shrines.

Both the Essenes and Nazarenes were a branch of magi who believed that they were designated to wait for the next prophet foretold by Moses. Moses had left the Essene magi with a message that the next true prophet would be known by certain sacred objects that once belonged to Moses. (*Deuteronomy* 18:14-18: *Copper Scrolls* 1, 12,-14). Later we will see how it was Jesus, through acquiring the Rod of Moses, who fulfilled this prophecy.

The Essene abode was centered at Mount Carmel, an area of Qumran near Mount Gerazim (Gipadri) where, it was believed, the gods visited and stored their secret treasures.

It is just south of Nabulus and the site of biblical Shechem, where the tomb of Joseph the Patriarch was located, and in 2001 it was totally destroyed by Arab mobs (see photo section). When the magi traveled the Old Silk Road to reach Joseph, Mary, and the baby Jesus, they were not in search of Bodhisattvas or a reincarnated Buddha, but a chosen, duly-elected king who would one day stand among them as an equal. Later, we will review evidence that these particular magi were actual blood relatives, uncles, and cousins of the child Jesus. They brought to him the Rod of Moses, which Joseph had with him when he fled to Egypt. It had been inherited through Mother Mary's ancestor Aaron. Later, in Kashmir, we will find that this rod still exists and can be subjected to scientific verification of its authenticity.

The magi were not exclusively a male-only boys club, but a vibrant system of learning and grooming for young kings and princesses, priests, priestesses, and administrators. Magi women were highly sought after as wives by ruling nobility because they were given educations equal to that of men. Kashmiri women were considered co-regents with their kings. They had to be as well educated and able to make important state decisions in the absence of their husbands. They had their own money and their own advisors and Chief Ministers. They enjoyed more respect, freedom, and equality than many women in the world experience today. What gave the magi such status and power to begin with? Here's one supposition:

*Gen.*6:1, 2.

> When men began to increase in numbers on the earth and daughters were born to them, the sons of God saw that the daughters of men were beautiful and they married any of them they chose.

*Ex.*4:16. And you Moses will be as Elohim to him Aaron.

Ex.22:28.

> Thou shalt not curse Elohim, or curse a ruler of your people (in this case Elohim seems to refer to human rulers descended from the Elohim)

Magi claimed they were the descendents of the Elohim, who they regarded as their fathers in Heaven. Based upon their descriptions, Jesus was also destined to be a magi-priest-king. Like Jesus, the magi believed that they were the princes, kings, and administrators who were these descendents from the stars. They were the children and grandchildren of the 'fallen angels' and they kept meticulous genealogy records for thousands of years to prove it. This is the bloodline of Jesus.

The next Biblical patriarch who has a strong presence in India is Noah.

Hale-Bopp: The Great Comet of 1997. Did amino acids, building blocks of life, seed the universe by riding it out on meteors and comets? Will other galactic life forms share a common DNA with us? When earth perishes our DNA remnants may also scatter across the universe and reappear in distant future worlds.
Photo Credit & Copyright: Jerry Lodriguss

Building the Ark

3. Noah

To further understand what led to descriptions of Noah and Jesus, and what influenced their lives, we turn again to Enoch. We know about Enoch primarily through the prolific writings of others who referred *back* to his writings. The Biblical Enoch lived during the 7th generation from Adam. However, the Sumerian Enoch goes back much further in time. He is equated with Emnenduranna's sage, Utuabzu, the seventh and last sage, who would eventually return to heaven permanently.

The Antediluvian king list is parallel to *Genesis* 5, which lists the ten patriarchs from Adam to Noah, all living from 365 years (Enoch) to 969 years (Methuselah). This adds up to reigns covering 8,575 years. It is possible that the 222,600 years of the Sumerian king list reflects a more realistic understanding of the huge span of time from Creation to the Flood, and the lengths of the dynasties involved. The first of the five cities mentioned, Eridu, is Uruk, in the area where the myths places the Garden of Eden, while the last city, Shuruppak, is the city of Ziusudra, the Sumerian Noah.

There are three key books associated with Enoch. *Book One* survived only in the Ethiopic language. *Book Two* survived only in Old Slavonic that dates back to the First Century, and *Book Three* was written in Hebrew. These surviving texts have been known by alternate names such as *The Book of Heavenly Palaces, The Book of Rabbi Ishmael* and *The Revelation of Metatron*.

The Essenes put great importance in the writings of Enoch and copies of the *Astronomical Book* section of Enoch were found among the *Dead Sea Scrolls* at Qumran. There are five divisions in the writings of Enoch, namely:

The Book of the Watchers-The Book of Similitude-The Book of Astronomical Writings-The Book of Dream Visions-The Book of the Epistle of Enoch.

Chris King, *the Apocalyptic Tradition:*

> (*The Book of Enoch*)… is a world view so encyclopedic that it embraces the geography of heaven and earth, astronomy, meteorology, medicine. It was part of Jewish tradition familiar to educated Greeks, but attempting to emulate and surpass Greek wisdom by having an integrating divine plan for destiny, elaborated through an angelic host with which Enoch is in communication through his mystical travels.

Enoch:

> And after I saw all the secrets of the heavens. Everything has a place and they do not change their orbits. The luminaries that are in heaven rise and set in their order each season…I saw their stately orbits…and they keep the law by which they are bound together (gravity)… The sun travels its path according to its rule.

The fragments found at Qumran that are known as the *Book of Noah* have been included with the *Book of Enoch* and the descriptions include an account of the birth of Noah. What follows here is the heart-rending confusion and lamentations of Noah's father at his birth;

> *And after some days my son Methuselah took a wife for his son Lamech and she became pregnant and bore a son. And his body was white as snow and red as the blooming of a rose, and the hair of his head and his long locks were white as wool, and his eyes beautiful….. And his father Lamech was afraid of him and fled, and came to his father Methuselah. And he said unto him: ' I have begotten a strange son, diverse from and unlike man, and resembling the sons of the God of*

heaven; and his nature is different and he is not like us, and his eyes are as the rays of the sun, and his countenance is glorious. And it seems to me that he is not sprung from me but from the angels, and I fear that in his days a wonder may be wrought on the earth. And now, my father, I am here to petition thee and implore thee that thou mayest go to Enoch, our father, and learn from him the truth…..And now, my father, hear me: unto Lamech my son there hath been born a son, the like of whom there is none, and his nature is not like man's nature, and the color of his body is whiter than snow and redder than the bloom of a rose, and the hair of his head is whiter than white wool, and his eyes are like the rays of the sun…

And his father Lamech became afraid and fled to me, and did not believe that he was sprung from him, but that he was in the likeness of the angels of heaven; and behold I have come to thee that thou mayest make

known to me the truth.' And I, Enoch, answered and said unto him:

'The Lord will do a new thing on the earth, and this I have already seen… and make known to thee that in the generation of my father Jared some of the angels of heaven transgressed …with women and married some of them, and have begot children by them… this son who has been born unto you shall be left on the earth, and his three children shall be saved with him when all mankind that are on the earth shall die… And now make known to thy son Lamech that he who has been born is in truth his son, and call his name Noah, for he shall be left to you.

One cannot help but ask if this was the experience of Joseph and Mary when Jesus was conceived and born. The circumstances seem nearly identical.

There is also the assumption that Enoch, which means 'one who initiates,' is a pseudepigraphical work that has been claimed to have been written by a biblical character but is actually a pen name. Most scholars believe this work of writing to be based on the life of the seventh antediluvian king Emmeduranki of Sippar. Whatever else it may be, it has had the most powerful and long lasting effect on the composition of virtually all *New Testament* texts that have followed. Its influence is especially evident in *Revelations*, the last book of the Bible.

Lao Tze and Confucius knew the writings of Enoch hundreds of years before Siddhartha Buddha was born. Lao Tze obviously drew upon knowledge of Enoch in his own philosophy and writing. It has been so notable that Martin Aronson wrote *Jesus and Lao Tze, The Parallel Sayings,* and Marcus Borg made similar connections in Jesus *and Buddha, The Parallel Sayings.* **(4, 9, 33, 49,)** Early Christians considered the writings of Enoch to be Holy Scripture. The early Second Century *Epistle of Barnabus* makes much use of the *Book of Enoch*. Second and third century Church fathers like Justin Martyr, Irenaeus, Origen and Clement of Alexander all made use of the *Book of Enoch*. Tertullian (160-230 C.E.)

specifically referred to the *Book of Enoch* as 'Holy Scripture.' The Ethiopic Church included Enoch in its official canon. After the Council of Laodicea in the fourth century, the *Book of Enoch* came under a ban from authorities and gradually passed out of circulation and was lost.

Many of the key concepts of which Jesus spoke came directly from the *Book of Enoch*. It is clear that Jesus not only studied the book but respected it highly enough to elaborate more fully on specific descriptions.

It is through Enoch that we discover religion is not about blind faith or meaningless rituals, remorse, and ablutions, but our intrinsic nature and eternal relationship with God. Discovering this relationship is the goal towards for which we strive. There are not many realities in the universe. There is but one and it is subject to many complex laws that science and religion struggle to grasp, and Enoch seemed aware of this. It is a great travesty that this was excluded from official Canons. It is through Enoch that we can best understand Jesus and his message because they both spoke from personal first-hand experiences. If we don't correctly understand their experiences, we can never correctly understand their real messages.

Chinese sketch of Lao Tze: They rode donkeys and cattle; they wrote eloquently of starships and galaxies. How did they know?

Noah in India

Noah-*Book of Jude* 1:14:

> My grandfather Enoch gave to me all the secrets in the book
> and in parables which had been given to him, and he put them
> together for me in the words of the Book of Parables.

Noah was so well known that the ancient Greeks and Romans
knew more about him than they did about David or Moses. To the
Greeks Noah was Poseidon or Neptune. He carried the same three-
pronged spear associated with the Hindu Manu. Noah was Ziasudra,
Nahashua and Xisubros.

It is interesting that China does not have any early flood sagas,
while India has three: the *Satyavarman*, the *Vaivasvata* and *Nahusha*
(who was best known for traveling in a vimana or flying car). The
Matsya Purana or fish chronicle appears in the *Mahabharata*. The hero
in this epic is Satya-varman (Manu-Noah) the 'protector of truth' or
'protector of righteous.' *Varnan* refers to the caste one is born into.
Originally caste referred to the divisions as priests, warriors and
commoners. The *Matsaya Purana* says:

> To Satyavaraman, the sovereign over the whole earth, was
> born three sons. The eldest was Shem (Manu) then Sham
> (Ham) and third was Jayapeti (Japhet, Jupiter)

From India is a set of law books called *The Laws of Manu*. Manu
is a social-religious position, not necessarily a specific name, and there
at least 7 manus in Hinduism. Hindus also believe there are 14 manus
born in every era. *The Book of Manu* was written about 200 B.C. and is
most noted for its controversial discrimination of women and shudras
(castes).

Jehovah was god of the sun, also known as Dyaus, Dioynius,
Bacchus, and Pitar. It is from the sons of Japheth that Buddha's family
of Sakyas was descended. They called this family the Yadavs (Yadus
from the word Jehovah; the surasena family mentioned in Bagavad
Gita.) They are descended from Emperor Yayati, mentioned as being a
Pandava in the Mahabharata, was therefore Jewish.

The Flood

Poseidon (Neptune, Manu, Noah)
The trident was originally a Jewish symbol

The story of Noah's Ark has always been about the ark as a boat, but an ark is not necessarily a boat. The word ark comes to us from the Greek 'arkheia' which means 'public records.' From this we get the word 'archive,' Ark of the Covenant, Ark of Testimonies and so forth.

The Ark of the Covenant was built specifically to house the *Laws of Moses*, the tablets inscribed with the Ten Commandments, and the Rod of Moses. Could it be that Noah's Ark was built for a similar purpose? We have seen in a previous chapter that Noah was believed to have brought the graves of Adam and Eve on the Ark, preserving them in order to rebury them later. This would suggest the use of bone jars or ossuaries began with Noah, although modern historians claim the practice was very limited to only around the first century. One of the main purposes for the ark was to rescue sacred relics and manuscripts, knowledge needed for all mankind if he had to start all over again.

In their book, *Noah's Flood, the New Scientific Discoveries about the Event that Changed History*, authors William Ryan and Walter Pitman **(58)** suggest that the flood actually occurred just over 7,000 years ago. They believe that the Black Sea was once a small fresh-water lake with large populations of people living around its shores. This inland lake was separated from the Mediterranean Sea by a land bridge. As this land bridge slowly weakened, it became saturated and could no longer hold back the sea. Once this deluge began, there was nothing to stop it. The entire ocean then began pouring through at a rate of millions of gallons per second. Today, this narrow opening between the Black Sea and the Mediterranean Sea is called the Bosporus Straights. The ocean currents still run in a northerly direction through these straights.

Oceanographer Robert Ballard made underwater films of the remnants of homes and communities that litter the sea bed. Evidence from mud samples plus dating of fresh water and salt water mollusks recovered from the sea floor, all support the idea of a fresh water lake that was flooded with salt-water about 7500 years ago. Ballard has documented a vibrant culture that once thrived here. Located just 20 miles from the Mediterranean, their tools, their homes, boats, and even their garbage, are precisely as they left them when they fled.

The Black Sea now covers an area of 750 miles long by 350 miles wide (1200 km by 610 km). It is bordered by Turkey, Bulgaria, Romania, Ukraine, Russia, and Georgia. Imagine people scrambling up the slopes trying to flee the rising waters over so vast an area. It is easy to understand how the flood saga would be carried by the survivors in many directions, thus becoming part of the oral history of many cultures. There exist worldwide more than 250 stories of this particular flood. Interestingly, they are all linked by people who share the same mitochondrial DNA.

Kurgan Graves and the Grave of Noah

It is absolutely astounding to think that men are still searching for the elusive Noah's Ark on the side of a 17,000 foot mountain in Turkey, yet historians are overlooking a grave purportedly belonging to the actual Noah. This grave, a thirty foot long barrow, or mound type grave, could conceivably yield an incredible amount of historical information if it is ever archaeologically documented. If it were not for the fact that it lies within close proximity to other Biblical graves along the Old Silk Road, it could easily be categorized as just a myth. It is known locally as the grave of Manuabost, the god Manu.

The oldest of these types of graves are found in the Ukraine and southern Russia, and in the Taklimakan Basin. These graves are unique to Indo-European cultures, and have revealed much to archaeologists. They are sometimes referred to as 'tumulus' graves. Tumulus is the mound of dirt and stones piled over a grave. These types of graves can be found from Iceland to India, and are linked to the same families through the artifacts and other identifying marks (tamgas-trademarks) included in the graves.

In Pakistan, about 20 miles above the town of Sialkot, is the small village of Tanda. It is here on a wooded hillside that one sees the outline of row after row of long narrow mounds neatly lined up the hillside, as though this had been used as a family burial plot for generations.

A local historian, Zaman Khokhar, documented these graves and photographed them. They appear in his local, self-published book *The Ten Yard Graves of the Beloved of Pakistan* **(39)** They are called 'ten-yard graves' because they appear as long narrow mounds, each about 30 feet, or 9 meters, in length. Approximately a dozen of these are arranged in neat rows ascending up the hill.

Noah as Neptune with trident, known as Manu with trident in India

It is from archaeological surveys of similar graves that we know they used the same language as most Indo-Europeans. They divided themselves into neatly structured divisions of labor, much like the caste system still retained (although not admittedly so) in India today. Many of the Kurgan graves were for poor laborers. They were buried with a simple knife or a pot. However, their chieftains had richly furnished graves that revealed they were members of a highly developed culture.

Frequently, double graves are discovered of a husband-wife buried together. The woman's remains are charred, which has led to the speculation that this could be the precursor of the Hindu custom of sati. According to Hindu scriptures, a widow is required to ascend the funeral pyre of her dead husband and be cremated with him. Even if the husband died at some distant place, the widow is none the less expected to be burned alive on a pyre by herself. A widow who accomplishes this is called a sati, one who is absolved of all sin and goes straight to heaven. Through her death, she would also absolve her husband of all his sins so that he may attain heaven with her help. Any woman who refused sati would, in effect, be 'unfairly' condemning her husband to hell. She would then have her head shaved and all her worldly possessions taken away. She was compelled to live in abject poverty and slavery, a beggar on the doorstep her own household.

Because the grave of Noah is so long, we can assume he was regarded as a man of great importance, a chieftain. There presumably must be artifacts in his grave that will help to identify him. As was noted earlier, the culture was also known for their use of tamgas, a sort of personal family brand or trade mark that appeared on their possessions, much the same way cattle are branded to make a quick and accurate determination of ownership. Tamgas were in continual use by each family for thousands of years, and this has enabled scholars to actually trace families, their genealogies, their migrations and movements for generations. If a positive identification is made at Noah's grave, then this will have a tremendous impact on the documentation of all the other Hebrew graves in close proximity.

From Noah's son Japheth, the names of his descendents included Gomer (who became the Cimmerians) Madai (the Medes) Javan (Ionians, Greeks) Tiras (Thrace) Ashkenaz (Scythians) Elishah (Cypress, Italy) Tarshish (Spain) Kittim (Cyprus) Rodanim (Rhodes). Many of these became maritime people, the Phoenicians.

In just four generations, not very far from here, Noah's great, great grandson, Abraham of the Chaldees, will also have a home and become one of the greatest gods in all of India.

Sarah, child of the Himalayas

4. Abraham

Sarah and Abraham In India

Egyptian history is divided into periods that roughly correspond to the thirty dynasties of kings listed by Manetho, an Egyptian chronicler of the third century B.C. Abraham was born under the new Sumero-Akkadian Empire of Ur-Nammu, the founder of the Third Dynasty of Ur (c. 2135-2025 BC). Ur-Nammu took the title 'King of Sumer and Akkad.' His mightiest work was the erection of the great ziggurat at Ur. Abraham would correspond with the Egyptian Old Kingdom. We know that one of the pharaohs from this era was Ramesses-Ramses. Although new Egyptian chroniclers have tried to reason that Ramses must have been Abraham, this is a theory not agreed upon by all Egyptologists. Abraham may one day prove be both a Biblical patriarch and an Egyptian pharaoh, but for now this is still being researched. Meanwhile we can include yet a third culture that embraced Abraham and Sarah as one of their own, this time as the gods Brahma and Sarasvati in India.

It is a certainty that Abraham and Sarah are the gods Brahma-Ram and Sarasvati. Long lists of historical comments refer to this obvious connection. Among these Voltaire said:

> 'This name Bram, Abram, was famous in India and Persia. Some learned men even allege that he was the same legislator whom the Greeks called Zoroaster (between eighteenth and sixteenth centuries B.C.) Others say he was Brahma of the In-dians. '

Cyrus the Great (590 B.C. to 529 B.C.) said he followed the same religion as Abraham. This suggests that Cyrus himself was a Hebrew, although as we've seen throughout, Hebrews and Zoroastrians seemed virtually identical in all respects. They obviously shared a common origin. Cyrus had a huge impact on the future fate of the Jews during the Persian Empire, for without his help and support, the Jews were on the brink of extinction as a distinct family and as a religion.

The author Gene Matlock, in *Jesus and Moses are Buried in India* **(44)** provides numerous examples that he believes support those claims. Matlock then goes on to say that Terah, the father of Abraham, originally came from Ur of the Chaldees, in that Chaldea is a contraction of Kaul-Deva or Holy Kauls. The Chaldeans were called Kaul-Devas, who were priestly castes living in Afghanistan, Pakistan, and Kashmir. The word Kaul-Deva means 'The Shining Ones of God.'

The Book of Judith 5:6-9 notes that Terah and Abraham fled Ur of the Chaldees because people were incensed when he destroyed multiple gods in favor of one God, Yahweh-Elohim. Among the gods rejected was the bull, or nandigan, called *Bhagirath.* The worship of this bull was also condemned by Moses. It is still believed today in India that God regularly descends in a reincarnated form whom people symbolically refer to as Nandigan (the Bull), the vehicle of God. This Nandigan (Bhagirath) is manifest in the Brahma (spirit of God). This is why it is against the law in India to kill a cow or to eat the meat from a cow.

Sarah and Keturah

Abraham had three wives; Sarah, Hagar, and Keturah. Of the three, Hagar was Egyptian and a maid servant in the household. When she left the household, she carried with her Ishmael, a son by Abraham.

Not far from the great Sarasvati cultural city of Harappa, home of Sarah, is Mohenjo-Daro, or 'Mound of the Dead,' an equally impressive city and once home to Keturah. The name refers to their ancient burial custom. Mohenjo-Daro is an Indus Valley civilization that flourished between 2600 and 1900 B.C.E. It was one of the greatest and first world and ancient Indian cities. The site was only discovered inn the 1920's and lies in Pakistan's Sindh province. The Dravids, descended from the people who built Mohenjo Daro claim they are descended from the same family as Keturah and have retained ancient records of their family line.

Sarah is best remembered in India as Sarai or Sarasvati of Kashmir (included in the Sarasvati culture) originally described as very fair and always clothed in white to represent her purity. Her presence has had a tremendous influence in India. There is an entire epic period of Indian history known as the Sarasvati (Sarah-Sindhu) culture that reflects this glorious civilization. The great Sarasvati River is also named after her. The 'Sarasvati School of Learning'

Seal from Mohenjo Daro

still existed in Kashmir until 400 CE, one of the oldest schools in continual existence in the world. In his book *Buddhism in Kashmir* *(62)* N.K. Singh discusses the famous scholar Gunavarman, a Buddhist who also 'kissed the cross of Christianity.' He was a student at the Sarasvati School in Kashmir when it still existed in 400 CE.

School children still invoke a prayer to Sarasvati to help them with their studies. It is called the '*Sharda Strotam hymn to the Goddess of Learning*.' It begins with the famous line: *Namaste Sharda Devi Kashmir Puravasini.*

From Vedic times, Goddess Sarasvati is regarded as the giver of wisdom. She is also referred to as Vak Devi (goddess of speech) and Sakala kaladhishtatri (goddess bestowing all the art forms.) The gold Sarasvati Yantra (charm) is still carried by students in India today as a good-luck symbol to help them learn and improve their studies.

Sarah excelled in Vak, that is, in eloquent speech and mastery of languages. In Hebrew this is the same as Vayika or Va-yikra, from a description in *Leviticus*, '... *and he is called,'* meaning, 'a priest of eloquent speech called upon to recite the holy words of the Torah,' with no distinction being made between male and female priests.

Vak (or Vik) is also a title attached to the names of kings, as in King Vikramaditiya, who was commemorated with a plaque at Mecca. In Sanskrit, Vikrama means valor, and 'Aditya' is son of Surya the sun god. The *atiya* ending represents the caste of Buddha, the Kashrtiyas (valor-warriors).

It was the first King Vikramaditiya who helped rebuild the Ram temple at Ayodiya. Thus, if Ram (Vik-*Ram*-Aditiya) was Abraham, then these kings represent descendents of Abraham. So a translation of Vak-ramaditiya (or Vikramaditiya) would be:

> '...An anointed king, gifted in learning and eloquent of speech, descended from Surya the sun god, related to the royal and noble Kashtriya family.' (Kashtriyas being of the family of Isaac)

The first king Vak-ram of Ujjain (in west-central India) ruled about 57 B.C. He is a hero of epic proportions in India, and as highly regarded as King Arthur in western literature. Thor Heyerdahl discovered that use of the word Vak in Swedish folklore is also associated with higher learning and the search for wisdom, and he attempted to connect the Nordic folklore and kings directly with myth and folklore of the Hindus and Hebrews **(32)**

Lin Yutang, the Chinese writer says in *Wisdom of India* that Kashmir was the place where China's great teachers in religion and imaginative literature attended schools of learning- the place of the world's most advanced teachers in trigonometry, quadratic equations, grammar, phonetics, and even chess. The inspirations for Boccaccio, Goethe, Schopenhauer, and Emerson have their roots here.

Sarasvati; goddess of beauty and intellectual pursuits. In Hindu art extra arms are added, each holds a symbol that god or goddess is known for. Books and music represent higher intellectual pursuits. Sarah holds prayer beads in one hand to convey her deep spirituality (as a priestess) and the gift of prophecy.

The city of Kurukshetra (now modern Thanasar) was in the heart of the thriving Sarasvati culture. It lies about one hundred miles north of New Delhi on the road to Kashmir between the sacred Sarasvati and Drishadvati Rivers. It was the site of the great wars in the *Mahabharata*. Many wars were fought here, for this is 'The Gateway of North India.'

From Ur of the Chaldees and the Sarasvati culture to the halls of the Pharaohs is but a journey of a few weeks walk along a branch of the Old Silk Road. It's a journey that many Biblical patriarchs made repeatedly during their lifetimes.

Abraham, Sarah, Isaac, Jacob, and Joseph were all buried in or near the Valley of the Kings. Their identity as possible 18th Dynasty Egyptian royalty has been the topic of heated speculation in recent times. Some have proposed the theory that Abraham was also the Egyptian Pharaoh Mam-aye-bra/Ay-Bra-ham. These Pharaohs were tall, many were over six feet. Could these be the race of 'giants' mentioned in ancient lore? The mummy of Yuya has striking bright yellow hair. That they were of the same race as the Tocharian mummies can hardly be disputed since we now have their mummies for comparison.

The Temple of Amun at Siwa used the Apis-Bull to represent the constellation Taurus. This was the same temple that Alexander the Great visited before setting off to the Himalayas in search of the ancient wisdom at Shambhalla. **(19)** It was the religion of these priests, centered on sacrificing animals and imposing restrictions on meat eating, which led to the great schisms between Hindus and Hebrews, between the Hebrews who became Jewish priests and those who became Brahmins in India. Today, Hindus worship the bull but refuse to eat meat. Jews eat meat but refuse to worship the bull.

Golden Nandi (calf or bull) and serpent protecting Shiva-lingam. Is this the 'Golden Calf' the children of Israel created when Moses made his sojourn to Mount Sinai and returned with the Ten Commandments?

Although Abraham appeared in Israelite writings as one of their greatest ancestors, it was the Davidic line from Isaac and Jacob that came to be regarded as the only accepted ancestor for any future king or messiah. Today, thousands of years after Abraham, all of the major dynasties, with the exception of Islam (who claim their roots through Ishmael, who has left no dynastic or genealogical records), have their roots with Abraham through Isaac, even Siddhartha Gautama Buddha.

This dynastic growth has been carefully chronicled for centuries, and is portrayed as the 'Kalpa Tree' or the 'World Religious Genealogical Tree.'

Names for Abraham

Attempts to break down Abraham's name have resulted in some interesting ideas. One such suggestion has been the Egyptian Ab-Ra-Ha/Ebra-Ay-Bra-Ham. In this instance, Ab is father; Ra is the Egyptian sun god, and Ham is a descendent of Noah. Brahm, in Sanskrit, also means to 'grow or multiply in number' as when God told Abraham his seed would prosper into the multitudes. Ram could be Amon-Ra, the ram given in temple sacrifice: Ram also means soul, thus Ab-Ram could be interpreted as 'father-soul.' Many of the Ram temples in India date back to the time of Abraham. Terah, Abraham's father, had first named his son Abram, not Abraham.

In Kashmir, the word Ram or Ab-Ram in the Sharda and Sogdian language means 'Divine Mercy.' Ram is also a title for a person of high rank. The chant 'om' is considered a sacred form of *amen*, said at the closing of each Christian prayer. It is a contraction of the word Abram, the father-creator, or God, written as *OM.* below:

Sanskrit om or amen

According to the research of M.M. Ninan, an Indian historian, **(45)** *om* never appeared in use in India before Thomas brought Christianity. Then om became synonymous with amen and now appears in temples and churches of all faiths throughout   India.

A-Braham could also mean 'not of Brahma,' meaning one who does not follow the religious practices of the Brahmin priests. The identities of Abraham and Sarah as Brahma and Sarasvati, interestingly enough, were even recognized and written about by Jesuit and Roman Catholic priests.

In Hinduism, Brahma (creator) Vishnu (preserver) and Shiva (destroyer) represent the trinity of gods. This concept of the Trinity in

Hinduism only appeared *after* Christianity and was based upon the concept of Trinity in Christianity.

Brahma on temple at Halebid, Karnataka, India. Courtesy wiki-pedia.org

Understanding Hinduism

It is difficult for many western minds to comprehend why there are at least 250,000 gods and deities in Hinduism. Unlike the Abrahmic religions that emphasized one god, Hinduism allows one to embrace many gods in many forms. In this belief system, God permeates all things and no form of worship can be 'wrong'. However, Hindus also believe in a supreme God and share with Hebrews and Christians the concepts of good and evil, angels, deities, and themes similar to Judaic and Christian scriptures. Hinduism differs from Christianity and other Western religions in that it does not have a single founder or prophet, a specific theological guiding system, or a central religious organization.

According to the religious historian Bhakti Ananda Goswami;

'The word Hinduism is derived from the name of a river in present-day Pakistan, the Sindhu (Indus)....invading armies called the place beyond the Sindhu 'Hindustan' and the people who lived there the Hindus - due to the language differences, the 's' was changed to 'h'. In the centuries that followed, the term Hindu became acceptable even to the Indians themselves as a general designation for their different religious traditions. But since the word Hindu is not found in the scriptures upon which these traditions are based, it is quite inappropriate. It is like calling the Abrahmic religions 'Jordanism' because they were all associated with an area around the Jordon River. '

Professor M.M. Ninan feels that it happened differently **(45)** He wrote

The British had occupied India since December 31, 1600 AD, The word Hinduism came into existence as the name of a religion when there were clashes between the British and Muslims over rule of India. All others who were neither Muslim nor Christian united under a third banner and called themselves Hindus.

Hindus believe that the Universe exists in cycles and that during each cycle, or Yuga, God (Vishnu) reappears in a new persona to fulfill his role as the preserver to save the world. Each individual who appears is unlike his previous incarnations. They are called 'Avatars,' appearing in different forms during different ages. Some are animal forms, like the cow, fish and tortoise incarnations. Some are semi-human like Ganesh, and some are fully human like Ram and Krishna. Ram and Krishna, the two primary incarnations of Vishnu, are Avatars of two different time periods, or 'yugas.' Ram (Brahma) is the Avatar of the second Yuga, and Krishna of the third. Melchizedek is believed to be an avatar of Seth (third son from Adam) and Shem (second son from Noah).

Vedas and Sanskrit

It is popular in India now to declare they are possessors of the world's oldest religion and language. However, they mat be erring ever so slightly in overlooking the prior 'Jewish-ness' of India. Sanskrit is a comparatively new written language. It did not exist in its present for until around the first and second centuries of this era. The word Sanskrit means 'that which has been refined.' Before Sanskrit became widely popular around the fourth century, all written forms of language used in India were forms of Pali and Prakrit. The Zoroastrian Zend Avistas were written in a form of Persian that was the same as the later Rig Vedas claimed to be written in the so-called 'Vedic' script. The word Vedas or Vedantas means "End of the Old" which indicates a new revision to older traditions. Thus Sanskrit, the 'refined' language that is referred to as 'Vedic' is actually based upon the 'Old Persian' and Panini-Brahmi, the languages that preceded it. (Parpola; **52,61, 73, 88, 98,104**)

Some Hindus say that the Vedas are even older than Abraham. This may well be correct if we could establish when they first existed, even as an oral tradition, but this has not been possible. Written Hebrew literature covers a period of about 3,000 years. The Indo-Aryan languages are divided into two groups: Indo-Aryan, and Iranian. There is no evidence that any of them are derived from Sanskrit. There is no mention of Sanskrit in the *Vedas*. Gautama Buddha did not use Sanskrit, even though he was a well-educated prince of India. In fact, Sanskrit did not appear until 500 B.C. in its earliest form. Its grammatical roots were in Panini, circa 5th century B.C., and Patanjali, circa 150 B.C. In its present form it wasn't in full use until the Gupta era, around 320 CE.

The Hindu faith begins with the four *Vedas (Vedantas)*. These are to Hinduism what the *Talmud* is to Hebrews. They are the *Rig-Veda*, *Sama-Veda*, *Yajur-Veda*, and the *Atharva-Veda*. Of these four, the *Rig-Veda* is considered the oldest surviving work of Hindu literature **(73)** The *Rig-Vedas* are primarily a liturgy of hymns and instructions for the priests. 'Rig Veda' often appears spelled as Rğ-Veda by dropping the 'i'. However, this is not necessary as it is simply an indication of slightly different dialects and pronunciation; a habit that is also common in the spelling of Krishna as Krśhna.

Brahmin priests say they are the *followers* of the teachings of Abraham, thus leaving little doubt about the impact that Abraham had on Hinduism. Nowhere do Brahmins say that they *taught* the *Vedas* to Abraham, but rather that they *learned* them from Abraham. Eupolemos has said that Abraham was regarded as the father of astrology who introduced the priests of Heliopolis to the study of all the sciences. It appears that before arriving in Heliopolis, Abraham had imparted his teachings to the Brahmins first.

Puranas

The historical information for Hindus is contained in the eighteen major *Puranas*. The word purana means ancient, or old, and the general themes of the *Puranas* are history, cultural traditions, and literature written as one person telling the story to another.

The *Puranas* talk about the creation and destruction of many civilizations. They also speak about life in the universe, in other galaxies, and on other planets. It is in the *Puranas* that we come to realize the Brahmins had acquired astrological-cosmology known to the Sumerians. They both spoke of the ability of life to travel from one form of existence to another. They spoke in similar terms about the ability to communicate between different worlds. Most of the *Puranas* obtained their final form around 500 CE. What is most interesting about the Puranas is that they are obviously based upon the Old and New Testaments. How do we know this? First because the stories are the same, and second because:

> 'The Puranas did not exist before the Old and New
> Testaments. It is in the Prathisara Parva chapter of the
> Bhavishya Purana that the true source of the Puranas, the
> Bible, becomes evident.' (M.M. Ninan **45**)

The *Puranas* serve as guide books for the whole of Hindu life and society. To be regarded as official *Puranas*, five topics must be covered in their texts. These are:

1.) original creation of the universe

2.) cycle of destruction and recreation

3.) manvantaras or yugas (eras)

4.) history of the lunar and solar dynasties

5.) royal genealogies

(note: Solar dynasties in the Puranas, like Lunar dynasties are similar to Biblical chronologies kept since the Elohim)

Mahabharata and Ramayana

The *Mahabharata* and the *Ramayana* are the two great epics of Hindu literature. Thousands of smaller stories about the gods and goddesses are buried within these two works. They represent the two longest running texts in the world, containing over a million words each. The *Maha-bharata*, meaning "Great India" was written down 540 to 300 BC, but has a much older oral history, dating back to Abraham; it has been attributed to the sage Vyasa. They record *"the legends of the Bharatas, one of the Aryan tribal groups."* the word *Bharata* is formed from the Sanskrit root 'Bhara', which under the sway of the rule of vowelization, may assume the form 'Ibhar', 'Iber', 'Ibhray', 'Ibhri', 'Ibri', 'Ibrini' etc., words which all have been equated with the term Hebrew (another meaning of the term Savitr, the Sanskrit form of the term Hebrew is Brahmana) **(73,76,104)**

The *Mahabharata* is an account of the strife between two warring families, the Pandavas (Pandu, king of Hastinapura and his five sons) and the Kauravas (family of Karu). In the early 19th century the religion-ist Godrfey Higgins speculated that an ancient secret religious order known as the Pandeists were well established outside of India, and they held Pandu (Pan means all/Deus means god) in high esteem, and that worship of him was known from India to Ireland. Was the founder of the Pandus Abraham? The wars in the Mahabharata are compara-ble with Biblical struggles of King David and his family.

The *Mahabharata* and the *Gita* have had a minimum of three major revisions according to Brahmin scholars. These revisions may have continued into the 13th century, and perhaps even into the current century. The scholar Rhys Davids, author of *Buddhist India* feels this constant editing and re-editing was done by the priests, first and foremost, to show the supremacy of the Brahmins over the nagas and Buddhists.

That the wars of the *Mahabharata* are connected with the Biblical wars of King David seems a certainty. However the constant rewriting, along with later insertions of fantastic mythology into this epic, have blurred the edges so much that accurate comparisons can no longer be found.

Yudhisthira and Pandera

Yudhisthira was the leader of his family, the Pandavas, during the epic war with his cousins. The name is similar to the Talmud Pandera/Pantira/Ben-Pantere. At first, the name would appear to be a variation of the Egyptian word for 'The God Ra' or 'Pa-Ntr-Ra,' so original intention of the word Pandava may mean 'son of the god Ra.' Pantira translates as 'Panther,' a nickname associated with Jesus' grandfather, Jacob.

Are Pandera, Pandava, and Pantira close enough to have been the same name? Could this name be a link between the *Talmud* and the *Mahabharata*? Continued research may prove they once had a common origin, but the Talmud is clearly in error when it declares that the name of Jesus' father (or Miriam the hairdresser they mentioned as his mother) was Stada. The Talmud scholar Gustav Dalman has pointed out that these claims were associated with Rabbi Akiva of the second century. Obviously this Rabbi, and the numerous Hebrew writings after the first century, were all events long after the facts, and made at a time when Christians had long since separated themselves from Hebrews. The Jews wrote insulting comments about this new break-away sect and their founder Jesus, and rarely got their facts straight in the few brief historical comments they made. Gustav Dalman tells us;

> 'It is possible to recognize in 'panthera' a mutilated form of 'parthenos,' which is Greek for 'virgin.' Thus this form would have arisen out of 'ben parthena' ('son of the virgin' using an Aramaic ending) which was the meaning of the word intended among the Christians.'

Yudhishtira-Yuhid is a word that means 'warrior.' To be very specific, Yudhisthira is a *Hebrew* warrior and in this particular case, it was apparently based upon the life of King David. The Jerusalemites were also known as Yehudiya or Judeans, which means 'warriors of Yah' (Jehovah). To this day in Kashmir there can be found names ending in '*oo*' such as 'Dunoo' (Yahood-Jew), further signifying a Kashmiri descended from Hebrews of Yudhisthira. The *Mahabharata* battles take place around modern Delhi between 900-800 B.C., or between the era of Abraham and King David.

After the battles, a victorious Yudhisthira then ascended to the throne. Thereafter only his bloodline would produce future leaders. All future leaders in Judaism would come from the line of David. To follow the king lists in India is to follow the descendents of Yudhithistira, thus we are following the parallel lineage of Jesus, and indeed this will become apparent when we later examine these king lists more thoroughly.

A scene from the great battles of the *Mahabharata*, Krishna and Arjuna.

Buddha also has a bloodline back to Yudhisthira **(17, 77, 99)** If David was Yudhisthira (Yahud, the Jewish warrior) then Buddha and Jesus shared the same Jewish ancestor, King David.

The weary Pandu brothers eventually retired to the Himalayas where they entered the blissful 'City of the Gods.' Could this have been the legendary Shangri-La, or perhaps the Kashmir Valley? Yes, that does seem to be the intended meaning of the passages. There is a grave in Kashmir for Tanook, who was a grandson of David.

The *Ramayana* (The Journey of Rama or Rama Chandra) is an India epic story about Ram, whose extremely beautiful wife Sita was abducted by her former suitor, Ravana, King of Lanka. There is a terrible war, complete with strange flying machines and weaponry, which some translators equate with nuclear weapons. Ram wins the war and Sita is returned, her chastity and high moral character intact. Ram is then crowned king of Ayodhya (Iodia-Judea). Ram is one of the most popular heroes of India.

The brother of Ram was the founder of the city of Magadha. Is this a reference to a brother of Abraham? Abraham and his brother, Nahor, were the sons of Terah by one wife, and Sarah and her brother, Haran, were offspring of Terah by his other wife, a daughter of the Semitic chief, Haran. The city of Haran was named after this chief, and there is a place called Harwan in Kashmir, where the grave of Aaron is located. We will return to this in more detail later.

. So close are the religious foundations and folklore of Hinduism, Judaism, Christianity, and Islam, that Hinduism should be regarded as the *fourth* Abrahamic religion.

The beautiful Drapati, mother of the five Pandava brothers in the Mahabharata. Is this their Jewish Princess Mother?

Krishna

The names of Christ and Krishna are so similar that people often wonder if they were the same. Krishna states he is the 'Supreme Lord' in the *Bhagavad-Gita*: "I am the source of all spiritual and material worlds. Everything emanates from me." In the *New Testament* Christ said it this way: "Whosoever believes in me shall not perish but have everlasting life."

In Latin, Christus (Greek, Christos) literally means 'anointed' (*chriein*). In Sanskrit, this translates to Kristos or Krishna, meaning 'the object of attention' (worship).

The author Kersey-Graves (1813-1883) made a study of the attributes common between Jesus Christ and Krishna. He found what he recognized as 346 shared elements between the two men, some too amazing to be mere coincidence. The *Mahabharata*, as stated earlier, takes place around the time of King David, and it was in the *Mahabharata* that Krishna first appeared. There are actually *three* separate Krishnas (or anointed ones) in the *Mahabharata*. By the time the *Bhagavad-Gita* reached its final form, around 500 A.D., a single Krishna figure had emerged and been elevated to a god, or a Christ-like figure. This may have a clear explanation in the fact that the final form of the *Bhagavad-Gita* was written during and after the life of Christ, who seemed to have a tremendous influence on the final version of the *Gita.*

There are 103 Sanskrit names for Krishna; one of these is Ishvara, or Isha (Issa) the name of Jesus in India. Christos and Krishna had obviously been used as descriptive *titles* that had been associated with different men throughout history. The word Krishna also means 'anointed one.' It could just as easily have been used as a title for Gautama Buddha or any anointed king. The origins for the names of Krishna and Christ both lay with Egypt. In Islam Krishna becomes Kahan or Kanhaya, but otherwise Islam barely makes note of any religions other than Hebrews and Christians, certainly nothing we can directly relate to Buddhism or Zoroastrianism, two prominent religions of the era..

Krishna is regarded as the eighth reincarnation of Vishnu. Krishna is the Hindu god most often compared with Jesus. For Hindus, this *is* their Jesus, the one who will destroy all pain, end all suffering, and bring love back into the world. He is the embodiment of love and joy and he will destroy all sin. Krishna was also physically, irresistibly, appealing. Ancient texts dwell at length on his exceptionally alluring countenance: a blue complexion soft like the monsoon cloud, shining locks of black hair framing a beautifully chiseled face, large lotus like eyes. He is always portrayed with blue skin, peacock feathers, yellow clothing, and holding a flute to signify his joy for life and creativity.

The reasons are lost in antiquity as to why the color of Krishna's skin is always blue. The closest anyone can come to an explanation is Krishna's association with the sky and/or with dark water (perhaps meaning the sea). Another legend has Krishna drinking poison to save the world, thus leaving his skin permanently altered. Interestingly, there is a similar story in several Eastern Thomasine traditions in India about the young Jesus. The Brahmins were amazed by his powers and decided to test him secretly. They gave him a dose of deadly poison, expecting him to die. His skin became an unusual color, but he survived, thus proving he was more god than man.

Jesus (in uncial Greek IHCOYC) is the Greek form of the Hebrew name Yeshua, which had also been the name of one of the High Priests during the Persian period. The name 'Yeshua', spelled Yod Shin Vav 'Ain, derives from the verb Yasha, which means 'He Saved'. The name 'Joshua' (Yehoshua') also comes from this verb, and is also rendered as IHCOYC in Greek. In Sanskrit, Yeshua-Joshua is Parshva.

Christos is related to the word 'chrism', meaning ointment. A 'Christos' was someone who was anointed. The word is a Greek translation of the Hebrew term 'Meshiach', which is derived from the verb Mashach (he anointed). The term 'Christian' is derived from the word 'Christos', the 'ian' ending being an adjective. 'Christianity' is more-or-less 'the Christian thing', and is probably the equivalent of Meshikhayutha in Aramaic.

'Krishna' is also interpreted as 'dark' demonstrated in all of the pictures of Krishna. The Greek equivalent could also be 'melos' or 'melanos'; Hebrew 'choshek' and the Syriac/Aramaic 'kheshuka' or perhaps 'kheshukaya'(a dark one). The name 'Yeshua' starts with a 'y' in Hebrew and Aramaic.

'Islam' comes from one of the secondary meanings of s-l-m, in this case, 'to submit' or 'to surrender'.

Krishna and Radha

In his early years, Krishna is lighthearted, sensual, and playful, even overly promiscuous. He's often depicted languishing seductively in some grassy meadow, playing a flute and enjoying the company of many beautiful young girls who beg for his attention. Gods in Indian mythology always have a consort, a companion. For Krishna, it was the sweet and beautiful Radha who stole his heart and helped him to turn inward. She opened the deeply spiritual within him, and he realized the great wisdom he had to share with the world. Radha became a role model of love, fidelity, and inspiration that most women in India today still hold up as the ideal woman and partner in life, and Krishna as the ideal man.

Shiva and shiva-lingams

The first use of the word Shiva (Mahadeva) appears in the *Rig Vedas* to mean something or someone 'auspicious.' Of the three major deities in India today, Brahma, Ram, and Shiva, Shiva has the largest following. Its origins apparently go back to the Egyptian priests at the Temple of Amun **(7)** The word lingam means 'form' and it is believed that the shape was chosen from a random shape appearing in nature that would signify God as 'formless.' That is not looking like man, or beast or any living thing that could be worshipped on earth. The name Isaac (Ishaack) means 'friend of God, Shiva.' Ishmael (Ish-mahel) means the great god or the great Shiva. Shiva's place of abode was Mount Kailasa and Shiva's consort was Kali.

Shiva is worshipped in the form of lingams, which are usually simple egg-shaped stones of all sizes that occur in nature, or are fashioned and polished from natural stones. Lingams are also associated with phallic symbols.

Shiva Lingam, oval-shaped stones represent God as the creator of universal seeds of life. Photo courtesy of Bob Keller, Private lingam collection, Phoenix, Az.

Shiva lingam: This type of linga is known as ekamukha (one-faced). In the rock- cut caves at Udayagiri. Photo by Dr. M.M. Ninan

Shiva Lingams made of stone, decorated with flowers by worshippers, Brihadishwara Temple, Tanjoor, India

Nandi-Chamundi Hills, Mysore, India. Huge Brahmin cattle roam freely and unmolested in the traffic of New Delhi, and are celebrated in the yearly Pola festivities.

A replica of Nandi the bull is usually placed near Shiva (lingam) during worship of a lingam to represent Brahma, or the soul of man being improved and protected while waiting for God. The shiva-lingam represents the primal energy of the Creator. In the Hindu views of the universe lingams possess the same powers of 'energy collection' as pyramids.

The Shiva lingam is also symbol of the pillar of fire. Like Abraham, Vishnu (as Brahma) went in search of the pillar of fire but was unable to trace it. It was at a temple of Siwa that Alexander spoke with the priests at Amun before setting off on his epic journey to the Himalayas.

There may also be an ancient origin for the shiva-lingam in the Benben stone. The conical-shaped stone is best known in Ireland, but the idea arrived there straight from Egypt, copied from the sacred rights at Heliopolis. The conical stone represents the seeds of life, or divine seeds of the cosmos being distributed to mankind.

Islam

Islam has come very late on the religious scene, certainly well after Christianity. We will examine its foundations in the same spirit and with the same scrutiny applied to other religions covered here, and see exactly where historical connections are, and where they are not.

We have already found Hindus and Hebrews connected in unexpected ways. Although Muslims claim they are one of the Abrahamic religions, actually they are not. These are recent claims to help them solidify their holdings on places they now have in their possession. In truth their origins are distinctly separate. They actually have their origins within paganism and Hinduism, not the more organized forms of religions such as Judaism or Christianity. Mohammed was well aware of this and spoke of it in the Qur'an. At the beginning of his life Mohammed naturally followed the religion of his tribe, which centered on the moon god Durga- Al-Ilat, the primary god of the 354 or so represented in the Kabba.

The religions practiced at the Kabba reflected many gods in the manner of the Hindus. Mohammed rejected the numerous gods in favor of one God. According to theologian Karen Armstrong (3) Mohammed wanted to emulate the practices of the Jews and Christians to raise his stature and business standing in their eyes even before he claimed prophetic visions from Gabriel.

Islam is connected with India and the shiva-lingam in unexpected ways. King Vikramaditiya, not Abraham, is best documented at Mecca. King Vikramaditiya, as noted earlier, was as famous and beloved in India as King Arthur in Europe. The Arabs at Mecca had even dedicated a gold plate to this king. Details of this plate were recorded in the *Sayar-ul-Okul,* which is now kept at the Sultania Library in Istanbul. Excerpts from the inscription on the plaque include these lines:

> '...The entire country (Arabia) was enveloped in darkness as intense as on a new moon night.... But the present dawn and pleasant sunshine of education is the result of the favor of the noble king Vikramaditya whose benevolent supervision did not lose sight of us- foreigners as we were... He spread his sacred

religion amongst us and sent scholars whose brilliance shone like that of the sun from his country to ours. These scholars and preceptors through whose benevolence we were once again made cognizant of the presence of God, come to our country to preach their religion and impart education at king Vikramaditiya behest...'

There were 354 idols in the temple of Mecca, almost one for each day and season of the year (based on the Arabic lunar calendar). These represented all the major deities of the traders who passed by on the main thoroughfare. This can be thought of as one of the first truly international and inter-denominational houses of worship in the world. Built by Brahmins, it reflected complete religious tolerance and sharing of worship and ideas with all faiths. The Vedic heritage of India was richly represented here. The main deity of the temple was Durga (Hubal), the Hindu moon god, who was the chosen deity of Mohammed's father and grandfather. This may have been historically based upon the Sumerian moon-god 'Sin' (Sinai means 'Land of Sin') the god who also used the crescent moon as his personal symbol.

Al-Lat, al-Uzza, and Manat, collectively known as al-Gharaniq or the Daughters of God (Allah), and Hubal, a martial deity, were well know to the Arabs. The matron goddess of Mohammed's tribe was the youngest one of the three sister goddesses, al-Uzza, her name meant "the mighty one". The father of al-Uzza and her sisters was "al-Llah", the moon god. "Verily they are the exalted maidens and their interces-sion is to be hoped for." (Quran) This is how the word Allah became synonymous with the word God, after the word Ar-Rahman (the merciful one) was first considered God by Mohammed, and then changed in favor of Al-Lah. **(80,82)**

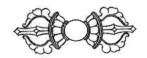

Allah in Arabic   Pakistan flag with emblem of Durga-Al-Lat

The god Neela khanda (blue throated Shiva) with sacred bull and guardian snakes, drinking of the poisoned waters of the cosmos to save the world; wears the crescent moon symbol of Durga-Al Ilah, the favored god of Mohammed's tribe.

The goddess Durga-Al-Lat recovered from a destroyed Vedic temple in Amman, Jordon (Picture Courtesy of Hindu unity.org)

Durga was represented by the crescent moon, a symbol that is still worn daily on the forehead of the followers of Durga in India. The crescent moon was the symbol associated with the primary gods worshipped in the Kaaba, which is why it has remained the symbol of Islam for Muslims. The words Garbha and Graha-Gabha mean Kabba, is the Sanskrit word for temple or Sanctuary. The word Allah is a contraction of Al-ilah, 'al' meaning 'the' and 'ilah' meaning 'goddess' or 'deity' in Arabic. Al-ilah does not come from the words El or Elohim. These words are of completely different and unknown ethnicity. The word Allah in Arabic now means one supreme God, and the word is commonly used to represent one god of Christians and Jews. However, in Sanskrit Allah signifies the mother goddess Durga (or Bhavani or Chandi). The Kaaba was dedicated to Al-lat and Al-Uzza both of which are forms of the Mother Goddess Shakti. The structure of the temple attested to the fact that it was based on the Tantric iconography of Devi Durga. Further, the god associated with Abraham is historically called *Elohei Avraham* meaning 'the god of Abraham, Isaac, and Jacob.' It has no relation to the words al-ilah.

Allah of Palmyra Picture Courtesy of Hindu unity.org

Sadhu in modern India. After thousands of years' traditions, they still paint religious symbols on their foreheads, including the crescent moon to represent the goddess Durgha. Allat is the moon God (lord Siva) and Allah (Goddess Durga) is the moon Goddess who is his heavenly (or Godly) wife.

Although Islam professes just one God, he can be manifested in 99 different names, which follows the Hindu concept of multiple manifestations of one God. For example, Krishna has 103 Sanskrit names.

Mohammed rejected worship of multiple gods at Mecca, aligning himself instead with the Hebrew concept of monotheism. According to Karen Armstrong, author of *A History of God* (3) this is when Mohammed also tried to identify with the Jews and converted to Judaism. He even proposed that he himself be recognized as a Jewish prophet. He was rejected outright by most Jews and Christians, primarily on the basis that he was not Hebrew blood, nor of the bloodline of King David. Their rejection then drove Mohammed back to the practices that were most familiar to him, learned from the Brahmin priests at Mecca. This is evident in the use of loan words from Sanskrit to Arabic, such as the word Islam, itself is a derivative of the Sanskrit word Isha-ayalem, which means 'Shiva's temple.' From this, we get the word Islam. 'Moshe-alayem' becomes 'Muslim.'

The wearing of white while circumnavigating the Kabba seven times is also an ancient Hindu practice that was never adopted by either Jews or Christians. Hindus recognize entire prayers taken directly from their sacred scriptures, word for word, and inserted into the Quran. There can be no doubt that it was Hinduism, not Judaism that had the biggest impact on shaping Islam, the religion of Mohammed. Curiously, although Buddhists were also well-known in the Arabian the world of Mohammed, he chose never to acknowledge them, and this has left Buddhism in a particularly vulnerable and low position in the eyes of the Muslim world. As we continue, we will come to know that Islam, like any other religion, has its fundamentalists, those who act out of unreasonable passion instead of 'reason.' This is having a devastating effect on world cultures, one we must eventually examine in this book, in relation to consequences at the tomb of Jesus, for these represent critical evaluations that have to be made regarding the future fate of that tomb and the artifacts that will identify beyond all doubt if Jesus is indeed buried at Roza Bal tomb. We will refer to this problem gradually throughout this book, as we first build up the background history of Jesus' family in India.

Islam is a religion that believes in rescuing people from eternal damnation through their conversion. Hinduism and Buddhism believe in letting the individual choose his or her path according to one's inner convictions and scale of evolution (karma-dharma or free will). Christians believe that Baptism is an absolute necessity, an outward sign of an inner conviction to follow God's laws (the Ten Commandments) and believe that Jesus died and resurrected for the sins of the world. The concept of resurrection and return is common to all four religions (ascensions, reincarnations, and resurrections of the dead in one manner or another).

The Graves of Abraham and Sarah

Genesis 23:1-2:

> Sarah lived one hundred and twenty seven years and Sarah died in Kiriath-arba (Hebron) in the land of Canaan. Abraham went in to mourn for her and he wept.

Abraham purchased the Cave of Machpelah and buried Sarah there. From the *Testament of Abraham:*

> 'Abraham lived all his years in quietness, gentleness, and righteousness, and was exceedingly hospitable. He received everyone both rich and poor, kings and rulers, the maimed and the helpless, friends and strangers, neighbors and travelers. God summoned his arch-angel Michael and said: 'Go down to Abraham and speak to him concerning his death, that he may set his affairs in order, for I have blessed him as the stars of heaven and the sands of the shores, and he is in abundance of long life and many possessions and is exceedingly rich.
>
> Beyond all men, moreover, he has been righteous, hospitable, and loving to the end of his life. Go to Abraham and announce to him his death and assure him thus: Thou shalt at this time depart from this world and shalt quit thy body and go to thy Lord. So Abraham finished seeing to the needs of the living and beloved. His family tended to his body with divine ointments until the third day after his death, and buried him in the land of promise, near the oak tree of Mamre. And Isaac buried his father beside his mother Sarah, glorifying and praising God.'

The Cave of Machpelah

The Cave of Machpelah is the world's most ancient Jewish site. It is also the second holiest place for Jewish people, after the Temple Mount in Jerusalem. The cave and the adjoining field are located in Hebron, and were purchased at full market price by Abraham. Abraham, Isaac, Jacob, Sarah, Rebecca and Leah are all buried here. They are considered the patriarchs and matriarchs of the Jewish people. The only one missing is Rachel, who died in childbirth and was buried near Bethlehem. (The nearby tomb of Joseph the Patriarch was completely destroyed by the Arab PLO on October 7, 2000 in an act of Archaeological terrorism).

The existence of this double cave has been a mystery for thousands of years. It was recently uncovered beneath a massive building constructed during the Second Temple Period by Herod, King of Judea. It was meant to serve as a gathering place for Jewish prayers at the graves of these patriarchs. The graves can still be visited today, providing one is *not* Jewish. Tragically, Muslims have built a mosque here, and with relentless and unreasonable religious intolerance, have effectively banned Hebrews from entry.

Clearly, this grave marks the end of a long journey for Abraham and Sarah, one that began from their ancestral home in the Himalayas. The cradle of Judaism has not been so small that it was confined to the deserts of Sinai and Egypt. It is broader in scope than anything previously imagined.

Whether you remember them as the gods Abraham/Ram/Brahma and Sarasvati-Sita, or whether you remember them as the Hebrew prophets Abraham and Sarah, their lives have had powerful and lasting influence on the destiny of mankind, an influence still determining the fate of the entire world today.

"Every man of the children of Israel shall pitch by his own standard, with the ensign of his father's house." - Num. 2:2

"And one of the elders saith unto me, Weep not: behold, the Lion of the tribe of Judah, the Root of David, hath prevailed to open the book, and to loose the seven seals thereof." Rev.5:5

Emblem of Jerusalem with lion. This symbol spread with the Jews. The Lion of Judah appears on the flag of Ethiopia, the flag of Sri Lanka, of Tibet, and on the heraldry of the royal families of Europe and Asia.

The tomb of the Patriarchs in Hebron was built over the cave of Machpelah by Herod the Great. This is the world's most sacred site for Hebrews. Here rest Abraham, Isaac, Jacob, Sarah, and Leah. Jews are now barred access and Christians are also discouraged from coming here, an act of religious intolerance towards others. Yet nearby at the Christian and Jewish historical sites, such as Church of the Sepulcher and the Wailing Wall, Muslim Arabs enter freely, and often work as guides for tourists.

4. Abraham

Tomb of Joseph the Patriarch being destroyed in October, 2003: smoke billowed from the tomb as Arabs burned priceless Jewish prayer books and other articles. With pickaxes and hammers they began to tear apart the stone building. Two days later the dome of the tomb was painted green to mock the Jews. This is identical with Wahabi-Taliban destruction of the Bamiyan Buddha, and what 'could' also happen at the tomb of Jesus in Kashmir.

The ancient sarcophagus of Joseph covered in black cloth and plastic for protection, as it looked when Jews cared for the grave.

The sarcophagus after the Arabs and PLO smashed it in an act of religious intolerance and cultural terrorism. Can this happen at Roza Bal tomb?

The Book of Joshua says, "Joseph's bones, which the Israelites had brought up from Egypt, were buried at Shechem in the tract of land that Jacob bought…This became the inheritance of Joseph's descendants." On April 2, 2002 armed Palestinian Arab terrorists forced their way into the Church of the Nativity in Bethlehem, one of Christianity's most sacred sites, and remained for 38 days, desecrating the Church and leaving human excrement in the sanctuaries. Ariel Cohen, *National Review,* said;

> *'Using priests and nuns as human shields in the most sacred location for Christianity is not just barbaric. It is a violation of the 1977 First Protocol to the Geneva Convention and is a war crime. Similar cases from the Balkan wars are heard today before the International Criminal Court in the Hague. Only brutal terrorists would desecrate religious shrines and hurt clergy...'*

The definition of terrorism, whether directed at civilians, culture, or archaeology, is defined as attacks against anyone or anything outside of normal government military in uniform.

"Violence, destruction of personal property, threats, or intimidation to achieve personal ends...." (Harper-Collins Dictionary, 2004)

"Religious intolerance may be purely religious, but can be a "cover story" for underlying political or cultural motives. Some countries retain blasphemy laws, forbidding defamation of religious belief, which are sometimes seen as a way of condoning religious intolerance, the connection between intolerance and blasphemy laws is most closely connected if the laws apply to only one religion." (Wikipedia)

The United Nations upholds the right to freedom of religious belief in article 18 of the Universal Declaration of Human Rights, while article 2 forbids discrimination on the basis of religion. Article 18 also allows for the freedom to change religion.

Above: Symbols of world religion

We have covered the importance of Enoch on the world religious stage, the grave of Noah in Kashmir, the roots of Islam in Hinduism, and the destruction of the tomb of Joseph the Patriarch. These acts of cultural terrorism will become relevant to the tomb of Jesus later in the book. For now, we look to Aaron and Moses and the significance of their graves in Kashmir, for it was at the homestead of Aaron that the Fourth Buddhist Council would be held and we will look for Jesus there.

We have learned about the importance of Enoch on the world religious stage, the grave of Noah in Kashmir, the roots of Islam in Hinduism, and the destruction of the tomb of Joseph the Patriarch. These acts of cultural terrorism are relevant to the tomb of Jesus. For now, we look to Aaron and Moses and the significance of their graves in Kashmir, for it was at the homestead of Aaron that the Fourth Buddhist Council would be held when Jesus may have actually presided over the events.

'Jewel in the Lotus' means wisdom can be found by understanding the small simple things first; This Thai script was connected with the Royal Gupta court of India, which used many Hebrew words and symbols

5. Moses

After a long history with the Egyptians and the Israelites, Moses stood at the threshold to the Promised Land but he did not enter. And from this very moment, we begin to look to Kashmir for the answers, and for his grave. He was 120 years old when he died;

> 'And Moses died there… in the land of Moab, by the word of God. And they buried him in Gai, in the land of Moab, facing Beth Peor, and man does not know his gravesite to this day. '

Deuteronomy, 34:6-7

We may have wrongly assumed it was a punishment of Moses because he didn't enter the Promised Land. What makes matters worse is that Beth Peor, according to the Jewish Encyclopedia, is associated with a primary, idolatrous god, Baal. According to the Jewish Encyclopedia, Peor was a mountain in Moab. In Hebrew, Beth means 'a house' or 'house of' and peor means a gaping or opening, as in a mountain. According to Eusebius this was once a city situated six Roman miles from Livias (or Beth-haran) near Mount Peor. According to another statement of Eusebius this mountain lay on the road from Livias to Heshbon. But no place corresponding to these descriptions has ever actually been identified, except in Kashmir.

Then to add further to the confusion, it was written in a part of the Talmud called the *Sotah*, 13b (The literature called Sotah is actually a chapter, called a Tractate, of the Mishnah) that 'Moses *didn't* die.' What does this mean? The Torah records his gravesite, then goes on to contradict itself.

According to Rabbi Israel Chait, Moses was referred to as a 'Sachel Nifrad'... 'a separated intelligence.' This means to say that Moses reached the highest level of any human; he operated completely through his intelligence and in complete control of his instincts. The Rabbinical conclusion is that God must have *orchestrated* the event of his death in order that there would be no possibility that Moses become deified.

There is a Midrashic (allegorical) statement that Rabbi Israel Chait also mentions as significant. After Moses died, wicked people sought out his burial site. When they were at the summit of the mountain, they saw his gravesite at the base. When they were at the base below, they saw it at the summit. They decided to break up into two groups: those at the base saw his site at the summit, and those at the summit, saw Moses' gravesite at the base. Then, they realized that what both groups saw was a *projection* built out from the mountain. This exactly describes the grave we are about to visit in Kashmir.

In the Himalayas, not far from the grave of Jesus, there are graves for both Aaron and Moses. The name of the mountain that Moses is buried on is called Bandipore, the Sanskrit version of the Biblical word Beth-Peor, meaning a gap in the mountains where the river runs through. Further, there is a place nearby known as Harwan (Haroon-Haran-Aron), which could be the same place mentioned above as

Beth-Haran (beth-house/haran-Aron). There are over 300 places in Kashmir and Judea that share the same name. Therefore, having a name is no assurance that we have identified the correct location. The Biblical Beth Peor could be the Kashmir location. There is no reason why *not.* **(27, 36,37)**

Birth of Moses

The life of Moses, interestingly enough, shares over 100 correlations with what we know about the life of Jesus. Near the time of Moses' birth, astrologers (magi) also witnessed strange lights in the sky. Deaths of all the male children were also ordered at the time of Moses' birth. Auspicious and 'unnatural' signs surrounded the birth of both Moses and Jesus. However, are there any unexplained and unusual events *outside* the Bible, or are the Bible stories unique to the experiences of mankind?

The answer is that from Pharaohs to common footmen, the unusual signs in the sky were witnessed and recorded by everyone. For example Thutmoses 3rd reigned during the period that is historically referred to as the 18th Dynasty of Egypt, a period associated with Moses. He is regarded as one of Egypt's greatest pharaohs during one of Egypt's greatest eras. Thutmoses ordered that hieroglyphs be made to detail what he and his army witnessed, something that left a strong impression upon them all:

> In the year 22 of the 3rd month of winter, a circle of fire was coming through the sky. As the days passed more circles appeared. When they gathered, they were brighter than the sun. The army of the pharaoh watched with him. Then the fires ascended higher in the sky and towards the south. Then they disappeared after several days.

The magi followed a star to find Jesus, the star that shepherds saw hovering over his manger. In *Exodus* 13:21 we are told about a similar star that behaved in a similar unnatural way as Moses led the Israelites during their Exodus:

> 'Yahweh went before them by day in a pillar of cloud to lead the way, and by night in a pillar of fire. They had light to go by day or night.'

In *Genesis*, one will find 362 verses describing flying objects as vehicles, as well as 162 verses describing specific flight patterns. Such independent descriptions also appear in the Vedic writings of India, and in China. The Chinese wrote of the *'12 Celestial Emperors'* who arrived from the stars. Their book, *Memories of the Sovereigns and Kings*, details how these sons from the stars would visit earth on vehicles of transportation.

An ancient Chaldean book from the *Sifria* (library or collection of literature) contains over a hundred pages of technical details for the building of flying machines. What Thutmoses 3rd witnessed was not an isolated incident. He was not describing worship or fearful encounters. He was describing something unusual in the sky, witnessed by many. He felt it was unusual enough to deserve special mention.

The translation in the NIV (*New International Version Bible*) describes Moses at his birth as *'not an ordinary child.'* The *Quran* (28:9) says:

> Pharaoh's wife said: (He will be) a joy to the eye for me and you. Don't kill him. He may be of use to us or we may take him as a son.

How could they have determined so quickly that this 'ordinary' Hebrew child could 'be of use' to them? Immediately we realize these were not ordinary circumstances. They knew exactly who he was and what his genealogy was. The mother of Moses was Jochebed (nobility of Jo/Ya). In the adjusted Biblical/Egyptian chronologies, she is also Queen Tiye, the mother of the Pharaoh Akhenaten. Tiye was the daughter of the Prime Minister Ya (Vizier Yuya) who governed Egypt during the reigns of the Pharaohs Thutmose IV and Amenhotep 3rd. If she was indeed the mother of Moses, then his birth is very significant. If his birth was 'auspicious' in the same way that the birth of Jesus or Noah was auspicious, then we immediately begin to understand why these children were set apart since birth. Could these be continued examples of interference from the Elohim? Remember that we still don't have an arrival and departure time for them, or a satisfying explanation for who they represent in Genesis, and so for the purposes of this book we will examine history with a mindful eye to their unex-plained presence in mankind's affairs.

Genealogies and Legitimacy of Birth

Because the pharaohs served in hereditary positions, legitimacy of birth was essential, hence the need for careful accuracy in keeping genealogical records (Josephus '*Contra Ap*'). In addition, the high priest could only marry an Israelite maiden (*Levi:* 21). Her birth on foreign soil was not considered a disqualification. All high priests had to be married. They could divorce, but as high priests they could not have concubines or multiple wives, a rule not imposed upon kings.

The keeping of genealogical records is really what the Bible is all about. It's one continual family record from Adam to Jesus. There is nothing else like it on earth. King lists and pedigrees of all sorts exist for individual families. A portion of Siddhartha Buddha's genealogy has been retained by the proud Sinhalese in Sri Lanka **(77, 99)**

Family records in India have also been retained, where it was a great source of pride to have a bard recites a family's history from scrolls made of cloth or paper. Some family records have been recovered from long inscriptions on stone. In western India, reciting a family history once a year is still practiced today. Kalhana calls these family records Prashasti Prattas, sources of great pride for those families who have retained their records. There are Hebrews who claim to have retained family records going directly back to King David. The search is on for records that would prove Jesus was married and had children.

As a hereditary descendent from Aaron for the priesthood, it was essential that the genealogy of Jesus should also be maintained. The Bible gives us two such possible genealogies, one being through his father Joseph, and the other through his mother, Mary. However, Jewish law required that high priests be descended directly through the father, *not* through the mother. By Jewish tradition then, women are never listed in the genealogical links.

With this in mind, there appears to have been an exception made in the case of Jesus, which would seem to strengthen the assumption that his father was *not* Joseph. The true father would have to have ranked at least as high as Joseph, and yet still be considered more important in the Hebrew lineage than even Joseph himself. Had it been otherwise, any illegitimate child of Mary's would immediately have been stricken from the records.

The Jewish laws were far too strict regarding these hereditary titles to allow for any child born of questionable genetics, to any mother of questionable loyalty to her husband, to be accorded such prominence as Jesus achieved. However, this would *not* apply to children of the Elohim. We saw at the birth of Noah, when his father lamented at the strangeness of the child, he knew immediately that this had been a creation of the Elohim, and he was counseled to raise the child with all due love and care as he would for any natural child.

Jewish rules established for the lineage of high priests included instructions for all to be anointed with sacred oils while wearing sacred garments. To the Jews, the high priest candidate becomes *merubbeh begadim* after wearing the pontifical garments. The first consecration for this priesthood was performed on Aaron by Moses. It was the high priest alone who could offer sacrifices for the sins of the people, including the other priests. He participated in ceremonies on the Sabbath, the New Moon, and other festivals. The high priest was also subject to the jurisdiction of the courts, and if accused of a crime entailing capital punishment, he was tried by the Great Sanhedrin. It was a High Priest alone who could refuse to give testimony (Sanh.18) just as Jesus had refused to give testimony at his own trial.

Moses established these laws of the priesthood, and these would later be the key issues raised at the trial and crucifixion of Jesus, the Sanhedrin, and the Hasmonean Jews all challenged Jesus' right to be referred to both as rabbi (kohen) and as king (through his lineage from King David). In actual fact, it was both Mary and Jesus who were put on trial that day.

Establishment of the High Priesthood

Aaron, of the tribe of Levi, was the 14th generation grandfather of Mother Mary. God designated Aaron as the first High Priest (ha-kohen in Exodus 28:1-2). The word Ko-hen means 'one who will stand firm with a strong base on earth.' The kohen stood as the mediator between man and God. He was the base rooted firmly in the soil, and his stalk stood tall and represented all the people before God. Succession was hereditary and passed directly through one of his sons, thus remaining in his own family.

Failing to have a son meant that the next eldest brother of the High Priest would assume the role. On the day that Moses anointed Aaron, the two eldest sons of Aaron, Nadab and Abihu, both young priests, died at the Tabernacle. It is their deaths that are remembered every year at Yom Kippur, the Hebrew time of fasting and atonement for sins.

Abihu is used in Sanskrit as part of a priestly title as in 'Abi-manyu' and 'Abi-Athar.' The king of Taxila, Gondopharnes, had a brother who bore the title Abdi-gases. This is based on inscriptions found on coins unearthed at Taxila dating to circa 55 CE. The name Iosha (Greek for Issa) also appears on coins of the same period. King Meghavahana (who may have been James, an 'abdigasses') was known as an Abi-manyu, according to the *Rajatarangini*. Meghavahana becomes an important name on the Kashmir king list because he lived during the years Jesus resided in Kashmir. Later we will return to look for further connections between this king and Jesus.

An earlier attempt to define Abraham's name suggested that the Egyptian translation of Ab is 'father,' thus Abi (father, or Abihu, son of) manyu is God or king. So a loose translation of Abiathar, Abdigases, Abihu, or Abimanu could be:

'the son of a father who was a son of God' or, *'a priest descended from God.'*

Civil authorities later usurped this law about hereditary priesthood in favor of the 'right of appointment.' This enabled Herod to appoint no less than six chief priests of his own choosing. However, it was the Sanhedrin who had the real power to decide who would be their high priest, for without their support, ruling would be very difficult for anyone in office. Before the exile, high priests were appointed for life. The minimum age for such appointments was twenty years, although Aristobolus was only seventeen when appointed by Herod. All this is being mentioned because a similar title appears on the king list in the *Rajatarangini* during the era of Jesus **(16,51)**. As noted, we need to return to this title later when we discuss it in Kashmir. For now, we are still gathering the background information about these names and titles.

Thy Rod and Staff Shall Comfort Me

The rods of Moses and Aaron figure prominently in Biblical stories, and the *same* rod will figure prominently at the tomb of Jesus, but first let us examine the history of rods in general. They are far more significant that being mere walking sticks or shepherd staffs. Rods were symbols of authority used to summon the gods. In India and China rods were described as 'parasols' casting a shield of power and protection over the bearer. In some instances in the *Rajatarangini* (in the Third Taranga **16,51**) parasols possessed the same magic powers as rods and staffs. They could not only be used to summon the gods, but they could even initiate flight from one place to another.

During the same period that rods and parasols identified positions of authority, the Tocharians and Scythians used tamgas, a special brand or mark that identified their individual possessions. The tamga forms remained unchanged for thousands of years, and this enabled scholars to trace entire family genealogies and movements. Thus, if rods or other relics are recovered from graves and tombs, it may be possible to make a positive family identification if a family tamga mark can be identified on the relic.

By the Middle Ages heraldry replaced rods in terms of family identity, whereas in the days of Moses, a man's rod was the most significant personal item that he possessed.

Ezekiel 19:11;

> Its branches were strong. They were used to make scepters for kings. It grew to be tall with many branches around it, and everyone saw it because of its branches.

Ezekiel 19:14

> And fire is gone out of a rod of her branches, which hath devoured her fruit, so that she hath no strong rod to be a scepter to rule. This is a lamentation....

Numbers 17:

> And it shall come to pass that the man's rod that I choose, shall blossom...

> And Moses spoke to the children of Israel, and every one of their princes gave him a rod apiece, for each prince had one, according to their father's houses. There were twelve rods, and among these was the rod of Aaron.

> And Moses laid these rods before the Lord in the tabernacle. And Aaron's rod sprouted and brought forth ripe almonds.

The Rod of Moses was so sacred that it was stored in the Ark of the Covenant with the Ten Commandments.

The *Jewish Encyclopedia* and *The Book of the Bee* **(105)** both say that Aaron and Moses performed miracles with this rod. After the death of Aaron, it was Joshua who next received it from Moses. From there, it was passed on to Phinehas. Then it remained hidden until the time of Jesus. After the visit of the magi at the birth of Jesus, Joseph then had the rod and brought it on his journey to Egypt with Mary and the infant Jesus. Author Peter Michas **(44B)** believes that, according to *The Book of Revelations,* this rod will reappear when the messiah returns.

Peter Michas and Robert Vander Maten, authors of *The Rod of an Almond Tree in God's Master Plan* **(44B)** have traced rabbinical stories suggesting that the rod came from an almond tree that was associated with the Garden of Eden, where it was first given to Adam. From there, it was passed down successively to Enoch, Shem, Abraham, Isaac, Jacob, Joseph, Jesse, David, Aaron and Moses in succession.

In an earlier chapter, it was suggested that Kashmir may have been the Garden of Eden. There are still almond trees in the sacred grove in Kashmir. This means we can speculate on a hypothesis. With this mounting evidence, it suggests that Adam was in Kashmir when it was like a Garden of Eden, and there he obtained the rod made from a tree in the sacred almond grove (the site still exists there today). What is most exciting is that the rod may actually exist in Kashmir today. This is not speculation. This is about the actual rod that was mentioned in the Bible. It was hidden in Kashmir 2,000 years ago in the tomb of Jesus. It can be examined, tested, and a determination can be made whether it is authentic or not.

Peter Michas goes on to say that, according to the *Midrash Yehlamdenu:*...the staff with which Jacob crossed the Jordan is identical with that which Judah gave to his daughter-in-law Tamar (*Genesis* 32:10) It is likewise the holy rod with which Moses worked

(*Exodus* 4:20) and with which Aaron performed wonders before Pharaoh (*Exodus* 7:10) and finally was with David when he slew the giant' (*Samuel* 17:40).

Revered by both Hebrews and Christians the world over, the 23rd Psalm is one of the most beloved, and well-known prayers in the world. The words have comforted and fortified men and women facing hardship and death. People who may not have known any other prayer in their lives at least know this one.

'The Lord is my shepherd, I shall not want...'

This segment of the prayer mentions the rod:

'Yeah though I walk through the valley of the shadow of death I will fear no evil for thou art with me; thy rod and thy staff they comfort me....'

It was the prayer most often recited in the Roman Coliseum as Christians were put to death by lions and gladiators. It is still invoked by ministers and priests as they lead the condemned down death row. The prayer is universally cited at virtually all Hebrew and Christian funerals. For men and women lost at sea, or languishing in dungeons, or being led to pyres of flaming fire, these words were their last, uttered in the belief that God would hear them in their final anguished moments on earth.

How quickly we race over the words, *thy rod and staff shall comfort me.* It is easy to visualize a simple shepherd holding a curved staff as he tends his flocks. We liken ourselves to those sheep being watched over, protected by a great father figure. Have we ever given any thought to the possibility that we could be wrong, very wrong, that it may not be simply an allegory, a myth? When we realize that Jesus had just such a rod hidden in his tomb, a rod that exists to this day, the significance of the words *thy rod and staff* becomes something incredibly important.

Scepters, rods and staffs have been significant since recorded time. They are always featured in the depictions of pharaohs and kings. The Hyksos kings used the curved staff (HYK) on their Egyptian glyphs to designate the title 'Hyksos' or 'Shepherd Kings.'

Ralph Ellis (*Jesus, The Last Pharaoh* **(19)**

> Abraham, Isaac, Jacob, and Jesus were not a family of poor downtrodden shepherds and barefoot prophets at all. They were nothing less than the Hyksos Shepherd kings.... This is why the stories from the Bible have been told and retold.

It should also be noted that rods and staffs are mentioned dozens of times in the Bible. More than any other personal possession, neither crowns, nor gold, nor even vimanas, held the significance of a single scepter, for without this, nothing else was obtainable. The most memorable rods of all the rods are the rods of Moses and Aaron. And we are told repeatedly that the rod was made from the wood of an almond tree, as though no other wood was comparable. What qualities did the almond tree possess that other woods did not have? That's a mystery the world has yet to solve.

In *Genesis* 43:11, Jacob wanted his sons to take the best fruits, including an almond tree, as a present to Joseph. *Numbers* 17:8 and *Hebrew* 9:4 say that Aaron's rod yielded almonds. In *Exodus* 25:33, Moses was directed to make certain parts of the candlesticks for the Ark from the almond tree.

> *Exodus* 25:3-4
> 'And on the lamp stand there are to be four cups shaped like almond flowers with buds and blossoms'.

Menorah- a special Candlestick for Hanukkah.
Many were originally carved of almond wood

The earliest known name for Mount Moriah is actually Luz, which is the word for almond tree in Aramaic, Arabic, and Ethiopic. This could be based on almond trees that may once have thrived there. The city of Luz was associated with an immense almond tree. The Hebrew word Lutz is translated as hazel or almond in the *King James Bible* (*Genesis 30-37)'*.

Sacred Almond Groves

Near the grave of Jesus in Kanyhar, is a hill that dominates most of Srinagar. It is known as Hari Parbat Hill, a name we shall later identify with Jesus. This hill was once the site of an ancient sacred almond grove and extensive gardens of exotic and imported herbs and flowers. Because of the importance of the rods in the Bible, and because the sacred almond groves are in close proximity to many patriarchs" graves, we can assume the rod of Jesse. The rod of Moses, the rod of Aaron, the rod of Jesus were all chosen from special almond trees found only in Kashmir.

Ancient neglected almond tree; men would travel very great distances to acquire a rod made from only the finest and most sacred of almond trees. The rod was highly prized and could pass down for generations within a single family.

The Emperor Ashoka once had edicts placed along the Old Silk routes asking travelers to bring rare and new plants to his kingdom for the benefit of his subjects. **(67)** Brahmins were noted for their love of planting trees and maintaining exotic gardens. It was under their care that the sacred almond grove and the gardens of Hari Parbat hill thrived. If Jesus knew anything about healing, then he was aware of the unique medicinal plants that were brought to Kashmir from around the world.

Edict from King Ashoka in Prakrit Language; according to the Gospels of Thomas of the Eastern Church, Jesus knew Prakrit and used it often.

Srinagar, Kashmir: Hari Parbat Hill and the Red Fort on its summit: Tomb of Jesus is near its base. This hill was once dedicated to sacred almond groves; garden paths were lined with exotic plants gathered from all over the world, and small shrines were located along the paths. This is still a sacred mountain for Kashmiri Pandits.

The First and Second Temples

As the story unfolds in Kashmir, and we follow the trail of the Rod of Moses, something else becomes significant linking this past with the present and future. It has to do with the Temple Mount in Jerusalem, the Book of Revelations, and with the coming of the messiah as predicted by the Hebrews.

The First Temple at Mount Moriah, in Jerusalem, was completed in 961 B.C. by King Solomon. It was the first permanent home for the Ark of the Covenant. This represented a major shift in the Hebrew world, for no longer would they be considered a nomadic people. Now they would have this fixed place on earth to be identified with. This great temple stood for 400 years until it was destroyed by Nebuchadnezzar in 586 B.C. The Second Temple was rebuilt on the same spot, standing for another 400 years until it was destroyed by the Romans in 70 CE. The Ark of the Covenant then disappeared, and its location has remained a mystery ever since.

The Ark of the Covenant was built by Moses based upon specific and detailed instructions from God. What made this ark so different from all the other arks, boxes, and baris of the period? First, this ark was garishly overlaid with gold, similar in design to chests that have been recovered from the tombs of pharaohs. This ark was not at all 'subtle' in appearance. Richly overlaid with gold, it was described as having mystical powers. Possession of this particular ark would not be an easy secret to keep. A 'cloud' occasionally hung over the ark, signifying the presence of God. It had properties that behaved some-what like a battery or 'super-conductor,' electrically charged and quite capable of terrible shock, or even death to anyone who mishandled it. This is what directly caused the death of two of Aaron's sons.

To connect the Ark of the Covenant with India may at first seem like a remote possibility. It was described as a large box that was used to hold valuable relics and scrolls, so one can think of it as an ancient bank vault, a safe deposit box that could be taken anywhere and kept hidden when necessary. This has led to endless speculation about its location. Why is this important? It has to do with the concept of end times, messiahs, and resurrection. Let's take a quick review of the major religious ideas about resurrections and messiah(s).

Resurrections Revisited

Hebrew prophesies have foretold that the Ark *will* be recovered and the third and final temple will be built. Only then will the messiah appear. The appearance of a messiah is believed in by Muslims, Jews, and Christians. Muslims believe it is Mohammed who will return, and he will lead Jesus in a great bloodbath to rid the world of all Christians and Jews. Jews believe the messiah will raise the Jews up to a glorified position and bring world peace. Christians, referring to the *Book of Revelations*, wait for Jesus to return and end all suffering and death.

However, for Hindus and Buddhists, these are irrational expectations. Souls are not 'hanging around' for millennia waiting for Mohammed, Jesus, resurrection, an Ark, or heaven.

The Hindus and Buddhists believe that the Universe is *infinite* and life in different forms exists throughout the Universe. The soul is constantly appearing and reappearing, growing and learning through many trials of life, until it is wise enough and perfected enough to reach 'moksha' or heaven, the end of all rebirth cycles. Concepts like eternal damnation, hell, sin, and resurrection, are not universal. No Buddhist or Hindu is expecting a catastrophic, world-shaking event like the return of a messiah. In their concept of rebirths and migration of souls, Jesus or any messiah may already have come and gone in several other forms.

However, that does not rule out the possibility that *something* may return in yet unexpected ways. With this in mind, we'll return to our search for the Ark of the Covenant.

Dome of the Rock

One of the presumed locations for the Ark of the Covenant has always been a secret cave or room deep under the foundations of the First and Second Temples.

When the Muslims conquered the Holy Land, they took over most of the existing Hebrew and Christian sites, forbidding Christians entry into their own churches and shrines, as happened to the Hebrews at the Cave of Machpelah. At the onset of Muslim expansionism, Christians sought help to protect their cultural heritage, and this is why the First Crusade was born.

It was the Caliph Umayyad who appropriated Mount Moriah from the Hebrews, thus taking one of their holiest places on earth away from them. At the time he was fighting with his rivals who had control of the Kabba. They were led by Ibn al-Zubayr. Caliph Umayyad had the golden Dome completed on Mount Moriah in 692. Some historians speculate that the real reason Mount Moriah was chosen was to create a destination that would draw pilgrims, and cash flow, away from his rivals at Mecca. It had nothing to do with the religion of Islam or the night ride of Mohammed to heaven on a winged beast. The *Quran* only states:

> Glory be to him who did take his servant for a journey from the Sacred Sanctuary to the *farthest* sanctuary. (*Quran*: Sura 17:1).

Dome of the Rock on Mount Moriah; the huge wall in front is the Western Wall, or Wailing Wall, where Jews gather daily to pray for the coming messiah, and for the third, and final Temple to be built. Solomon built the first permanent Jewish temple here in 650 B.C. (Photo courtesy of Wikipedia)

Obviously, historically it could never have meant Mount Moriah. The *Kitab-al-Maghazi* (a Muslim historical book) identifies the *true* Al Aqsa location could only be on the Arabian Peninsula, not anywhere near Jerusalem or Mount Moriah, especially since no mosque existed there at the time of Mohammed. **(82)** The Jewish claims, on the other hand, leave no doubt to their historicity. This complex religious and political backdrop is over a mere 35 acres of buildings that are known as the Temple Mount.

Both the Old Testament and the New Testament affirm that a new Temple will once again occupy this exact space, which then raises some interesting new questions. One of the questions now raised is how will any of this be relevant to Jesus in Kashmir? There are several reasons. The Jews believe that the messiah will appear (Christians interpret this to mean the second coming of Christ) after the Third and final temple is rebuilt on Mount Moriah. The messiah will use the Third Temple as his headquarters. This is predicted in the *Book of Revelation* (Rev 11) and in Paul's second letter to the Thessalonians (2The 2:4). The Torah has several strict requirements for the building of the third temple; one that includes the ashes of a pure red heifer for temple sacrifice. So certain are the Ultra Orthodox Jews, and even many Christians, that these end-time predictions are unfolding, that a breeding program of pure red heifers was begun several years ago. This is to insure that a pure red heifer will always be available at whatever moment the Temple sacrifice will take place.

Al Aqsa mosque and Dome of the Rock occupy the 35 acres of Mount Moriah today. This means that these would have to be torn down and replaced by the Third Temple *before* any Jewish messiah can appear. It is hard to imagine under what circumstances this will happen, or how these prophesy will be fulfilled. But all Jews, and most Christians, believe it is predestined to happen. Even Muslims have acknowledged its fulfillment before their own prophet can return, and they believe he will. Whatever is revealed about the tomb of Jesus in Kashmir will relate directly to the predictions, hopes, and expectations of three major religions. Against this tense backdrop, the research, archaeology, and necessary scientific analysis that could help every-one reach the truth and prepare for their future gets bogged down.

A Prophet Like Moses

The Nazarenes and Pythagorean Essenes were branches of Therapeuta magi. It was the Essenes that anticipated *the prophet whom Moses foretold.* This prophet would be identified through arti-facts once belonging to Moses. Perhaps they were marked with an identifying tamga, a 'family logo' of some kind, as mentioned earlier. These artifacts were believed to be hidden under Mount Gerazim, just outside of Jerusalem. Those who possessed 'knowledge of the secrets of the interior parts of the earth' knew where these treasures were and how to access them. The Rod of Moses, according to the rabbis interviewed by Peter Michas and Robert Vander Maten **(44B)**will reappear as the Rod of the Messiah.

Messiahs, Rebirths, and Reincarnations

Moses' word about this prophecy has never been doubted by either the Hebrews or Christians. To the Jews, Moses has been the greatest prophet, priest, teacher, savior, and lawgiver. None of the other prophets came close to fulfilling so many roles. In one of his most specific predictions, Moses declared that God would raise up another Jewish prophet whose life would closely resemble his own (*Deuteronomy* 18:15-19.)

Jews acknowledge that Jesus is descended from the House of David, and that he *did* fulfill most of the prophesies. However, he did not bring world peace (the hoped for freedom from Roman rule) and he did not free the Jews from oppression, therefore he could not have been the prophet foretold by Moses.

The Grave of Aaron

The Biblical death of Aaron took place when Moses led Aaron and his son Eleazer up the hill known as Mount Hor. Aaron was then over 100 years old. He gave his priestly vestments to his son and died soon after. (*Num.* 20:23-29. *Deut.* 10:6; 32:50).

Then he was gathered unto his people and mourned for 30 days.

Of the two summits on Mount Hor, the place where Aaron is believed to have died is now marked by a Muslim shrine. A shrine or resting place, however, is not the same as the *final* resting place, the actual grave. The Biblical, the physical death of Aaron may be quite accurate. However, that is *not* the complete story, because there is a final resting place for Aaron in Kashmir, a place he had returned to enough times in his life that a substantial permanent home exists for him there, a home that was passed down through his great granddaughter Mary to her son Jesus. How do we know this? Because when the Fourth Buddhist Council was convened, it was led by Parshva and held at the ancient homestead of Aaron. Aaron's grave is still there, and once it was clearly marked with an ancient stone slab. Parshva is a Sanskrit version of the name Yeshua or Joshua, the original name of Jesus.

The unique thing about these resting places and final resting places is that they may *all* be true. It was a uniquely Jewish custom to retrieve the desiccated bones of relatives and bring them to new locations closer to family homesteads. People often died far away, in wars, or while on long journeys. By making every effort to locate them and retrieve their bodies, they could be reburied closer to those who loved them most in life.

It was believed that this was an odd Hebrew custom that only existed around the time of Jesus, but we know from the story of Noah and the graves of Adam and Eve that this custom is actually very ancient. Further, when we discuss the life and death of the apostle Thomas in India, we will discover that his bones were moved several times and finally came to rest in several different locations, all far from India and from any of his family roots.

On March 28, 1980, a construction crew in Talpyiot, Jerusalem, uncovered a tomb that contained 10 limestone bone boxes, or ossuaries. Five of the 10 discovered boxes in the Talpyiot tomb were inscribed with names believed to be associated with key figures in the New Testament: Jesus, Mary, Matthew, Joseph, and Mary Magdalene. A sixth inscription, written in Aramaic, translates to "Judah Son of Jesus."

In addition to the "Judah son of Jesus" inscription, which is written in Aramaic on one of the ossuaries, another limestone burial box is labeled in Aramaic with "Jesus Son of Joseph." Another bears the Hebrew inscription "Maria," a Latin version of "Miriam," or, in English, "Mary." Yet another ossuary inscription, written in Hebrew, reads "Matia," the original Hebrew word for "Matthew." Only one of the inscriptions is written in Greek. It reads, "Mariamen e Mara," which can be translated as, "Mary known as the Master." DNA has purportedly been recovered from at least two of these ossuaries, which is good news if, in future, it can be compared with DNA of Egyptian pharaohs and Kashmir tombs.

It is the custom in Israel, because so many old bones are constantly dug up by construction crews, that the ossuaries be cleaned out and stored in warehouses, and the bones reburied where they were found. The bones in ossuaries from Talpyiot were first found in the 1980's and routinely reburied. Apparently they can never be recovered in a pristine condition for further DNA testing today.

Theoretically, the bones of family members could have been divided, and then carried great distances. The stone ossuaries found in Talpyiot may have been constructed to hold a few bones gathered from each deceased family member. Those who died in different places and at different times could be brought together again at last. However, the Romans drove many of the Jews out of Jerusalem by the 70's AD. It must have been impossible for Jews to maintain the tombs thereafter. But it was not impossible for them to carry a few bones from each ancestor and bring them to the new family homesteads for reburial.

The grave of Aaron in Kashmir is located in the town of Harwan (Haroon-Haran), a pleasant 25 minute bus ride from Srinagar. On a grassy hill far above a lake are the remains of his ancient settlement. The sign board from the Indian Government proclaims this as the site of the Fourth Buddhist Council held here in 79 CE. Many ancient stone ruins cover the hillside, remains of the homes that sheltered the 800 Buddhist monks, the Council members for that year.

Ruins of Aaron's home, where Kanishka and Issa/Parshva (Pravarasena-Jesus) convened the Fourth Buddhist Council in 79 AD. Parshva led this council. Ruins of Buddhist cottages seen on the hill behind. Wall construction is ancient 'diaper and pebble' technique found only here and in Syria. Photo by author.

Buddhism in Kashmir by N.K. Sing **(62):**

> The country from remote times was distinguished for learning, and priests of high religious merit and conspicuous virtues, manner, and talent were far different from the ordinary class. The Council sat for six months and made strenuous efforts to bring order to the scattered sayings and theories of various doctors of the Law. The Fourth Buddhist Council can be regarded as an epic event in Buddhism. By the time of the annexation of Kashmir by the Mughals (1339) the Valley saw one of the darkest periods in her history. Under Haider (1472-1484) images were removed from temples and leading non-Muslim Buddhists were cruelly tortured.

All that remains of Aaron's main house is a large stone foundation. The exterior was paved with small round stones in a style called 'diaper and pebble,' a style of construction found only here and in Syria. On the floor were once clay tiles (some that dated to between 3,000 and 2,000 years old) that have recently been removed and sent to museums in Delhi and Srinagar, to protect them from looters. I saw those stored at the Srinagar Museum. These tiles are unique for showing the ethnic types of dress and ornaments worn by the men and women of different eras. Some are dressed in a Greek style. Others are wearing a style of shalwaar-kameez (shirt and pants) that are still worn today in the Punjabi regions of India and Central Asia. Another style, uniquely associated with the Jaulian monastery of Taxila, is similar to ancient styles worn in the Alps.

Off to one side of Aaron's home, near the rushing mountain waters of the irrigation channel, is a large berm of earth outlined with a low rock wall. This is a typical barrow-culture grave with a simple stone marker on one end. The oldest photographs of this grave have revealed that there was a large stone slab that originally covered this grave. An inscription was clearly carved on the stone, but no one has made an effort to either locate the stone, or decipher the words. It, too, was removed and is now believed to be somewhere in Jammu or New Delhi. If this is indeed the grave of Aaron, it becomes vitally important to locate that stone and determine what was written on it to positively identify this gravesite. **(1,27, 36, 37)**

Later, we will revisit this place when the Fourth Buddhist Council was convened here. It is intriguing to realize that Jesus probably inherited this ancestral home from his great great grandfather Aaron through his mother Mary. There is no other way to explain how he showed up here generations later to convene the Fourth Buddhist Council. It is too much to be mere coincidence.

The Grave of Moses

The grave of Moses is a greater distance, and a very different kind of trip from Srinagar than a visit to the grave of Aaron. It is in the mountainous, heavily wooded hills that stretch into Pakistan. Here, the town of Bandipore is believed to be the same word as 'Beth-Peor' in the Bible. Beth is Hebrew for 'home' or 'house of' and Peor means a hill or mountain, thus 'a home in the mountains.' **(1, 27, 36)**

During troubled times when the countries are on the brink of war, the borders here become porous and dangerous, and trouble travels along the faint alpine trails in both directions. These mountains are neither a safe nor a comfortable journey during such times.

There are actually two sites associated with a physical grave for Moses, plus four sites known as 'a place of rest' for Moses. The first is near Auth Wattu (*Ayat Maula*, the sign of God) in Handwara Tehsil. The next is at the junction of two rivers, the Jhelum and Sindh near Shadipur, also called Kohna-i-Musa, and a third is at Pisgah.

The best known and most widely accepted location for his grave is on Nebu baal (Mount Nebo), about eight miles from the actual town of Bandipore, followed by a long trek of several hours over faint mountain trails.

There were numerous Army check points along the main roads, and no assurances that anyone would be permitted through. There are no signs, no directions, and one must have a reliable local guide who knows the trails. This requires several hours of walking. At the summit, there is a large enclosure that contains four graves. One of them is for Sang Bibi, a Sufi hermitess, and two of the graves are for her disciples. These are in the traditional Muslim north-south direction. The fourth grave is in the Hebrew east-west direction. Down the hillside, one can see many stone markers for ancient graves, none of which have ever been studied further.

Two trees were planted next to the Hebrew grave about 400 years ago by Hazrat Makhdoom Shaikh Hamza. They have overtaken and almost completely obliterated the grave site. All that remains is a rock, barely visible, embedded in the ground at the edge of a large tree root. This is traditionally where most pilgrims are taken when they ask to see the grave of Moses in Kashmir. And yet, after all this, this author felt certain this was *not* Moses' grave. It didn't match the Biblical description close enough.

There is one more possible location, however, even more difficult to get to than this. It is in the mountains quite a distance from Lake Wular and almost on the edge of the Pakistan border. After passing through Bandipore on the main roads, the border area between India and Pakistan is still very sensitive. Vehicle are stopped at Army checkpoints every few miles and rigorously searched.

After a distance of about 20 miles or so, there is an unmarked turn onto a rough logging road. Driving along for another few miles, the dirt road stops abruptly in front of a huge pile of fallen trees and boulders at the edge of the Jhelum River. The only way to continue from here is to cross the hand-made rope and wooden bridge. One then needs to find a volunteer, a brave and willing local villager who knows the mountain trails that lead to the grave.

The last group of Europeans, three men and two women who made this trek over twenty years ago were all killed by militants. This is hardly rated as a prime tourist destination. Sometimes, when trouble flares up, the Army checkpoints every few miles will not let anyone pass through. I was fortunate on the days that I made the journey with my guides; they were able to convince the Army to let us through. It was an incredible personal journey. I will treasure the memory for the rest of my life. The Himalayas were at their finest, the small Alpine village was beautiful, and the people were wonderful. Having an entire day at the alleged grave of Moses led to a day of deep reflection. However this remains a difficult and dangerous undertaking because of continued tensions between India and Pakistan and the porous borders here.

Resting on the trail with companions. Colorful prayer flags called wind horses continue to mark the place where 'four holy people' rested while visiting Moses' grave centuries ago. One was presumed to be Jesus; he also visited the grave of Shem. Author's photos

Bringing supplies across the bridge at alpine village near Moses' grave. Author's photos

There is a forest clearing lined with rocks and projecting out from the side of the mountain overlooking the river below. Here is the large, but unremarkable barrow-type grave an east-west alignment, a Hebrew grave. It projects slightly outward from the valley below. The only marker is a rock slab deeply embedded in the dirt. A few wooly monkeys live in the trees around the clearing. The clearing is lined with colorful prayer flags, or wind horses, which comes as a surprise up in these isolated mountains. Traditionally this is a piece of colorful scrap cloth, or even cloth torn from one's own clothing tied to sticks or tree limbs. The whole area was draped in these bright strips of fabric colors. People were still finding their way here in spite of the obvious dangers.

To one side of this clearing there is a separate area that, according to legend, 'four holy people' rested there while visiting the grave of Moses.

Author at Moses' headstone; Mountain gap and river below are just past the trees

It would be a stunning achievement in archaeology if this grave could be positively identified as the real grave of Moses. Until then, the Bible gives us the final word about the grave of Moses:

Deu. 31:2

'And Moses said unto them I am one hundred and twenty years old this day: I can no more go out and come in. And the Lord said unto me, Thou shalt not go over this Jordan. Moses died in Moab and he was buried in the valley opposite Beth Peor, but to this day no one knows where his grave is. Of his sepulcher God hid from the Israelites to prevent their superstition and idolatry, to which he knew their great proneness.'

SHEM

One of Noah's five sons: possibly an abbreviation of the Egyptian name Senerkhet (thoughtful friend) He is also known in ancient Egyptian Records as Semsem, 7th Pharaoh of the 1st Dynasty. The '*Jami-uf-Tamark*' Volume 2 mentions Jesus' visit to the grave of Shem. A title of the Essene priesthood was 'The Order of Shem.' The Apostle Paul had this title.

6. Solomon

"Kings of the earth come to hear Solomon's wisdom." 1 Kings 4:34

The next Biblical figure that has strong associations with India is King Solomon. The closer we get to the era of Jesus, the more Biblical ties to India remain intact such as temples that Solomon and Hiran Abif collaborated on building and restoring. However, it is the Throne of Solomon and the Ark of the Covenant legends that have the strongest links between Solomon and Jesus. We'll examine some of the background in India that leads eventually to Solomon and to Jesus.

'Now when the queen of Sheba heard of the fame of Solomon concerning the name of the Lord, she came to test him with hard questions. She came to Jerusalem with a very great retinue, with camels that bore spices, very much gold, and precious stones; and when she came to Solomon, she spoke with him about all that was in her heart.'   *1Kings 10:1-2*

King Salassie of Ethiopia- direct descendent of Makeda (Queen Bilque) and Solomon.

The Bible mentions Ethiopia as Abyssinia forty-one times, so important was the history of Ethiopians linked with the history of the Hebrews. They were the same people and the same religion. The *Book of Enoch* was recently rediscovered in Ethiopia, included with the original Ethiopic Church texts. Graham Hancock wrote in *The Sign and the Seal* **(26)** *t*hat it was Anayar (Aryan), a grandson of Noah, who brought this religion to Ethiopia.

Solomon and Makeda, through their son Menelik, would be the founders of a dynasty that would last until the dynasty of Haile Selassie was overthrown in 1974. This dynasty was also known as 'The House of Solomon' or 'The Lions of Zion.' The descendents of Menelik are called Falasha Jews, and many have been granted the right of return to Israel based upon DNA results that have exhibited a strong Jewish marker. Now we'll look at the Temples in Kashmir built by Solomon, and then see how these may be linked with Menelik and the Ark of the Covenant.

Tahkt- i- Sulaiman and the Sun Temples

Moses and the Israelites had no permanent or safe place to store the Ark of the Covenant until King David purchased land for the building of the first temple. It was Solomon and the King of Tyre, Hiram Abiff, who then built the First Temple to house the Ark. He used Phoenician craftsmen chosen by Hiram Abiff, and a temple style similar to other Phoenician temples of the same period. This style was duplicated in the temples built in India during the same period.

Two significant temple ruins that are still standing in Kashmir are the Martand Sun Temple, and the Tahkt-i-sulaiman, or the 'Throne of Solomon'. Both are associated with building projects of Solomon and Hiram Abif. Both were locations of far more ancient temples. Both of these temples face east and both have been associated with sun worship since ancient times. They have been rebuilt several times on the same holy ground dating back at least 4,000 years **(35)**

According to the Brahmin historians of India **(35)** these temples are often called Pandav Palaces because historically they are associ- ated with the Pandava dynasty of prolific temple builders. If David was Yudhisthira, a Pandava, then Solomon, his son, must have been a Pandava, and Solomon most assuredly was a great temple builder. The father of David was Jesse. The Rod that we mentioned earlier called the Rod of Moses, has with it an ancient 'genealogy' record of sorts. It lists the names of the owners of this rod, and Jesse's name appears on the list. So we can assume that the cherished family rod was always returned to Kashmir until it was decided who would take possession of it next. And it is because of Solomon's great building projects in Kashmir that places were made available to store and hide these artifacts, for generations if necessary. We'll discuss this again as we move further down the historical trails.

Tahkt-i-Sulaiman, the Throne of Solomon, was also known as Jayesh- theg-vara temple, meaning the temple for 'the people of the sun.' *Vara* is both 'sun' and 'Sunday' in Sanskrit: Jayestha is a figure based upon the Indian zodiacal calendar, and the scorpion was meant to represent the astronomical location of the star Antares (Alpha Scorpio) the brightest star in the Milky Way (the symbol was originally the eagle, and was later changed to the scorpion for unknown reasons). Thus the oldest surviving name for the first temple on the hill was associated with astronomy and the star Antares, so how did it go from *that* to associations with the throne of Solomon? We will soon find out.

According to the research of Navaratna S. Rajaram in *Vedic Aryans and Origins of Civilization* **(56)** another name that was often used for these temples was Sakadvipi or maga (magi) sun temples. Today this refers to an order of Brahmins. Sakadvipa magi (Saka-of Issac) are the founders of aryuvedics (homeopathic medicine), sun worship, and astronomy in India. Remember the eighteen magi families whom the Brahmins invited to build Magadha and share their knowledge? This knowledge arrived with them.

These sun gods are alternately referred to as Suryas (best known as Iranian sun gods). Thus they would have been well known to Solomon. The Iranian Suryas (sun god) wear a long coat, sacred stringed girdles, and knee-high boots, seen often on old coins, mosaics and cave paintings. (The word Sakya, or Shakyas, is derived from the name of Issachar, or Isaac, from which we also get the word 'Saxon.')

Interestingly, the statutes of the ancient sun gods that have survived in India are dressed just like the Zoroastrian (Persian) and Hebrew priests, (modern Jewish rabbi in picture is wearing the same traditional garments and 'girdled' with knotted fringes). The attire worn by these priests is still in use by rabbis and Ethiopian priests today. The knotted fringes are mentioned often in Indian literature to distinguish these priests from Brahmin priests.

Martand

In addition to Solomon's Temple on the hill in Srinagar, there is another temple strongly associated with Solomon and Jesus in Kashmir, and that is the Temple of Martand. The magnificent ruins of Martand can be found just a few miles south of Srinagar. The temple stands upon a high plateau facing east. Its trefoil arches form graceful frames for the mighty panorama of the snow-capped Himalayas beyond. This temple is so old that the five Pandu brothers of the

Mahabharata wars are said to have worshipped here. **(35)** That would be none other than King David and his brothers. The Masonic geometrical figure of the triangle super-imposed upon the square appears on several of the stones and pillars.

Dr. James Ferguson said of Martand:

> This temple is a very small building only sixty feet in length and thirty eight feet wide, the width of the façade is eked out by two wings as adjuncts, which make it sixty feet. It also realizes the problem the Jews had so earnestly set themselves to solve, that is how to build a temple with three dimensions equal but not yet cubic. Small as the Jewish temple was, it was twice as large as this one. At Jerusalem it was 100 cubits, or 150 feet in length, breadth, and height. At Martand these dimensions were only sixty feet. But in the Kashmiri temples it is one of the points of interest that they produce, in plan at least, the *Jewish temple* more nearly than any other known building.

Philostratus had provided us with a description of the *Temple of the Sun* where Apollonius worshipped, and it closely resembles this temple. In fact it could have been a reference to this temple because Apollonius spent thirteen years as a student in Kashmir.

Apollonius wanted to continue the work of Pythagoras, whom he described as his *spiritual* ancestor. Five centuries before Apollonius, Pythagoras had made the same journey to Kashmir to study the ancient wisdom. Philostratus described the wise men here as

> 'Sages who dwell on earth yet are not of this earth, who possesses nothing, yet all things.'

When Apollonius left Kashmir he wrote a farewell letter to the sages that said;

> "Iarchus and the other sages, greetings from Apollonius. I came to you by land, and with your aid I return by sea, and I might even return by air, such is the wisdom you have imparted to me." According to his traveling companion Damis (or Demas) Apollonius had indeed *ascended* with the sages at least once.

The Sword in the Sun Temple

It is difficult to accurately date Martand. The very first Martand temple that is officially on record at this site was mentioned in the *Mahabharata* and built by King Ramadeva (Rama-Abraham) This king was coronated at Ayodiya, and the dates vary from 4,400 B.C. to 3,000 B.C., to as late as 1100-1200 B.C. He is also described as a great-grandson of Noah. It is realistic to assume that Noah himself visited here, since his grave that we visited earlier in Tanda is within easy distance of Martand.

In the *Rajatarangini*, we are told that Solomon and Hiram Abiff came here specifically to remodel this temple. Their new design for Martand appears to have been an exact half-size replica of the First Temple in Jerusalem that was being built at the same time. When King Lalitaditiya ruled from 724 CE to 760 CE (just before the arrival of Islam) he also had Martand restored.

Martand lays in impressive ruins now, victim to one of the greatest stories of madness and destruction the world will ever know. Mahmud of Ghanzi, who was made famous for burning the great libraries at Kabul and Taxila (we will meet him again shortly) began his attacks on India between 1001 and 1027. He conducted seventeen successful attacks in a very short period of time. As he ransacked each city, he destroyed every temple that existed.

Following Mahmud of Ghanzi came the warrior Sikander, who declared himself 'Emperor of Lodi' (from1489-1517). Within a few months of his arrival, it is estimated that nearly five million people in India died directly or indirectly through his efforts.

A Muslim historian, Hassan, wrote in *History of Kashmir an* account of what he witnessed. He said that Sikander initially arrived with 300 men to enforce the orders for 'conversion.' Many fled, but many could not flee, and so they accepted death rather than dishonor or conversion. This pleased Sikander, who delighted in watching the torture of men, women, *and* children. When he heard the sounds of their screams, it was like sweet music to him because he took such delight in their suffering and death. A witness to one of these massacres, Hazrat Amir Kabir, was horrified by this cruelty, and in an effort to curtail Sikander's excesses, he suggested that Sikander impose taxes on them rather than kill them and lose a good source of revenue and labor.

At Martand, Sikander gathered great piles of wood and old shoes from the dead, and set a huge bonfire inside the temple. The massive cedar beams then burned, causing the collapse of the great golden-domed roof. Then, stone by stone, the temple was dismantled and the stones were used to build mosques and homes. Narender Sehgal wrote about the final death and destruction of the Martand temple in *Converted Kashmir-Memorial of Mistakes: A Bitter Saga of Religious Conversion;*

> 'The demonic gaze of Sikander fell on all the sacred and spiritual centers. All writings were thrown into Dal Lake and buried under piles of clay and stone. It took a year to fully destroy Martand.'

One brave Buddhist monk decided that when his turn came to be forced to convert, he would not give up his faith or his name and heritage. He gathered about twenty of his family and planned their immediate escape. They attempted to cross through a Himalayan pass that led to the Buddhist capital city of Leh, in Ladakh. They didn't have time or the room to gather enough food and warm blankets for the journey, but the children, the grandchildren, and the parents each hoisted a large basket onto their backs and each basket was filled to the brim with priceless ancient manuscripts and relics hastily gathered by the monks from local temples. Their bodies were found huddled together the following spring. They had frozen to death when they were caught in a sudden early winter storm in the mountains (from *Buddhism in Kashmir* by N.K. Singh). No one knows how many more must have perished while trying to escape.

Within one or two generations, all traces of Kashmir antiquities and culture were wiped out. All traces of having been a Hebrew, a Buddhist, a Jain, Zoroastrian, Brahmin, a Pandit or a Christian were gone. Entire family names and genealogies that had proudly survived intact for generations suddenly disappeared, to be replaced with foreign people and foreign names associated with the conqueror's identity. Most Kashmiris today have only a vague idea of who they were and what a rich history they had prior to Islam. **(35, 50, 57, 60, 62, 64, 73, 75, 78, 81, 88, 98)**

Kashmir to Ladakh route where the Buddhist family perished

6. Solomon

Remains of Martand sun temple; Jesus (Issa) probably officiated here as High Priest during winter solstice ceremonies, according the Eastern Bible and writings of Thomas. This is also mentioned in traditional gypsy songs of Kashmir. This temple is a half-size replica of the First Temple simultaneously built in Jerusalem by Solomon and Hiram Abiff. (Author's photo).

The Winter Solstice-Let There be Light

When Jesus lived in Kashmir during the first century, Martand was
still in year round active use as a temple. The great winter 'festivals of
lights' associated with Diwali (Deepvali), Hanukah, and Christmas
were celebrated here. People gathered for the week-long festival of
gift-giving, songs, feasts and prayers. Food and warm clothing were
distributed to the poor. Each night the high priest led a candlelight
service of song, chants, and prayer. The week long celebration either
ended or began on the longest night of the year, the winter solstice.
The services were so well-known that kings and princes from all
religions in surrounding satraps (jurisdictions) would make the winter
trek to be at Martand for the annual 'festival of lights.' When Jesus was
in Kashmir as a High Priest, he would officiate at these services.

James Tabor **(66)** says of December 25th as Jesus' birthday:

> December 25th as the date of the birth of Jesus can be traced
> back to the early 3rd century A.D. and achieved universal rec-
> ognition in the late 4th century. It is often asserted that "Christ-

mas is pagan" and that it originated because of the popularity of the Roman winter festivals of Saturnalia (Dec. 16-24) and Sol Invictus that marked the Winter Solstice (Dec.21st) or 'birth of the sun,' It is indeed likely that the celebration of such winter festivals in various cultures where Christianity spread might have contributed to the seasonal popularity of Dec.25th, and there is no doubt that lots of Christmas customs (decorations, trees, Yule logs, mistletoe, gifts, parties) developed from such celebrations. However as far as we can tell the designation of December 25th as the date of the birth of Jesus has nothing to do with pagan customs. Rather it was based on the chronological calculations of early Christians such as Julius Africanus (c.200 CE).

Anyone who spent even a minimal amount of time studying the movement of planets around the sun would arrive at the awareness of a winter solstice. The earth is actually nearer the sun by three million miles in December and January than in June. During this time the earth leans slightly on its axis. Astronomers have even calculated the exact tilt. It is 23 degrees and 27 minutes off the perpendicular to the plane of the orbit. This planetary tilt is what causes all the variety in our climate and seasons. It determines exactly how many minutes and hours each hemisphere receives in sunlight.

The recognition and celebration of winter solstice can be traced back thousands of years in all cultures. It's not just about Christmas. It is about a celebration of the human spirit in recognition of great cosmic events. Some of the most memorable temples and monuments in the world, such as temples to Horus (as the son of the sun), or in Egyptian tombs, or at Stonehenge, or the Aztec pyramids, these were all built with an understanding of the planetary alignments during this one auspicious week of the year. In the most sacred prayers and ceremonies of Buddhists, Hindus, and Jews, one faces east to the direction of the rising sun and temples were always built facing east.

The *Candlegrove* website specializes in gathering traditions about winter solstice and offers this information:

In Iran there is the observance of 'Yalda' in which families keep vigil through the night and fires burn brightly to help the sun (good) battle darkness (evil).

Winter solstice celebrations are also part of the cultural heritage of Pakistan and Tibet. In China, where the calendar is based on the moon, the day of winter solstice is called Dong Zhi, 'the arrival of winter:' it's observed with a holiday spirit called JuDong, or, 'Doing the winter.'

Hanukkah, the Jewish Festival of Lights, occurs around this time of year. It is tied to both the lunar and solar calendars and begins on the 25th of Kislev, three days before the new moon closest to the winter solstice. It's a celebration of the Maccabee's victory over the Greeks, and a rededication of the temple at Jerusalem. But in fact its alignment with the winter solstice suggests a deeper significance, a celebration of growing light and a commemoration of spiritual rebirth.

Celebrating the winter solstice may not be called 'Christmas' by everyone, but it is understood none the less by people everywhere. It is not about 'worshipping' lights or fire or stars so much as it is a celebration of the reassuring continuance of the cycles and delicate balances that allow us to live on earth. Rituals are reassuring and important to mankind. In those moments of celebration and renewal, whether lighting a menorah for Hanukah, or a hand-made clay mustard-seed lamp for Diwali, or a string of electric lights at Christmas, these are celebrations of the cycles of man in harmony with the cycles of the natural world. The birthday of Jesus is celebrated on December 25th and this may have been determined by his fame as a priest and his particular fondness for leading the celebrations for winter solstice. That this sometimes took place in a temple built by Solomon in Kashmir is adds to the lore and mystery surrounding this as the chosen date to celebrate the birth of Jesus.

The Throne of Solomon

There are two large hills in Srinagar that face each other across Dal Lake. One of these hills is called Hari Parbat. Here stood the sacred almond groves lovingly tended by the Pandits. The shrines to Sarah and the sun were once on its summit, where the huge fort of Akbar now stands. The other hill also has a small temple at its summit, facing east, and this temple is Tahkt-i-Sulaiman or the Throne of Solomon.

6. Solomon

King Suleiman ruled Kashmir circa 2,629-2,644 B.C. (*Rajata-rangini*) and it's assumed he was the first to build a large and permanent temple on this site. This could not be Solomon, son of David, because he is presumed to have been born in 848 BCE, and died at age 52 in 796 BCE. However, King Solomon also built a temple on the same site as the predecessor who bore his name. Following the king list in the *Rajatarangini*, we are told that Gonanda 1st ruled after Suleiman. His son was Damodara, by a princess of the House of Yadu (Royal House of Hebrews.) She bore an auspicious son with 'the marks of divine signs' similar to the remarkable features of Adam and Noah. A great grandson of Gonanda, Gopananda 2nd was considered

'The sprout on the dynastic tree burned by fire'

Compare the *Rajatarangini* description with *Isaiah 11:1-3* describing Jesse and King David;

'And there shall come forth a shoot from the stump of Jesse, and a branch shall grow out of his roots.'

This grandson wore the traditional kakapaksa (uncut sideburns, a traditional Jewish custom) until he was coronated by his grandfather. The temple hill was then called Gupkar or Gopadri, or Gopa Hill after this grandson. It seems obvious immediately that these were Hebrew rulers in India, and they parallel Biblical figures.

Several kings then ruled without producing a son. Each ruler was chosen from a strict list of eligible candidates. In the eighth century CE, another Gopa king repaired the temple Today it is known as Shankacharya hill.

The name comes from Adi Shankaracharya, a great writer and philosopher who united a feudal India into one country. He established four *muthas* (or monasteries) in the four corners of the united Hindu land- Kashmir in the North, Dwaraka in the West, Puri in the East, and Sringeri in the South. These institutions are operational into the present day. These *muthas* have held India together as one nation for more than twelve centuries. All the heads of these institutions are today known as Shankaracharyas and wield tremendous political power in India. To distinguish these pontiffs from the first preceptor, Shankara is referred to as Adi Shankaracharya or Jagadguru (Universal teacher).

Shankacharya, the great and gifted teacher **B.688-d.710 C.E.** He ordered all holy men, women and sadhus to meet once every twelve years to share their views and discoveries in religions and philosophies. Many walk the great distances from their Himalayan retreats barefoot and often naked to show their total austerity and freedom from worldly attachments. This tradition is known as Kumbha Mela and results in the largest gathering of humans on the planet; attended by 15 million people in 1989 and 25 million people in 2001. Miracles and special feats are performed by the most advanced teachers there.

This hill has been the site of a shrine or temple almost since the first inhabitants arrived in Kashmir. Solomon remodeled or rebuilt here in the same period of time that the First Temple was being built in Jerusalem and the Martand temple was being built in Kashmir. The First Temple in Jerusalem was built specifically to house the Ark of the Covenant. We know from 2 *Chronicles* 35:3 that King Josiah had the Ark put into Solomon's Temple in about 623 B.C., so by this date we can also date the present Martand and Throne of Solomon temples.

Three sacred things were placed inside the Ark. These were Aaron's sacred rod, which was used to perform miracles in front of Pharaoh; manna, which God gave the Israelites to eat in the wilderness; and the Ten Commandments written on tablets of stone.

There were, in fact, *two* sets of sacred vessels used in the Biblical worship of God. The first were used in the Tabernacle after God showed Moses how to make the Ark of the Covenant and other holy vessels. In about 1446 B.C. Moses instructed Bezalel (Bezaleel ben Uri) to build everything exactly as God commanded. Bezalel's name appropriately means, 'In the Shadow of El (God), the Son of my Light.' The original vessels disappeared when King Solomon made new, more ornate ones for the First Temple.

These vessels were later carried off to Babylon by Nebuchadnezzar after he destroyed the First Temple in 586 BC, but were later restored to the Second Temple. In 70 AD, the vessels were again lost, this time they were stolen by the Romans when Titus destroyed the Second Temple.

According to ancient writings dating back to the First Temple period, King Solomon built a secret subterranean tunnel under a small room in the temple where the wood for the sacrificial fire was stored. The priests were instructed to hide the Ark of the Covenant there if Jerusalem should come under siege. That may explain why the Ark of the Covenant was not in the temple when Nebuchadnezzar conquered Jerusalem. Interestingly, when I visited the Temple of Solomon in Kashmir there was a similar ancient stone room located underground and near to the temple. It appears they may once have been connected via a tunnel. Now two stone steps lead down to a solid stone wall, very unusual and seemingly significant. One day archaeologists in Kashmir may take an interest in investigating this temple further.

The Ark of the Covenant disappeared *before* the destruction of the First Temple. It was hidden by priests who foresaw the coming desolation, and its whereabouts has been the source of myth, mystery, and legend ever since. The obvious question is this: If Solomon built such an elaborate hiding place for sacred relics from the Jerusalem Temple, would he not have duplicated these hiding places when he built temples in Kashmir?

Arch of Titus Detail: Spoils of Jerusalem

This relief is an image of the Romans' triumphal procession, returning with spoils from the Jewish Temple in Jerusalem. Especially prominent is the sacred Menorah and the Table of the Shewbread.

Author and the the Church of Our Lady of Mount Zion in Axum, Ethiopia; Is the Ark hidden here?

According to one theory circulating among scholars and archaeologists, the Ark of the Covenant and the sacred vessels of the Tabernacle may be hidden in a secret tunnel somewhere between the Temple Mount and Qumran, where the Dead Sea Scrolls were discovered. However, the Temple Mount is currently off-limits to all faiths outside Islam, so searching for the Ark there is impossible. The site is currently controlled by a waqfi. It becomes necessary to bring waqfi into this discussion about relics and tombs and control of religious sites because a waqfi similar to the one controlling the temple Mount also controls the Tomb of Jesus. So let us take a quick look at just what a waqfi is.

The Ark of the Covenant. The shape of the touching angel wings is the design that also appears on the dome of Solomon's Temple in Kashmir (see photo next page). Coincidence? Or did Solomon deliberately remodel the Kashmir temple to hide the Ark until it was removed by Menelik?

Throne of Solomon today, and antique picture; the summit is 1100 feet plus 224 steps, plus additional 18 steps to the temple door. Menelik removed the 'great golden throne' of Solomon; four inscriptions were left here by Thomas and Jesus in 45 A.D. Were the Rod of Moses and the Ark hidden here? Was this location actually serving as a secret Jewish storage vault?

6. Solomon

Antique pictures of Throne of Solomon looking across the floating gardens of Dal Lake, it is on the highest point of the mountain (picture; Ken Lee at 'elevenshadows' website where he has more pictures of the tombs and temples

Definition of a waqf (source; wikipedia)

'A religious endowment in Islam, typically devoting a building or plot of land for Muslim religious or charitable purposes. It is conceptually similar to the common law trust. *A wqaf* were among the most important owners of property in the Islamic world until recent times, and remain significant. The practice of declaring property as waqf gained considerable currency due to the practice in many Muslim states of expropriating the properties of important... places... or persons, especially officials, when they died or were disgraced. By declaring his estate as waqf and his descendants as trustees, a rich man could provide an income for his surviving family.

The Muslim administrative body responsible for the Haram al-Sharif in Jerusalem is often referred to as "the waqf".

Both the tomb of Jesus and the Temple Mount are controlled by waqf. In the situation at the tomb of Jesus, the property was seized under this law of Waqfi and the court documents from the fourteenth century onward remain available for public inspection today. This has had a devastating impact on the tomb of Jesus. As an example, consider what is happening under the Temple Mount.

The waqfi controlling the Temple Mount decided, around 1997, to dig up the south eastern area under the Temple. Their reasons are unclear. They may have been looking for the Ark themselves, or for other secret chambers built by the Hebrews long ago. In doing this, they seriously damaged the very foundations of the site. Truck loads of Hebrew antiquities were blasted out from under the Temple and carted off as shards and smashed rubble to a dump near the Mount of Olives. Archaeologists sifted through the rubble and realized that priceless antiquities were being destroyed. They even found small priceless emblems dating to King David. Archaeologists then accused the waqfi of carrying out the excavations as a malicious attempt to destroy evidence of any Jewish presence on the Temple Mount prior to Islam.

So what we know up to this point is that Hebrews valued their relics and sacred artifacts and scrolls and went to great lengths to hide and protect them. Sometimes they were successful, as when the Ark of the

Covenant remained well hidden when the First temple was destroyed. Sometimes they did not succeed, as when the Romans looted the Second Temple and carted off its treasures. But they didn't get the Ark.

In anticipation of the need to keep their sacred relics well hidden, Solomon had built secret rooms and vaults and tunnels under his temple sites. He did this in Jerusalem, and he built identical temples in Kashmir, thus we can reasonably expect to find secret chambers in Kashmir, too. This will help explain why the patriarchs kept returning here time after time. Think of it as making a trip to the local bank to make deposits and withdrawals of valuables.

A well-known theory places the Ark in Axum, Ethiopia. **(26)** This came about through Solomon's relationship with Bilque, the Queen of Sheba, and their son Menelik. It is Menelik who is suspected of spiriting the Ark to Ethiopia without the knowledge or permission of Solomon **(26, 51)** It's hard to imagine how something as significant as the Ark of the Covenant could be 'stolen' from Solomon without his knowledge, unless it was taken from a secret vault some distance from Solomon and the watchful eyes of his court and priests.

In the Rajatarangini **(16, 51),** we learn that Menelik had visited Kashmir and removed a great golden throne or bench that belonged to his father. We are not told if Solomon was still alive and knew of this, or if Menelik took this large 'bench' after Solomon died. Either way this may tie in with the legend that Menelik obtained the Ark and carried it back to Ethiopia without his father's knowledge. On the other hand, the whole business of the Ark disappearing into Ethiopia may have been well planned and thought-out by Solomon long in advance. Either way, Menelik definitely appeared in Kashmir at Solomon's Temple, and definitely removed a large golden bench. Archaeologists in Kashmir have never really examined this site properly, and it's doubtful they were looking for secret chambers in their cursory glances around the hill. We can also very definitely place Jesus and Thomas at this temple. In fact, the Historical Division of India Museums may be holding in their care the very pillars removed from the Temple of Solomon that Jesus and Thomas left their 'graffiti' upon. In addition, there are carvings in nearby Taxila that record visits by Thomas and Jesus. The photos of these inscriptions show us what was once there, **(21, 27, 36)**

Jesus in Sanskrit

Khwaja Nazir Ahmad, author of *Jesus in Heaven on Earth* *(1)* deciphered an inscription that he found at Taxila. It was part of a larger memorial pillar, engraved in Aramaic, the language of Jesus during the first century of the Christian era. The few remaining words that were left legible on this pillar are about a high official named Romadota (Aramaic for Rudradeva, a sun-god) and two others, Naggaruda (Aramaic for carpentry) and Priyadars *(*referring to a "Peridesia" which means a foreigner). The inscription refers to a palace (Mahal) of ivory and deodar (a type of cedar tree native to the Himalayas) that had been built at Taxila. **(13)**

As K.N.Ahmad interprets this, we are reading about a carpenter in 45 CE who came to Taxila (from a foreign place) to help build a palace for the king (Gondopharnes) and this carpenter was accompanied by a sun-god or holy person. This perfectly describes Jesus sending Thomas to India to help Gondopharnes build a new palace or temple. Looking deeper beneath the surface of Sanskrit names like Gondo-pharnes, surprising twists and turns become apparent in their relation-ships with Jesus. Why aren't scholars rushing to interpret more of these inscriptions about Jesus in India? For the very simple reason that no one is looking for Jesus in India, especially not after his cruci-fixion in 33 CE. The pillars that Jesus and Thomas left inscriptions on at the Temple of Solomon were removed in recent times by the India Government when the Temple was turned over to a Hindu shrine to the God Shiva. Thus it is probable that historians can still locate these pillars in a dusty museum storage room in Delhi and evaluate their authenticity.

Ethiopians: Moses' Ethiopian wife Merriam-
Nefertiti: Modern Ethiopian Amharic woman: Last
Ethiopian King, Salassie, descended from
Solomon: Axum, Ethiopian Priest, descended
from Hebrew magi-priest kings, proudly known as
Falashas 'Sons of Zion.' They are remarkably
intelligent and handsome people, with distinguish-
ing high cheekbones and sharply defined features
that can be recognized anywhere in the world.

In one version of the story, when Menelik was a mature young man he traveled from Ethiopia to visit his father. Solomon was more impressed with this son than with any of his other children, and considered Menelik the most handsome and the most intelligent of all his sons. After a visit that lasted several years, Menelik prepared to return to Ethiopia. Solomon then provided him with twenty royal magi families to serve as administrative assistants. Some sources believe these magi were specially chosen to accompany the Ark to a new hiding place in Ethiopia. Others believe that Menelik or his companions stole the Ark from its hiding place, and Solomon was unaware they'd taken it. (Graham Hancock, *'The Sign and the Seal'* **26**)

It was a group of between eighteen and twenty magi families who are credited with founding the city of Magadha in India as well, which then spread to encompass the entire Magdian Empire. This became the center for the Renaissance period of India. Magadha was founded by a magi prince, a brother of Ram. If Ram represents Abraham, then it would be one of his two brothers, Nahor or Haran. As we saw earlier, it was King Matagalpa (Magda-Migal- 2,445 B.C) who was the great builder of ziggurats and established them as part of religious ceremonies. Did the Magdian Empire have its roots with this king and his religion? If so, who was he? Did he also have an identity as another name in the Bible? His era coincides with the era of Shem. In Ethiopia we have yet another coincidence where there is a temple of Magdha in an area associated with Queen Bilque, the Queen of Sheba.**(100)** Were both Bilque and Magdalene associated with these temples? If this can be proven someday, it enhances the continuity of Hebrew religious practices and customs of Hebrew females (especially as priestesses) as well as the Hebrew males.

The word Haran is quite close to the word Harwan, location of the grave of Aaron in Kashmir. With this as a backdrop about the magi, it's understandable why they accompanied Menelik back to Ethiopia to put into effect some grand building plans.

In the Ethiopian version of the story, Menelik returned to Ethiopia with this group of twenty magi families. Several among his friends had 'stolen' the Ark from Solomon and brought it to Ethiopia. In an effort to cleanse Menelik of any wrongdoing, some versions of this story say that even Menelik did not know they had the Ark with them, although that seems an impossible object to successfully steal and carry on a long journey undetected..

However, the version of these events in the *Rajatarangini* tells us quite a different story. It states that Menelik came to Kashmir with a group of friends on the pretext of 'repairing' his father's temple. We can presume this happened *after* Solomon died. Recall the similar story about Thomas and Jesus who came to 'repair' this same Temple. When Menelik left Kashmir, he took away a great golden throne or bench. Menelik claimed that it had belonged to his father and was now his by birthright. The real purpose of the 'repairs' to Solomon's Throne now becomes obvious. This temple functioned as a Hebrew safe-deposit bank vault and these journeys for 'repairs' represented regular deposits and withdrawals of holy relics and manuscripts, whether authorized or not. It must have been a very closely guarded secret, and a very well built chamber or vault to have kept its secrets all these centuries.

This also explains how this hill got the unusual name, 'The *Throne of Solomon*' hill. Otherwise, why would a simple temple on a hill be so specifically associated with a famous 'throne' or bench? In this case, there is an obvious reason why. There was a throne, or a bench, or perhaps even the Ark itself, hidden there. There is no other reasonable explanation for associating this hill with something as famous as the Throne of Solomon. The large, bench-like appearance of the Ark could easily be mistaken for a large bench or throne. Is the Ark still there, hidden under Solomon's Temple in Kashmir? Yes, there's a slim possibility that Hebrew relics may still be found there some day. Long after Menelik left with his golden seat, mention of it appears once more in the *Rajatarangini*.

We are told that King Pravarasena (whom we'll later identify with Jesus) entered the country of Saurashtra (modern state of Gujarat) to demand the return of a gold throne that was stolen from his family. Saurashtra was then a powerful nation. It was mentioned in the *Mahabharata,* and was ruled by Yadav kings. It was also an entry port for Solomon's navy in India. It is located on a main link to the Old Silk Road near the Ajanta Caves. Pravarasena recovered this golden 'Lion Throne' of his ancestors, claiming that it had been stolen from the city of King Vikramaditiya. As mentioned previously, it was a later king from the same dynasty (of Vikramaditiyas) who was honored with a silver plaque at Mecca.

Was the Lion Throne retrieved by Pravarasena the same golden bench carried away by Menelik? Could these be references to the Ark of the Covenant again? If these legends are actually about the Ark of the Covenant, then this means the Ark was moved around several times including stays in Kashmir. Today it may still be in Ethiopia, or hidden somewhere in Kashmir. After Pravarasena retrieved it from Saurashtra, we can follow the trail back to Kashmir where it disappeared from the history books once again.

Graham Hancock wrote **(26)** what he believes to be the history of the Ark in Ethiopia. He mentions that there are literally hundreds of duplicate Arks in Ethiopia. He said; "The best way to hide a tree is within a forest." He believes there are duplicate Arks hidden in different places, but all the locations are in Ethiopia.

We have seen that since the days of Moses it was not unusual to have duplicates made of the most important holy relics in Judaism. Even when Moses 'broke' the original Ten Commandments written on stone, he was able to obtain a duplicate set without difficulty. Aaron and Moses had several duplicate rods they shared between them. It becomes a very real possibility that the duplicates, and/or the originals, may one day be discovered in Kashmir.

The *Talmud* states:

> The Ark was hidden by King Josias in a most secret place, prepared by Solomon in case the temple might be taken and set on fire.

The patriarchs had to have a plan for every contingency. If fire was a major concern, then rock caverns and stone rooms are the only fireproof way to protect valuables. During this author's frequent journeys up to the Throne of Solomon in Kashmir, what becomes immediately apparent is the amount of rockwork; the massive walls and the platform built on the summit are supporting one comparatively small temple located in a remote area with a sparse population. The quarry for the temple stones seems to be the barren rock precipices located directly behind the temple site.

As I described earlier, behind the temple on the path leading to the TV satellite antenna and the Army offices, there is an oddly out of place door built right into a dirt hill. It leads to just one underground stone room. The room is like a cellar for storage, and a small twelve by twelve feet in size. Its stone ceiling is supported by beams made entirely of solid stone, each beam about ten feet long. On the under-side of one stone beam this author found an ancient inscription carved into the rock and only visible by lying down and shining a light directly up under the beam. The script appeared to be in early Phoenician or Brahmi script. **(52)**

Inscription (highlighted by author) carved in rock at Solomon's Temple; photo by author

It seems apparent that a tunnel once linked this underground room with the main temple. Oddly out of place are two stone stairs that end abruptly in front of a solid stone wall. How or why these steps are blocked off with a solid rock wall is a mystery. Future explorers will have more work to do to unravel the mysteries surrounding the Throne of Solomon in Kashmir.

Today, the tomb has gone through yet another transformation. All traces of Solomon, the Zoroastrians, Jesus, Thomas, and the Christians are gone. The pillars that Jesus and Thomas carved their names into are also gone. The temple has now been 'reincarnated' as a Hindu temple for Shiva. Inside the small rotunda there is a Shiva lingam guarded by a replicas of the hooded cobra and Nandi, the bull. The Hebrew ghosts of religions past must be aghast!

The Army has a barracks on the hill to guard the transmission tower again possible terror attacks. The temple is of only moderate interest to the occasional brave and hearty tourist who can climb the steep steps to the summit. I made the journey many times. The views are beautiful from that height, although the view of Dal Lake is some-what disappointing now; over a thousand houseboats clutter its mucky, littered and polluted shores. The Army base up there throws its refuse and plastic bags and bottles down the hillsides. Never the less the temple still evokes wonder about its place in history, no less haunting than the history of the Great Wall of China, Glastonbury, the Pyramids, or the Sphinx. This magnificent little temple hidden in this magnificent little valley may still be keeping the best of the world's ancient secrets very well, thanks to the clever tertons and tektons of long ago.

7. Buddha

Sanskrit: *Awakened or Enlightened One: from Sanskrit*
'Budh,' to know.

Gandhara Buddha-mark in forehead represents insight or
'third eye.' Many first-second century figures called
Brahma or Buddha may actually be intended to represent
Jesus. Metropolitan Museum of Art, New York

 Siddhartha Gautama (563?–483? BC) is not in the Judaic Bible at all and probably never ventured as far as Judea. More than 500 years before Jesus was born—and at about the same time that Confucius was teaching the Chinese how to lead the good life—this prince became famed in India. In the chronicling Kashmir connections with Jesus, it becomes important to discuss Buddha and Buddhism because there is so much speculation about the links between Jesus and Buddha, and between Buddhism and Christianity. What may surprise you to discover is that they were actually related through their common ancestor, King David.

As we have touched upon earlier, if King David was Yudhithistira, and we have the genealogy of Buddha from the Kings of Kalinga list **(77, 99)** we know the Buddha was of the Pandava line through his grandfathers. This becomes a vital clue to the real relationship between Jesus, Buddha, and the similarities in their teachings. To study Buddhism is to study a form of Judaism, the religion that Buddha was actually closest to and most familiar with. There may have been Brahmin priests at the palace, but there certainly were also Hebrew priests identified through their specific Hebrew names and customs and the stringed girdles that they wore.

Isabel Elder, *'Buddha the Israelite,'* **(17)** believes the first Buddha (Sakya Buddha, the original Buddha, was the Saxon Wise One; he was also known as Jakku, son of Jacob) can be identified as Buzi, the Aaronite (of the tribe of Levi) father of Ezekiel. Buzi-Buddhi-Bukkhi; the change of one letter does not alter the word. She has identified the common shared elements of Buddhism and Judaism such as the lion, the trident, and the wheel (as described in 1 Kings 33 the wheels depicted in Solomon's Temple). She believes the second 'Buddha' must have had knowledge of his ancestor's prophetic teaching to abolish idolatry in favor of an imageless God, abolishment of the caste system, and to acquire knowledge as the way to religious liberation. The earliest Buddhist mission was to revive the older original religion, to refute brute worship and demand equality, goodwill, and moral excellence from men and women, priest and lay person alike.

7. Buddha

Although 'Buddha' is not his full and correct name, for the sake of this book I will use 'Buddha" when referring to Prince Gautama Siddhartha. He was the son of the king of the Shakyas (a tribe or family) and he was born a Kashtriya (the warrior-king caste- Shakya, or Sakyamuni, meaning 'of Isaac,' one who is 'capable' or 'able'). The Sakyas (Saxons) are also mentioned in the Mahabharata as one of the descendents of the 'solar race' (iksvaka) through the legendary Ok-kaka (Isaac). There were two branches of Scythians, the nomads and the royals.

Buddha was born in Lumbini, a city near Kapilavastu, a place the 'Acts of Thomas' said that Jesus spent considerable time. Buddha died in Kusinara, a town in the kingdom of Magadha, another place associated with both Magdalene and Jesus according to 'The Acts of Thomas.' It will surprise most to know that Siddhartha Buddha had typical Indo-European features, a blend of Asian and Greco-Roman Europeans, the marriage of 'occidental' to 'oriental'. The dates commonly accepted for his life are 563 B.C. to 483 B.C. (some historians argue that he may have lived a full century later).

The Sakyas southern capital city was Kapilavastu. Here is where Buddha spent thirty years of his life. Both the Church of the East, and the Gospels of Thomas make mention that Jesus traveled there several times. It was a place where he was known and loved, a place that gave him shelter and refuge during his travels. The ruins of Kapilavastu are quite impressive. To visit there is like stepping into a time capsule, it is so far removed from the hustle and bustle of modern urban life. Through the impressive ruins, stupas, and temples, life seems little changed and one feels a connection to life as it must have been here over 2,000 years ago. This is one of the holiest sites of Buddhism, comparable to the Holy Land of Hebrews and Christians.

Kapilavastu is located near the banks of the holy Ganges River in southern Nepal, and from here it is a short trip south through Magadha, then on to the port at the Bay of Bengal. Just thirty miles over Adam's Bridge (a sunken thirty-mile land bridge) is the island of Ceylon, or Sri (holy) Lanka (island), location of Adam's Peak. Lanka was once ruled by a Yaksha king named Vaisravana, who was also called Kubera. When the last old king of Lanka died childless, a letter was sent to King Sumitta requesting that he send a new king from his family. The king's youngest son, Panduvasudeva, was sent to rule, and all in his court were given Pandu wives, providing a strong link with the Pandavas of the Mahabharata epic and suggesting their Jewish ethnicity. Many of them bore the Jewish name 'Tissa,' referring to a parsha (section) of the Torah. The early Lankan kings were of the same ruling dynasties as the Greco-Persian kings. Thus, we find in several apocryphal works the stories of kings of Ravanna who visited Jesus, because they were in all probability related.

The genealogy of Buddha has been faithfully recorded in *The Mahavamsa* or *'Great Chronicle of Lanka from 6th Century to 4th Century BC'* (**17, 77, 86, 99**)

The family names include Suppadevi (the Lion of Judah) Sinahu (from the root word Sinai) Jivatissa (Tissa refers to a parsha or section of the Old Testament) Pandava and Panduvasudeva (the family of Yudhist-hira, or King David, from the Mahabharata) and Jayasena, the famous saint; Sena is a name we have followed since the Egyptian dynasties of the Pharaohs Harise and Ra-Sena that have led us to Jesus and the Hari Rasenas and Prava Rasenas. These genaeologies criss-cross with the ancient Egyptians, Hasmoneans, the Ptolamys, the Pandavas and most prominent ruling families of Rome, Greece, and India. One can always discover new places where their genealogies criss-crossed through the centuries and there is much work yet ahead as new discoveries will be made. (**19, 24, 48, 57**)

These rulers were also called the 'Sun' Dynasties, followed later by the 'Moon' or Lunar dynasties that would eventually lead to the gods worshipped by the Arabs at the Kabba during the reign of King Vikramaditiya to whom the Arabs donated a commemorative plaque. Now this is not to say that all kings who ruled India and Lanka were Palava or Greco-Persian kings, for many were not. However our intention is only to identify those we can connect directly or indirectly with the families of Buddha, Jesus, and the Jews in India, and there are many such connections.

Herodotus mentions several practices of the nomadic warrior Scythians that are identical to the Kashtriya warrior clans of Siddhartha Gautama's family. Among these characteristics, the women made a paste of pounded cypress, cedar, and frankincense to apply all over their bodies. When taking the plaster off the following morning, their skin would be clean, smooth, and very sweet-smelling. These were a very passionate people who would cut their hair as a show of mourning their dead. This period of mourning lasted forty days.

7. Buddha

The Sakya men usually wore full beards and were often described as having intense, deep-set blue eyes. Descriptions of the Buddha were well-preserved by the monks and by those who had met him. He was quite remarkable in his appearance. He was tall, strong, healthy, vigorous, athletic and very handsome. Buddha is perhaps one of the few sages for whom we have mention of such impressive physical characteristics. He stood at least six feet (180 cm) tall and had a strong enough body to be noticed by a visiting king who asked him to join his army as a general. He is also said to have had *'The 32 Signs of the Great Men.'* One of these notable signs was his blue eyes.

The Scythians (and Kashtriyas) were among the earliest races to wear trousers, probably because they were avid horsemen at least since the days of King Solomon. (Avristan/Avra-horse/Sthan-place of= Arabia, place of the horses, originally meaning the thoroughbreds of King Solomon). They wore soft leather boots with heels in the style found at the excavations at Taxila. They used local dialects of Indo-European languages, primarily Prakrit, Greek, and Aramaic. They were brilliant craftsmen, noted for their intricate and elaborate scrollwork, especially with gold. Many examples of their goldsmith skills are currently on display in museums around the world. Riding fast horses, dressed in riding trousers, possibly having blue eyes, being tall and strong and handsome, these are not the traits we normally associate with Buddha. However, by all accounts, this is what the real Buddha accurately looked like. He was a tall, handsome and vigorous man who traveled widely and spoke eloquently.

Pittsburg Museum:
Central Asian
Scythian gold art
circa 100B.C.

The mother of Buddha was Maya Devi, which means 'the goddess (holy) mother.' According to Dr. D.B. Spooner, she was of Persian-Iranian descent and a follower of the ancient religion of her ancestor Buzi-Buddhi. She has also been identified a s a Kashmiri by the distinctive jewelry she wore. She died within days of his birth. Gautama was then raised by her sister, who also lived at the Palace. At the age of sixteen, he was betrothed to his cousin, the princess Yasodhara. They wed and had a son named Rahula.

Princess Yasodhara was beautiful. The hair of Princess Yasodhara was like a crown, full and shining, and reaching the floor (in modern India, women who can grow their hair to the ground are still held in high esteem). During the years that Gautama Buddha wandered and preached, he was separated from his wife and son.Yasodhara waited faithfully for his return to the Palace. When he returned, to show her loyalty and complete acceptance of his teachings she cut off all of her hair as an outward symbol of her inner 'non-attachment' to earthly vanities. She became the first Buddhist bhikkhuni (nun) to do this. This is why even today, in places like Nepal, Sri Lanka, and Thailand, one still sees the Bhikkhus and Bhikkhunis with their uncovered shaved heads. Not all Buddhists, however, have to shave their heads.

The word bhiksu is the same as the word 'monk.' It refers to members in a Buddhist sangha, or society. The word literally means 'to beg.' Regardless of the previously held positions in the working world, when one enters the Sangha they must adhere to vows of poverty and chastity just like the nuns of the Catholic churches. Even the piece of cloth that is wrapped around their bodies must be old, preferably made of several torn pieces of cloth that have been sewn together. In Kashmir and Tibet the cheapest color cloth available has always been red and so it is that these monks still wear red or maroon robes today. In other Buddhist areas, the robes might be in grey (Japan), yellow, or black, depending on local customs.

While there are many paths of Buddhism that are not open to monks and nuns, such as working in society, helping the lives of others, being a yogin or yogini, these are also considered esteemed paths of Buddhism. **(29,34,62,71,73, 81, 86, 94)**

The Jew in the Lotus

Highly significant sculptural remains have been found at Pandre-than, a village near Srinagar in Kashmir. The sculpture is of Maha Maya, Gautama Buddha's mother. She and her sisters are depicted wearing the traditional and unique style of Kashmiri earrings called dejeharu, a style that is still worn by some married Kashmiri women today. However, this style has now become limited to a few shepherd girls, because girls in villages and towns regard it as too old-fashioned. These exquisite little jewelry pieces can now be purchased for a few rupees in local shops in Srinagar who are anxious to dispose of these valueless and outdated remnants of a time past.

By all these indications Gautama Buddha's mother was from Kashmir. And yet repeatedly we are told in the *Rajatarangini* that *only* Jews were permitted to live there. Thus it is not hard to establish the fact that Gautama, being of royal Hebrew blood himself through the Pandu clan and Yudhithistira, had a mother from Kashmir who would be of royal Hebrew blood. Through these complex bloodlines buried under Persian, Greek, and Sanskrit names, we can manage to dis-cover links between the family of Buddha and the family of Jesus.

Arjuna (in the *Mahabharata*) had chosen a wife from among naga (Kashmir) princesses. He married the naga princess, Ulopi. When he was wounded and left for dead in the city of Manipur, it was a naga maiden who knew how to restore his life. Gautama Buddha was a naga who belonged to a naga kula, a specific religious community. The first king over all the nagas was Nila or Neela (the Sumerian king Enlil). The *Nilamatapurana* mention 527 different naga kings who were known in Kashmir.

It would be of interest to mention here a story from the *Mahab-harata* that, according to the translation by the scholar Dayanand, describes how, shortly after the coronation of Yudhisthira as emperor, he, Arjuna, and Krishna all went to America. This conclusion came from an Indian scholar! If the *Mahabharata* is being correctly under-stood, then, according to Dyannand the word 'Paataala' is 'America.' They traveled there in an 'Ashwatari' (a special vehicle capable of traveling through sea and air) King Pandu was married to Madri, the daughter of the King of Iran (Persia). Several current researchers are still examining evidence for conclusive proof that Hebrews and Phoenicians had established colonies in the Americas and it will be interesting to see what they come up with.

If these princes were choosing their brides from among Kashmiri Hebrew princesses, who were also their cousins, then they were obviously all the same family. They were *all* Jews obeying the laws of Moses and choosing only Israelite brides, especially those from Kashmir, who seemed to represent the most royal and the most desirable lineages.

Thus Buddha's genealogy includes Yudhisthira, several Pandavas, and Hebrew Persian kings and princesses, including his own mother, with Jewish names like Tissa. They would definitely not have used names that had made other dynasties prominent, preferring instead to proudly promote their own family names.

The *Mahabharata* mentions this saint, Jayasena, and Arjuna refers to him at Malleswara. The Malleswara temple was founded by one of the Prava-rasenas. Now all these names and family groups will become vitally important to us soon, because of the three kings mentioned in Kashmir that could be Jesus, one of them is Pravarasena. This would be a direct connection between the genealogy of Jesus and the genealogy of Buddha. This startling revelation seems to establish that Buddha and Jesus shared a common family bloodline. As we continue to seek out direct links from the family of Buddha to the family of Jesus, even Magdalene may have been related to them. She was a princess from the kingdom of Magadha, the kingdom that was also the home of Prince Siddhartha.

As mentioned Gautama Buddha was also a naga who belonged to a naga kula, a religious community comparable with the Essenes and Nazarenes. Nazarene means 'little fishes' and refers to followers of the constellation Pisces. The Buddha's naga-kula was a forest-dwelling order of ascetics who gave up worldly pleasures for austerity. This immediately brings to mind Mahavir (Vardhamana 599-527 BC, or 549-477 BC.) He was the founder of the Jains. He was also a son of King Siddharta and lived as a prince. This makes him an uncle of Buddha. The king of Magadha, Shrenik, and Mahavir's maternal uncle, Chetak, supported him and believed in his reform movement. They were all regarded as Aryan (Persian) princes. He was about thirty years older than Siddharta Buddha, and it is believed that, for a time, Buddha followed the same severe austerities practiced by Mahavir. This may be the austere influence that so alarmed his father and the atsrologers when predicting Buddha's future. Buddha later rejected these austerities and concluded that man lives best on the middle path, moderation in all things. King Ashoka would continue to support the Jains and Buddhists with donations for ashrams and schools because, as he said,

'I myself am of the same blood.'

However, as we shall discuss soon, Ashoka *was* Greek on his father's side of the family! So speaking of Mahavir and the Jains and Buddhists as *of the same blood*, was he referring to the Greek side of their families? Based on what we now know, then why not?

Among the priests of these special orders were many magi and nagas who formed their own naga-kulas. They wore long white robes and string girdles in much the same style as the Essene and Nazarene communities. They considered themselves members of a fraternity called the 'White Brotherhood.' The female nagas and magi were members of the naga fraternity called 'The Circle of Mothers.' This may have been inspired by the Hebrew story of the three mothers- aleph, mem, and shin, who are mentioned in the kabalistic book of *Zephyr Yitzira* or *Book of Formation.*

The men and women of these orders identified themselves with royal scepters based on the design of the scepter of Nila (Enlil?) the first naga king. It would be of extreme interest if some future scholar can determine if the word naga actually came from the word 'Ninhursag.' Sumerian records have shown that Nila and Ninhursag were a Sumerian brother and sister. **(24, 63)**

Royal scepters had an image on the filial that some have interpreted to be a snake, while others have thought it might be a dragon. The Indian historian-philosopher-teacher Dyanand makes it clear however that these were never originally symbols of snakes, and that nagas never worshipped snakes. According to Dyanand, there is no historical evidence for this belief. It began as myth,a rumor, and complete misunderstanding of the signs.

South-East Asian Hebrews

The Himalayan kings were also called the Raj Nagas, or royal nagas. These rulers were roughly divided into two families, the northern Pala kings and the southern Palavas. Their style of rule was more oriented to democracy and social justice for all, in stark contrast to the Brahmin emphasis on caste as social boundaries. During the first century of the Christian era, these kings were losing ground to the Yueh-Chis (northern Mongolians) of Central Asia,who had been aggressively overtaking them and driving them out.

Many of the Palas and Palavas gravitated towards Europe, but others moved further and further south where they had established thriving seaports and trade centers. For centuries these Pala (northern) kings had been establishing ties with South East Asia and China through the southern Silk routes and maritime trade. The Jewish names given to their favorite places were reused where ever they had a presence. Judea became Ayodhya in India, and Iudea in Siam (Thailand) a very large, well- laid out city since 2,000 years ago, soon after the migrations began

From these dynastic migrations of kings and royal families out of India sprang the early dynasties of Bangladesh, Cambodia, Viet Nam, and Thailand. Their royal houses are descended from these Pala kings. The Cham kings of Cambodia were the old Champas of northeast India and the Himalayas. The main Cambodian city of Kamboja was named after a city in Gandhara. The Khmer kings of Cambodia were the Kamara Pala kings. Both the Royal Pongsavata scripture of Nokor Khmer and the Kham scripture of Thailand were based on the Magadha scripture of the Gupta court. . **(6, 25, 31, 34, 40, 41, 54, 56, 60, 62, 64, 67, 73, 75, 81, 86, 87, 88, 94, 98, 104, 106)**

In Thailand, the longest reigning monarch in the world today is King Bhumibol Adulyadej. Like most Thai kings he was coronated with a name from his family's glorious ancestors. He is Rama IX.

As these ancient Indian dynasties migrated, they carried with them a mixed cultural heritage influenced by three religions. Although by this time they were predominantly Buddhist and Christian, many ancient Hebrew customs and symbols were retained. Even today, evidence of their Hebrew influences can be found as far away as the royal families of the emperors of Japan. *The Bible Mysteries* website offers the following facts about Hebrew influences in Japan:

'In the Nagano prefecture, there is a large Shinto shrine where a yearly festival called Ontohsai celebrates the story about Abraham and his son Isaac. The festival of Misakuchi is a celebration about 'mi-isaku' or Isaac, the son of Abraham. The word is based on the Hebrew word Yitzhak (Isaac).

The crest on the Imperial House of Japan is the same crest found on the gates of Jerusalem. The Shinto shrine used by the Royal family has the Star of David, or crest of Manai-jinja carved onto the lamp posts, a symbol that has been used in Japan since ancient times.

The Shinto shrine used by the Royal family of Japan has the Star of David, or crest of Manai-jinja.

Rama IX, His Majesty King Bhumibol Adulyadej of Thailand (Buddhist king) from kings out of India came early dynasties of South-East Asia; descended from Pala kings. Scriptures of Thailand were based on the Magadha scripture of the Gupta court.

The 'Code of the Samurai' resembles the 'Code of the Rajputs' of India. This, in turn, reflected the Code of Ethics of the Kashtriyas that was later adapted in China, and from there evolved again with the Samurai, the Japanese Knights. They carried swords that bore inscriptions in Sanskrit. The Japanese priests known as Yamabushis wear a phylactery on their foreheads, a little black box called a tokin. Yamabushis and Hebrew rabbis are the only priests in the world who retain this custom today.

China

The southern Silk routes led through South-East Asia, whereas the northern Silk Roads reached far into Russia, China, and Mongolia. It was near the end of the Chou dynasty (1050 B.C. to 250 CE.) that some of the most profound philosophers of Chinese thought made their appearance. The Chinese had become among the most advanced and spiritually developed people on earth. The great philosophers of China had extensive knowledge about Buddhism, Socrates, Aristotle, and Plato. Confucius (551 to 479 B.C.) introduced a philosophy that was a neo-Platonic form of Socialism, still widely adhered to in China today. Lao Tze ('Old Master' circa 600 B.C.) introduced a more sophisticated version of traditional worship called Taoism, commonly known as 'The Way.' In China, these teachings were combined into a book called *The Tao Te Ching or 'I Ching'*. The outburst of great Chinese philosophical thought coincides with the great burst of religious and philosophical development then taking place in the western world. Socratic philosophies would continue to dominate the Chinese political structure into the 20th Century.

Their writings also reflected knowledge about the teachings of Enoch, with many of their quotes and philosophical ideals coming straight from *The Book of Enoch.*

R.H. Charles, author of *The Book of Enoch* (1912);

> *The Book of Enoch* is, for the history of theological development, the most important pseudepigraph of the first two centuries B.C. Some of its authors - and there were several - belonged to the true succession of the prophets, To describe in short compass the *Book of Enoch* is impossible. It touches

upon every subject that could have arisen in the ancient schools of the prophets, but naturally it deals with these subjects in an advanced stage of development. Nearly every religious idea appears in a variety of forms, and, if these are studied in relation to their context and dates, we cannot fail to observe that in the age to which the Enoch literature belongs, there is movement everywhere.

In 379 CE, Mahayana Buddhism, blended with components of both Confucianism and Taoism, became the official religion in most of China. Christianity (often in the form of Mani-ism) was the next most prevalent religion. By 900 CE, however, Buddhists in China would be persecuted almost to extinction. Tibet, because of its remote location, had managed to stave off religious and political change. Then, In October 1950, soon after China completed roads into the region, 40,000 Chinese soldiers invaded Tibet and annihilated the remaining 8,000 Tibetan soldiers. Tibet then came under Communist China rule. In November 1950 the Dalai Lama, only 16 at that time, had to assume full authority as Head of State. China regarded all Buddhists as primitive, backward, superstitious, and in need of 'development.'

Tibetans have been second-class citizens in their own country ever since, especially since all obstacles were removed. Then nothing prevented millions of Chinese farmers and laborers to flood into Tibet. Ninety percent of all ancient relics, books, scrolls, records, caves and monasteries that still remained were destroyed on orders from Chairman Mao during the Cultural Revolution. According to yearly reports from the TWA (Tibetan Woman's Association report from Dharamsala, May 1999) forced sterilizations and abortions are still routinely performed on Tibetan women without their consent. In effect, Tibetans as a distinct land, culture, and race are rapidly disappearing from the face of the earth.

India, ever the safe abode of the persecuted (they had welcomed the persecuted Zoroastrians and Jains before) now gave the Dali Lama shelter. He now runs an entire 'Tibetan government in exile' from Dharamsala in India. 'Tibetans' as an ancient and distinct culture and race will probably never live in Tibet again.

His Holiness 14th Dali Lama

The name means 'Oceans of Wisdom'

"Who is the creator? How do we choose a religion? What would you ask Jesus if you met him? Is there life after death? What is the mind in the universe?" The Dali Lama was asked these questions by a Christian. He answered, "You will know the way for yourself by 'Luminous Cognizance.' Insight is the key to liberation, regardless what religion we profess. We are all on a quest for the way things are."

The Oriental Jewess

Buddhists and Brahmins

The concept of caste was never part of naga or Persian history and is unique to the world of ideas that the Brahmins introduced. Being born into a low caste was a fate worse than slavery. Slaves can always be set free and rise to greatness, but a low caste at birth meant a low caste at death, and all the money or education in the world could not change that. Your caste, just like your color, was determined by your parentage and your birth. Only by learning through cycles of rebirths, sometimes as a content person, sometimes deeply troubled and plagued with sufferings, could one's caste be determined in the future. A great king in one lifetime may be reborn as a sickly beggar in his next cycle. A very saintly person may choose to return to help the less fortunate. This is one's personal karma.

That the Brahmins adhered strictly to the caste system has been substantiated through modern DNA studies. A peculiar HAL polymorphism in the males of upper caste Indian Brahmins showed HAL proteins to be most common to Caucasoid groups from the Ukraine and the Portuguese Basques (based on *Y-Chromosome study from 1999: Indian Statistical Institute of Kokata*). The Brahmins, it would seem, originally entered India as wealthy Phoenician merchants and traders, and encountered the northern and southern populations already established there. This seems to validate what the philosopher-historian Dyanand had said previously, that the very first inhabitants of north India were Scythians who arrived from the Himalayas to settle largely uninhabited lands. The Phoenicians, those who became identified with Brahmins, were not directly connected with Scythians, although their families would eventually connect through conversions and marriages. The ruling families remained genetically distinct from the general population.

A clear example of these ancient conflicts between Brahmin-Phoenicians and Hebrews would be the meeting of the Hebrew prophet Ezekiel and Jezebel *(Deuteronomy)*. Jezebel was a Phoenician queen. Phoenicians were abhorred by Jews because they worshiped a swarm of gods and goddesses just as Brahmins still do today. Prominent among these were the sacred bull and Baal (Baal at first represented not one but many demonic gods).

7. Buddha

It was the naga-magi priests (Isvaras or messiahs-'anointed priests') who established the kingdoms of Magadha, Kapilavastu, and Iodea (Ayodiya).Gradually, the Brahmins' bid for acceptance and power succeeded, and it was the Brahmin influence upon these centers that eventually prevailed.

The chief languages were Abhira (Kubera) and Pali (Paulastya). The root languages were in the Magadhi and Prakrit dialects. It was the kingdom of Magadha that used a dialect called Ardhamgadh Prakrit, which was similar to Aramaic. All were languages that were familiar to Jesus. It was not until around the first century that use of Sanskrit really began to take hold.

Gautama Buddha did not think Sanskrit was worth considering because it was not in wide use. King Ashoka never used Sanskrit on his stone edifices. He used Greek, Aramaic, and a Brahmi (Phoenician-related) script. This is no surprise. His grandfather was Chandragupta Maurya, who was well known to the Greeks. It was common for people of the era to assume both Greek and Egyptian names, and later names in Sanskrit or other languages were added to their identities.

Chandragupta (d.297 B.C.) was educated at Taxila, and was the first to use the title 'emperor' in India, styling himself after his cousins, the Ptolemy and the Roman Emperors. His empire reached as far as Magadha. Although himself a Jain, he seemed strongly influence by the Brahmin priests. Later, he became very superstitious and seriously paranoid of all those around him. He 'reformed' the caste system so that instead four castes, there were now seven. It was because of such paranoia and excesses that his grandson Ashoka rejected the Puranas and the Brahmins, and instead embraced Buddhism and made it the national religion.

Another kingdom adjoining Ashoka was ruled by Turamaya (285-247). He was Ptolemy 2nd, also known as Philadelphos (Phillip) of Egypt, famous for getting the great library of Alexandria built and subsidizing the philosophers and scientists in his kingdoms. Some researchers believe they will soon find further direct links between these families and the family of Jesus (Ralph Ellis among them)

Magus of Cyrene (350-250) once ruled next to the Kingdom of Ashoka. Cyrene (Cyrenaica) became part of the empire controlled by the Ptolemaic dynasty from Alexandria in Egypt, and later passed to the Roman Empire. Cleopatra, who died in 30 B.C., was the last Ptolemy to hold such high office in the Roman Empire.

The rulers of India were none other than the Egyptians, Greeks, and Romans. It's as though India were a suburb of Rome and Alexandria. This was the world as the parents of Jesus knew it. This was the extended family of Jesus. **(6, 20, 25,34,40,41, 56, 60, 62, 73, 75, 81, 86,87,93,98, 104)**

NAME	Date B.C.	Persian Name	Bible Name	Bible Back grou nd
Cyrus	539-530	Koorush	Cyrus	Isaiah 45, Daniel, Ezra 1-3
Cam-byses	530-521	Cambujieh	Ahasru-erus	Ezra 4-6
Pseudo Smerdis	521	Berooyeh Doroughi	Artax-erxes	Ezra 4:7-23
Darius the Great	521-486	Darryoosh	Darius	Ezra 5,6
Xerxes	486-465	Khashayarshah	Ahasure-rus	Esthe r 1-10

Farsinet.com

Buddhist traditions were recorded all over India, but the best records were kept by the Lankans of Sri Lanka, or Ceylon. They carefully recorded most of the events from Buddha's life and teachings. These records were kept on leaves written in the Pali script. These were then carefully packed into three large baskets and delivered to the Fourth Buddhist Council in 79 CE. Ever since then, these canons have been known as the Tripitaka (meaning the three baskets of wisdom) the name still used today.

At the Fourth Buddhist Council there was a serious debate regarding the appropriate language for Buddhist teachings. The Brahmins had requested the freedom to translate the texts into Sanskrit, but many Buddhists were against this, especially because Sanskrit was completely unknown in the south and in Lanka. Finally the Buddhists relented and allowed official Sanskrit copies of the canons. As a direct result of this decision, the Brahmin priests began incorporating many of the Buddha's ideas into their religious practices. This led to a blending of the two religions until they became almost indistinguishable from each other in India. Prior to this decision, several translations had begun appearing in China, translated from Sanskrit, which indicates there had been 'unofficial' if not 'official' translations were being made prior to the Council decisions.

What sets Hinduism apart from all other religions is the complete lack of what could be regarded as official 'temple' or 'church' cannons and texts. There is no central creator or guiding force in Hinduism. It was not created by a 'prophet' like Abraham, Mahavir, Buddha, Christ, or Mohammed. Writings in Hinduism were subjected to the personal expressions of individual Brahmins, until the final form was reached some time in the third and fourth centuries of this era. This has led others to perceive the Vedas as neither holy, nor divinely inspired scriptures. A Hindu may not perceive the Talmud or the New Testament as infallible scared scripture either. The Vedas would not be regarded as sacred scripture to a Christian. The differences become a decision of theology verses mythology; personal decisions based upon cultural and historical preferences. The west has chosen not to make gods or prophets of Socrates or Plato as they have with Abraham or

Moses. The east has chosen to raise the status of Buddha to a near god. It is as much a philosophical choice as a religious one.

Buddhists do not teach the concept of 'one supreme creator God for all' nor do they worship images. Although many Christians and Jews have forayed into Buddhism and gained valuable insights, no Buddhist has ever forayed into Christianity or Judaism or Islam and been able to make the same claims. To Buddhists, these others use God as a crutch, a way to not take responsibility for our lives.

Gautama Buddha completely and deliberately avoided discussions about God. In the Buddhist view of things, prophets and priests are simply teachers, nothing more, and certainly not the object of worship or religion. There is no 'one size fits all' when it comes to religions, perhaps because we vary so widely in *not* comprehending religion at all. Buddha understood this weakness in man's search for a path to God, and that is perhaps why he strenuously avoided creating any such traps for his followers.

Buddhists believe that the entire universe goes through cycles, and these cycles affect all living and all spiritual beings, including the gods themselves. His approach to the concept of reincarnation reflects the Jewish mystical influences called Gilgul, taken directly from the Kabala. It pertains to the 'cycle' of souls.   Hindus have no teachers for their priests or lay people. Each person must, therefore, guide himself. If a guru or sadhu (ascetic who has given up all worldly pleasures) reaches a form of enlightenment that he considers valuable and wants to share, he sets out to find followers who, in turn, will support his views and support him as he imparts his wisdom and blessings upon them. One is free to choose the teacher one wishes to follow. Hopefully one would use wisdom and good judgment when making choices about a religion or a teacher. Unfortunately this rarely happens. People can be locked into a certain belief system because of family and cultural traditions and the taboos against 'different' or outside choices, Or people can be led astray, even to committing cruel, outrageous and illegal acts in the name of their favorite religion or leader, because they passionately believed in a popular and very persuasive person, prophet, or idea that was incompatible with the prevailing laws and rights of the human race. So determining what is a 'religious' right from what is a 'social' or 'moral' right becomes a significant decision in one's lifetime.

7. Buddha

' 'As a man can drink water from any side of a full tank, so the skilled theologian can wrest from any scripture that which will serve his purpose.   The Gita (250 BC-250 AD)

The meditations and the spiritual path of Gautama Buddha have been adopted by Jews and Christians alike. Knowing that Buddhism is centered on the *path* and not the God in much the same way Socrates and Plato showed us paths to advanced thinking and living (Buddha is not a God, but state of being) its teachings are often adopted *without* having to convert, or let go of any other beliefs. Thus, in an odd way, Jews and Christians can follow many of the practices and beliefs of Buddhism, yet remain Jews and Christians in outlook. In Islam, it has been the Sufi branch that most comprehends and embraces Buddhist philosophy. In reality, the highly philosophical and metaphysical views of Buddhism and Judaism are very close. Considering that Buddha has his own roots in Judaism, this should come as no surprise. **(3, 9, 14, 17, 29, 31, 33, 55, 62, 71, 73, 74, 75, 80, 81, 88, 103,)**

Buddha, Socrates and Jesus

Hannah Arendt (1906-1975) Jewish-German philosopher said:

> 'Of all the great minds that have influenced contemporary thought, Socrates, Buddha, Confucius, and Jesus have had the most profound and lasting impact. When it comes to broad, en- during influence over many hundreds of years, these four are so far above the others that they must be singled out if we are to form a clear view of the world's history.'

To understand Buddhism, we must broaden our scope into Greece during the time when Socrates and Buddha both lived. Active commerce always existed between the Greeks and Indo-Aryans. The philosophies of the two men, Socrates and Buddha, bear such striking resemblances to each other that they are often compared. Although the truth may now be lost in time, there is no doubt they were aware of each other's philosophies **(33, 59)**. To understand Jesus' relation- ship with Buddhism, one must first understand Buddhism's relationship to Socrates and the Sophists (a school of philosophical teachers).

As the Buddha story goes, after six years of searching for peace through asceticism (deprivation and near starvation) Buddha was in the town of Uruvela in the kingdom of Magadha, not very far from the Palace of his father and the home of his wife. Magadha, like Taxila, was a center of great learning. Even the poorest ascetic roaming the village streets there with a begging bowl knew the greatest philosophies of the day. Gautama was assimilating this knowledge too, but at a much deeper level of understanding. After forty-nine days of intense concentration and deep introspection, this is where he had his *eureka* moment It's that sudden instant glimpse of eternity that may only last a few seconds. And yet it forever alters every life and it takes a lifetime and a million words to explain. Often that is not enough time. He became a Buddha, an 'enlightened one.' This moment has all the deep religious significance in Buddhism that Jesus, on becoming the Christ, has in Christianity.

The use of this term, 'Enlightened One' is considered a modern misnomer, first appearing in eighteenth century translations by the British. The original term implies knowledge and wisdom. Unfortunately, it was striving to make the Buddha appear like 'a perfect English gentleman' in the sense that eighteenth century enlightenment was understood, that the term stuck, and today 'enlightenment' is the buzz-word of Buddhism. The Greek world Gnosis and the Sanskrit term Bodhi have exactly the same meaning; 'knowledge.' Gnosticism is derived from Gnosis, and Buddhism is derived from Bodhi.

Karl Jaspers, like Hannah Arendt, was a great philosopher. He was also a physician and psychiatrist. In *Socrates, Buddha, Confucius, and Jesus* **(33)** he expresses the exact similarities between Buddhist philosophy and Socratic thought:

> '(Socrates) was filled with an awareness of his vocation, his divine mission. Like the other prophets, he was certain of his calling. Unlike them, he had nothing to proclaim. No God had chosen him to tell men what he commanded. He had no faith in anything, but demanded that through thought, questioning, testing, man should refer back to himself. His life was a conversation with everyone. He does not hand down wisdom, but makes others find it. Death is equivalent to nothingness, without sensation of anything at all, like a dreamless sleep: then all eternity seems no longer than a single night. Or else death is the migration of a soul to another place. Whatever the truth about death

may be, for a good man there is no evil, neither in life nor in death.' **(4, 9, 14, 17, 22, 23, 25, 29, 31, 33, 40, 48, 54, 55, 56, 68, 69, 71, 74, 80, 81, 86, 93, 94, 98, 103, 104, 106)**

Socrates and Buddha may have lived approximately the same time and been aware of each other's philosophies. At a time when man was struggling to understand and explain the meaning of life and society, these great thinkers left us ideas that we still depend on today for our comprehension of the world.

The Royal Cities as Ivy League Colleges

Before and after the birth of Jesus, it was India, not Rome, which had the largest economy in the ancient world, controlling 1/4 to 1/3 of the world's wealth. That Jesus went to India as a youth, and remained there for up to eighteen years is generally not disputed. What is unknown, however, is why he went there in the first place. To understand this, one needs to look no further than the great schools at Taxila and Magadha, for it was these great centers of learning in India that were so well-known and emulated by the Egyptians, the Romans, and the Greeks (see *Taxila* and additional sources by Dr. Ahmad Dani and Sir John Marshall). The site includes numerous related buildings, fortifications, settlements and monasteries, and shows architectural influences for the length of its role as a Buddhist training center, between the 5th century BC through the 2nd century AD. The capital was conquered by several groups, including Alexander the Great in the 4th century BC. As a result, Persian, Greek and Asian influences are visible in the ruins of the city. They sent their sons and daughters to Kashmir and India as a status symbol. These were the most coveted educations available at the time. These schools were the equivalent of the modern Harvards and MIT's, the Cambridge and Essex Universities of today, and indeed the core curriculum, and method of learning, have changed little since then.

Varanasi (Benares or Kashi) is regarded as the oldest seat of learning in India with a known history of over 3000 years. The most prominent of the great university centers were at Kashmir (also site of the largest Sharda library in world), Taxila, and Magadha. Both Takshashila University (Taxila is the anglicized version of this word) in present day Pakistan, and the Nalanda University in north central India existed at least since 700 BCE. This date is assured because Greek historians like Strabo and Megasthanese were the first outsiders to refer to them. **(13)**

204

"Education of Jesus" by Newell Convers Wyeth (1882-1945)

Located at National Museum of American Illustrators

Taxila University

Taxila (Tackshashilla) is important in our search for Jesus in India because we can unequivocally place him here at least once, and, quite conceivably, several times in his life. A wealth of material has been excavated from Taxila, which is now classed as a World-Heritage site. Christians would no doubt find a wealth of previously untapped history about the early church there.

The word Taxila comes from Takka (Taksa-Saka-Isaac). In Sanskrit, Takshacila means 'Prince of the Serpent Tribes' (meaning; Prince of the (naga) Sakya Tribes) Taxila was known as Ambhi or Omphis in Greek. In one historical explanation of the word, it was associated with naga-carpenters.

Between fourteen and sixteen, children were prepared to be sent off to schools of higher learning. Wealthy families would pack them off to relatives, often with a tutor and a nanny, so they could begin higher education and gain preparation for adulthood. Good tutors (*upadhya*) of a brilliant, well-rounded student who graduated with high marks could expect handsome rewards upon their return, even being awarded homes and land grants if their pupil impressed his school masters. **(13)**

Dr. Ahmad Dani was in charge of excavations at Taxila for over thirty years (before this Sir John Marshall did extensive research there). He has intimate knowledge of the thousands of artifacts and edicts recovered there, and understood the day-to-day routine of life there at the time of Gautama Buddha, Socrates, and Jesus. In his book *Taxila* **(13)** he states there were nearly one thousand schools spread out over a vast area covering nearly thirty miles, and these sustained close to ten thousand students in any given year at Taxila. The students came with their entourage from as far as China, Japan, Rome, Greece, Ethiopia, Libya, and even Britain. Priests representing dozens of religions gathered there. Up until the 10th century, almost every province in India could boast a massive centre of learning. The fame and might of a king was often measured by how many poets, mathematicians, and learned men he kept at his court.

7. Buddha

The remains of the Jaulian Monastery near Taxila have revealed a wealth of information. Many stupas, statues, coins, and relics have been uncovered. One of these statutes has been positively identified as either Jesus or Thomas, clothed in the specific style associated with that monastery. They were dressed in the boots and pants and cloak of horsemen accustomed to traveling great distances. According to the research of the famed archaeologist Sir John Marshall, the name Jaulian is from Julian of Nisibis, who accompanied Thomas to Taxila. According to Dr. Marshall, the name has no relationship to the Julian calendar era that began with Julius Caesar in 45 B.C.

Often the Jewish teachers at Taxila were identified as smri-tis (smerdis) which meant 'an assembly to discharge the legal respon-sibilities of the community,' and from this we also get the word 'Semitic' (teachers descended from Shem). The word is also retained in Hindu-ism as the 'Smritis', the canonical texts of Hinduism. It is the same as the word 'guru' which means 'teacher' or tutor. As Jesus traveled about in India, his actions as both a Jew and as a spiritual leader were constantly observed by these Hebrew teachers and priests, and always subject to their approval.

Women were educated alongside the men, having more rights and equality than many women of the world today. If they were from royal families, they were expected to be competent managers. Women usually had separate inheritances and financial accounts, their own advisors and Chief Ministers. It was crucial, therefore, that a woman of high breeding be deemed competent to manage affairs of state in her husband's absence. History is replete with legends of such women. Cleopatra is one of the more outstanding examples.

Women did not participate in activities like wrestling, sword skills, or target practice with a bow. Men would not take courses on child care or managing domestic servants.

A strong, healthy, well-built body was essential, so a healthy diet and participation in sports was required by everyone. Bathing pools as large as today's Olympic size pools were utilized for both sports and bathing. Martial arts were taught. Astronomy, painting, music, archery, knowledge of geology and jewels, antidotes against poisons and basic pharmacopeia (called vishpaharana or toxicology) geometry, mathe-matics, science, the art of war, animal husbandry, elephant and horse lore, and geography were among the subjects covered. Students were required to contribute their own compositions in the writing contests (called kavyashastravinoda) and eloquent speakers were held in high regard.

The Brahmins also had schools at Taxila. They taught the Four Vedas and the Eighteen Arts, which included law, medicine, study of warfare and famous battles, and skills that included archery and hunting. The Brahmins referred to the graduates of the other schools as Brahmabandhus (those not of our faith).

Students were expected to be good public speakers, able to express themselves on all the great philosophies known to man. Students would also be exposed to languages like Aramaic, Prakrit, Latin, Greek, Persian, Phoenician, and dozens of local dialects from other countries. Between the birth of Buddha and the birth of Jesus was the era of the greatest philosophical movements in the world. Much emphasis was given to explaining concepts of good and evil, right and wrong, the existence of a soul and its relationship to the state, the community, and the universe, and debating upon the value and of God. From these great debates emerged the great religious and social foundations that govern our world today **(59)**.

Some of the greatest known historical figures attended schools here- the Sanskrit grammarian Panini; the political theorist Kautilya (who became chief advisor to the founder of the Maurayn dynasty), the Ayurvedic healer Charaka, the Greek philosopher Apollonius of Tyana, who has been relentlessly compared with Jesus, these are but a few historical men who attended schools at Taxila.

Death came to Taxila in the 13th century. We met Mehmood of Ghazni previously, back at Martand when we first saw how Sikander wreaked havoc on Kashmir. The library at Taxila is said to have housed 600,000 manuscripts, comparable to the great library at Alexandria. When Mehmood of Ghanzi was conquering India, upon arriving at any of the great learning centers, he was reportedly a little 'confused' as to what to do with the libraries. After thinking it over, he came to the conclusion that all writings could be classified only in two ways- either against Islam, or in favor of Islam. If they were against Islam, they *had* to be destroyed, and even if they wrote something favorable toward Islam, they were to be destroyed, since *nothing* else was important beyond the *Quran*. Accordingly, he ordered all libraries and their contents to be burnt. **(35, 60, 78)**

Tragically, this attitude continues today in a form of archaeological terrorism unprecedented in the world. One of the most striking recent examples would have to be the deliberate destruction of the Bamiyan Buddhas, the '9-11' of Central Asia. The elaborate Bamiyan Buddha monastery complex took over a hundred years for the monks to build. As Jesus passed here, they were finally nearing completion and applying the outer decorations, paintings of birds and butterflies and flowers adorned the surrounding rock walls and the robes of the huge stone Buddhas. Copper masks defined their faces and hands. One wore red robes, and the other wore blue. The two colossi must once have been a truly awesome sight, visible for miles. Jesus would have marveled at such a wonder. Yakut was a Chinese historian who passed through Bamiyan just to see these fabled Buddhas. In his geographical dictionary, written in 1218, he said;

> 'There one sees a structure of an elevation prodigious in height; it is supported by gigantic pillars and covered with paintings of all the birds created by God. In the interior are two immense Buddhas carved in the rock and rising from the foot of the mountains to the summit. One cannot see anything comparable to these statues in the whole world.'

2,000 year old Bamiyan Buddha, monks built it as a residential school; its face and arms were hacked off, the same fate of religious intolerance dealt to mummies and the Sphinx in Egypt; Wahabi-Taliban finished destroying this Bamiyan Buddha in 2001. It is now a pile of rubble. Photo was taken in 1979: by G.R. Lasko.

7. Buddha

Taxila today: Pakistan Government tries to save historical ruins of Taxila, always under attack from violence, extremists, cultural terrorism, and illegal black-market looters. Every year hundreds of archaeologists and historians from around the world come to Pakistan to work and study archaeological ruins. Photo by Asghar Khan, Gulf News, December 2006

The Graduates

Gautama Buddha, Jesus, and women of royalty like Mother Mary and Mary Magdalene were educated in the most extraordinary schools in the most extraordinary of times. It would not be unreasonable to say that their educations far exceeded what most of the world aspires to today. It would be both impossible and impractical for them to be 'ignorant shepherds' and 'simple carpenters,' and yet be able to lead and to communicate in profound and complex subjects eloquently and with such complete mastery.

It was not only by divine revelation that Gautama Buddha and Jesus achieved enlightenment. By the time their minds were 'enlightened,' they were already working like fine-tuned instruments, honed by years of internalizing complex ideas. As people thirsted for knowledge, these were the men who would fill their cups to the brim.

Jesus used parables and short stories to express complex ideas, but not because he lacked words or the necessary imagination. In fact, it was quite the contrary.

✳ "Parables and proverbs are short sentences drawn from long experience," said Miguel de Cervantes.

Jesus could say in one or two sentences what Gautama Buddha might have said in five hundred. By the time Jesus returned from India and resumed his life in Judea, *Mark* was able say of him (1; 22-27):

> And they were astounded at his teachings, for he taught them as one who had authority, not as one of the scribes.

The teachings of Enoch were as influential to mankind as the teachings of Socrates, Confucius, and Buddha. *The Books of Enoch*, in one form or another, had already spread across the entire known world. Parallel Enoch sayings are found in Lao Tze and Confucianism. There are also parallel Enoch sayings in Hinduism, Buddhism, and Christianity. The ancient Nasorian sect of Judaism believed in 'The Path' or 'The Way' which paralleled Enoch. The Sanskrit word bodhi-sattva is translated as nazir and in Hebrew means "one who abstains"

and is generally a word used for monks. Jesus too is referred throughout the Greek New Testament as a Nazarene. According to the
description of Nazirs in Numbers 6:1-2, it was not a permanent vow,
but a temporary vow that gave man time to be free of daily cares and
enter a meditative state that could vary from a few days to weeks or
even months.

The teachings of Enoch were as influential to mankind as the teachings of Socrates, Confucius, and Buddha. *The Book of Enoch* in one
form or another had already spread across the entire known world.
Parallel Enoch sayings are found in Lao Tze and Confucianism. There
are also parallel Enoch sayings in Hinduism, Buddhism, and Christianity.

Enoch was the Melchizedek, the High Priest of Israel who ascended with the gods in order to continue his studies.

'The Way' was at the heart of the teachings of Manichaeism and
Tsabism (star-based teachings) that have been practiced, in one form
or another, over virtually the entire planet. The study of astronomy was
impossible without studying Enoch, for he was considered the father of
both astronomy and astrology. Enoch was the Einstein of the ancient
world. We would not have a 'Space Age' without the basic awareness
he left for us to build on.

Jesus never went to India to become a Buddhist, and yet Jesus'
philosophy, even unto death, was quite similar to Buddhism. Jesus
spoke of a supreme God. Buddha did not. Buddha believed there was
a supernatural energy outside ourselves, and that all sentient beings
could be shown a common path to attain those powers.

Jesus had personal experiences with God and eye-witnesses to
his ascensions. Jesus and God spoke to one another on a highly
personal level. Buddha never claimed such personal experiences with
God. And yet both men seemed to have arrived at the same personal
understanding about the supernatural and religion in general, even
though they arrived by quite dissimilar paths.

Great ideas are meant to serve as springboards for more great
ideas, and there is no better proof of this than the impact of men like
Socrates, Buddha, Confucius and Jesus upon mankind. The very
same arguments continue today between creationists and evolution-

ists. Nearly three thousand years later, and we still don't have the absolute undeniable evidence either way. If we're extremely intractable and unfortunate as scientists and religionists, these arguments may well continue for another three thousand years. Let's hope not.

Soon after Buddhism began to spread, elements of miracles and the supernatural crept into the stories of his life. The Buddha himself believed he was teaching a philosophy, a proper way for mankind to discern his place in the universe and live decently and equally, without prejudice or caste or in fear of superstitions. Like Socrates and Plato he taught human-based philosophy, not God-based religion. It was not at the command of God, nor to impress God that he spoke. And yet his spiritual concepts were masterfully comprehensive and eloquent.

> 'I have given each being a separate way of seeing, and know-ing, and saying that knowledge. What seems wrong to you is right for him. Purity and impurity, sloth and diligence in worship, they mean nothing to me. Ways of worshipping are not to be ranked as better or worse. .. It's not me being glorified in the act of worship. It's the worshipper. I don't see the forms they use, or the words they say. I look on the inside, and seek the humility.'

Excerpt from *God Sees Beneath the Forms* by the Sufi poet Jalaluddin Rumi (1207-1273- born in Afghanistan)

Struggles of Buddhism in India

Just as Christians and Jews suffered under Roman persecution, so, too, Buddhists suffered under Brahmin persecution. It was the Brahmins, through the Rajputs, who rose to hold the strongest position in India, one that survives to this day. Buddhism was adopted as the national religion (or more appropriately, national philosophy) by King Ashoka, a reflection of his abhorrence at divisions of people in castes, and the gods and rituals being constantly absorbed into Hinduism, turning it chaotic. Ashoka was not a Brahmin. His grandfather was a Jain, and mostly Greek. On a rock stupa, Ashoka left us this message:

> 'What lies at the heart of true religion? Not abstinence, or going naked or shaving head, or wearing rough garments and thorns, or offerings to priests, or rituals of worship, or sacrifices in the name of God, can ever cleanse a soul.'

However, rituals to the sun were like daily meditations. They were always an integral part of Ashoka's daily worship. It was Ashoka who rapidly helped establish Buddhism by supporting monks as teachers and missionaries. Ashoka's son, Jalok, built many schools and residences for foreigners studying in Kashmir. They both maintained very close ties with Greece and many Greeks lived in Ashoka's kingdom **(50,60, 67)**

There was constant competition between Brahmins and Buddhists for the supremacy of their different philosophies. When Brahmins finally succeeded in gaining full control of India, there was a lot of persecution and prejudices against Buddhists, until Buddhism declined in India almost to extinction. However, it can also be said that Buddhism owes a lot to the Brahmin Hindus, who protected them and their holy sites from Islamic invaders.

After the conquest by Islam, Rajputs began producing incredible, yet fake, genealogies to impress their new conquerors and gain their favor. The word Rajput comes from two Sanskrit words, rajanya and tatpurusha compounded as rajaputra, meaning 'son of a king.' This is a Hindu caste who originated in what is now the Indian state of Rajasthan. They claim their origins are from the Kashtriyas.

The Rajputs have been likened to the western King Arthur and noble Knights of the Round Table. They even followed the ancient magi tradition of gathering at a round table, a practice that was in existence long before King Arthur. Instead of being called 'Knights of the Round Table' this was called the Parisad (pari, 'round', sard, 'to sit'), a large round conference table used for meetings between the magi and officiating priests (Purohita) of the temples and sanctuaries (Tirtha). The members of these conclaves were referred to as Tarangas or Parsadas.

Although Rajput lives were devoted to war, they lived lives of chivalry, generosity, courage, patriotism, loyalty and honor, and gained world-wide respect and notoriety. Kalhana refers to them as

> 'The greatest triumph of human breeding in beauty, form, intelligence, and grace unequaled in the world.'

However, the rigidity of the old Brahmin caste system was strictly enforced by the Rajputs, one of their sadder legacies. Swami Dharma Teertha made these observations about the Rajput era:

> '(Christian and Buddhist) Monasteries were demolished, monks were banished, and books were burned. By the end of the tenth century, Buddhism and Christianity were stamped out of India. Had the Rajputs learned to work together instead of bickering among themselves, they could have defeated the Muslim hordes. They adulterated the sacred literature so much so that historical unreliability has become the characteristic of the entire Sanskrit language. The best historian cannot tell where facts end and fiction begins.'

Taj Mahal India one of the most beautiful structures in the world is now the subject of ownership-dispute between Muslims and Hindus, a reason why retaining accurate records of the past is still important.

it goes the way of the way "
"everything goes away "

Sri L. M. Joshi said:

> Great Buddhist contributions to ancient India lay in the social
> harmony and racial integration they brought on a national
> scale. It was through Buddhist and Christian influence of social
> harmony and tolerance that foreign invaders such as the
> Greeks, Pahlavas, Kusanas, and Huns were so easily assimi-
> lated into Indian society.

The Three Baskets

Theravada Buddhism was the earliest form of Buddhism. Translated, it means Old (thera) Way (vada). This has also been translated
as 'The Doctrine of the Elders.' Theravada Buddhism takes the Pali
Canon as its main source of authority. Earlier, we saw how the three
baskets of religious cannon arrived in Kashmir for the Fourth Buddhist
Council.

The first basket, known as the Vinaya Pitaka, contains the rules of
monastic discipline. The second basket, the Sutta Pitaka, contains all
the discourses of the Buddha, his essential teachings, the details of his
life and his approaches to meditation and morality. The third, the
Abhidhamma Pitaka, the most complex of the three, contains the
psychological and philosophical interpretations of the Buddha's teachings. Theravada Buddhism is still practiced in such countries as Sri
Lanka, Burma, and Thailand.

What is most amazing about all of this is to find the influence of
Jesus on Buddhism, and not the other way 'round as so many have
wrongly speculated. After the Buddhist sayings and traditions were
written down on leaves and brought to Kashmir, it was Jesus, as
Pravarasena-Parshva, who helped the Buddhists assemble these
traditions into their final form. We'll learn more about this shortly.

Caves

The Ajanta Caves have a special relationship to our search for Jesus in India. These particular caves were near Solomon's seaports. The caves served as home to dozens of monks and their extended families, just like the caves at Bamiyan, and they were well concealed off the main roads. They were supported by two families, the Hari Senas and their cousins, the Pravarasenas. Both were of the Vakataka dynasty. A later Pravarasena (270-330 CE), who may have been a great grandchild of Jesus, became the best known of the six or so Pravarasenas in India's history of kings. **(46)**

Caves served as hiding places for food and weapons and as storage places for trade goods. They also represented a virtual standing army of well trained and well-disciplined monks. They served as a rapid relay system for messages speeding along the entire Silk Road.

Men would soon know if a king had fallen, or a wife was unfaithful, if a war party was mounting, or who had been declared the next Caesar of Rome. For worshippers, caves were a place of solitude. For artisans, they were a blank canvas, and some became as elaborate as any palace. For John the Baptist, and for the Essenes of Qumran, caves were places to live, and places to hide sacred texts like the Dead Sea scrolls. For Jesus, supporting the monks at the Ajanta Caves and elsewhere may have been a great tactical maneuver, providing a support network for apostles and for persecuted Jews needing safe haven.

Jesus was certainly the most famous persecuted Jew. He was crucified and by this action and the implications surrounding this event, an entire religion has become devoted to his suffering and death. But what if.........what if he didn't die then? What if he survived the crucifixion and lived for nearly a hundred years? It's an alternative explanation for the unexplained. Could anyone have survived a crucifixion? If Jesus survived and remained on earth, there must have been witnesses. Where is it written? Who were they? We'll examine the evidence next.

7. Buddha

Tomb of St. Luke, Ephesus, View looking south at the remains of a circular structure that is said to be the Tomb of Luke (author of the gospel and Acts of the Apostles). At one time this structure may have served as a church. As well as Jesus and Mary Magdalene, the following people have been associated with the city of Ephesus: Paul, Priscilla, Aquila, Apollos, John, Mary (the mother of Jesus), Luke, and Timothy. Government of Turkey has no interest in these sites, and they are rapidly falling to ruin and disappearing from memory. *(Courtesy of Carl Rasmussen, 'HolyLandTour')*

Entrance to the Talpiot tomb discovered in Jerusalem in 1980. It contained ten ossuaries, many bearing the names of members of Jesus' family. This has become known as the tomb of Jesus, which is still being disputed by many scholars. The symbol of a pyramid with circle or 'eye' on the tomb may be linked with family symbols of both Egypt and modern Masonic brotherhoods.

Clues to the Crucifixion

Could Jesus, or anyone for that matter, have survived crucifix-ions? If Jesus did survive, then where are the clues? Can clues be found in Kashmir?

There can be no doubt that Jesus was betrayed and crucified. *The Mechilta* (Midrash) writings of the Hebrews outlined all of the rules to follow for finding a man 'guilty as charged' and condemned to death. The United States form of government and the laws of the Supreme Court are based upon these ancient Hebrew laws that were first written by King David. *The Archoka Volume* known as the *Archaeological Writings of the Sanhedrin and Talmud of the Jews'* (located at the St. Sophia Library in Constantinople) details the accounts of the High Priests 'concerning the execution of Jesus.' Chapter 7 is about 'Caiaphas to the Sanhedrin concerning the resurrection of Jesus.' It seems out of character that the Jews would write anything that sub-stantiated Christian claims about Jesus and yet this is what was written;

> 'Jesus of Nazareth was crucified, and at that hour there was a terrible earthquake, and a mist rose and covered that area for three hours. His mother was said to be a virgin, and as a child he was taken by the magi into Egypt. As a man, Jesus per-formed many miracles....'

George Carey, the Archbishop of Canterbury, said:

> "Belief in the resurrection is not an appendage to the Christian faith. It is the Christian faith."

Theologians and critical thinkers outside the Church have pointed out that throughout Christian history the resurrection was not treated as central to the faith, but something that developed *in recent times*. When the four canonic Gospels were written, from 70 C.E. to 110 C.E.,

Christians still believed that Jesus rose from the grave in his original body and by his own power. This can also be interpreted as having survived his wounds and the crucifixion.

Surviving Crucifixion

Crucifixion comes from the Latin word *excruciatus*, meaning 'out of the cross' and from this we get the word 'excruciating.' Beliefnet.com describes crucifixion this way:

> Crucifixion was not so much an execution as a torturing to death. The procedure was very simple: the victim was tied, hanging to the crossbar, while his feet were supported on a block at the base of the cross. His feet were also usually tied at the block, although at least one example recovered by archaeologists reveals that a nail might also be driven through the ankles. The Romans often tied men to crosses or tree limbs without the use of nails.
>
> The weight of the hanging body made breathing very difficult and could be managed only by constantly pushing upwards with the legs and feet to relieve the tension in the chest. Eventually, of course, weariness and weakness overcame the ability to keep pushing. When this happened, the body slumped, breathing became impossible, and the crucified person died—by asphyxiation. This was reckoned to take about three days. As an act of mercy—only the brutal Romans could come up with such a definition—the legs of the victim were often broken and so deprived of any strength whatsoever to maintain the weight of the body. The body would drop, and death by asphyxiation was rapid.

The symbol of a ladder being used to ascend to a very high cross makes little sense. The cross or pole that he was mounted to may actually have been just high enough to insure that his feet cleared the ground. There was no reason to raise someone any higher than a few inches in order to achieve the same end. In fact, in many depictions of early crucifixions, just a single pole or tree limb was used, without even the necessity of a cross-piece.

Patibulums are the upright portion of the crosses and these were often permanently mounted just outside the city walls. The condemned were not made to carry an entire assembled wooden cross because the logs of necessary size would have weighed over three hundred pounds, impossible for any man to carry alone. When nails were used, the Romans preferred five to seven inch square spikes. The condemned was made to lie down on the ground, and then he would be attached to the 'stipes,' meaning the cross-bar, in whatever manner the guards chose. He would then be hoisted up, and the cross beam would be tied to the patibulum. His feet could be nailed by rotating one leg painfully over the other, in order to hold both feet in place with one spike instead of two.

 Hands were usually tied tightly to the stipes, whether or not nails were also used. Death might take hours, or even days, depending on the exact methods used, the health of the crucified man, and other environmental conditions. Someone would be expected to die much faster in freezing rain than in sunshine. 'Beliefnet' continues:

'Breathing problems (asphyxiation) was not the sole cause of death. The combination of beating, circulation being cut off as the result of hanging from ropes that were tightly bound to support a man's weight (as nails alone were not sufficient enough to hold most human bodies) and exposure to the weather, all resulted in death by hypo-volemic shock. This means death through extreme pain, excessive bleeding, severe trauma, and exhaustion.'

Even if we are to assume that Jesus survived all of this, the wounds of crucifixion alone would have rendered him crippled for weeks. If nails were driven through his hands and feet, then some bones may have been broken. It's probable that a skilled Roman executioner would know how to inflict either the minimum or maximum damage to the condemned.

Jesus would have limped for weeks while his feet healed, and only walked with the aid of a stick. His sandals would have to be lined with thick lamb's wool pads inside to help cushion his walk. He would not have appeared to the apostles 'whole' again in a mere three days; alive, even upright, yes, but 'whole?' No. Unless, according to Pilate's orders and the personal sentiments of the soldiers, no one held the belief that Jesus was deserving of this punishment and death. This does not indicate a 'crucifixion plot' in which Jesus was actively involved in a deception, but rather that sympathies were for Jesus and his family, and against a few arrogant and haughty priests.

There are other logical reasons that could help explain his unique survival and recovery. When we closely examine the method of the crucifixion used on Jesus, we first come to realize that no *mortal* wound of any kind was ever inflicted upon him. The thrust of the spear was not made to give Jesus the death stroke. It may not have been inflicted high into the rib cage, but lower, just above the hip bone. It may have been just a poke, just enough to gauge if the 'corpse' showed any automatic reflex reactions to new pain. Nothing further was required.

His arms and feet would have been secured with thick, hard cords wrapped so tight that these limbs would become numb due to diminished circulation. Even if nails had been driven into his hands, this may not have produced any great expression of pain, and there would have been very little loss of blood. The ropes would have impairing his circulation so much that it could even lead to fainting, or a deep apoplexy to the heart and brain. In other words, he would probably have slipped into a coma.

Both of the thieves who were crucified with Jesus were still alive, and showed outward signs of life. This is why their legs were broken by the Roman soldiers. Jesus was already exhausted from the scouring, whether that was mild or severe, it reduced him to a more weakened state than the other two men who were crucified with him.

However one approaches the events of the crucifixion, there is a message worth reflecting on. To have died on the cross may not have been the message of the crucifixion. The message may have been more about survival, about strength and true grit, and overcoming evil against all the odds. To *survive* the crucifixion may be the real miracle and the real message of the cross, and we missed the point God was making when Jesus survived.

In order to prove that Jesus survived crucifixion, we would not only need medical information to rely on, we would also seek verification from sources *outside* of the Bible

If Jesus survived the crucifixion, it may not have been under the *most* horrendous circumstances that one could possibly imagine. There may have been friends and family frantically working behind the scenes to avert an unjust and unfair tragedy. Even Pilate himself seems to have been in on the secrets to his survival. He rose to the occasion because he realized the treachery of the accusers against Jesus, whom he had repeatedly declared an innocent man.

Pontius Pilate

There is an interesting incident about Pilate told by Josephus the Jewish historian. This is a very small matter, barely worthy of historical mention, and yet it may be one of the keys to understanding everything about the trial and crucifixion of Jesus. This concerns something that happened shortly *after* the crucifixion.

Josephus recounts that during the Procuratorship of Pilate there was an anonymous Samaritan who had gathered a following. He led a small group to Mount Gerazim, where he claimed that he knew the Samaritan secrets and the very spot where Moses hid the holy vessels on the mountain. (*Antiquities* 18.85) He was going to reveal this secret hiding place and stand before the people as their new messiah.

When Pilate heard what this man was up to, he sent a band of cavalry and footmen who intercepted them at the village of Tirabatha. Some of them were killed and some were taken as prisoners. Their leader escaped and Pilate issued a death sentence for him. Why would certain relics of Moses hold any interest at all for Pilate? Why would he 'rescue' the relics of Moses from this crowd?

Some say that the name of this leader was Taheb and that he wanted his followers to believe that, in fact, *he* was their expected Messiah and not Jesus. This leads us to ask how did Taheb learn about this secret hiding place? Why now, right after the crucifixion of Jesus, would it be of special interest for him?

Gamaliel, a Pharisee, mentions a man named Judas as a failed messianic leader. In Christianity, Judas is known as the Essene treasurer who turned Jesus over to the authorities. Judas is also mentioned in the *Book of the Bee* as the man whole stole the Rod of Moses from the family of Jesus. Now there seems to be a lot more to this whole crucifixion plot against Jesus than what has originally appeared on the surface.

After Pilate was able to gain control of the gang that set out to steal the relics of Moses, he issued a death warrant for their leader, who was never captured. Soon after this incident, the Samaritan authorities appealed to the Syrian legate Vitellius, claiming they were being unduly harassed and, in fact, they were just 'poor refugees' suffering under the harshness of Pilate. They had made it appear that Pilate used too heavy a hand on them through some 'misunderstand-ings.' Vitellius suggested that Pilate travel to Rome and personally explain the details to Tiberius. However, Emperor Tiberius died before Pilate could make the journey. Tiberius died quietly in a villa at Misenum on 16 March A.D. 37. He was 78 years old. This suggests that neither Vitellius nor Tiberius felt any urgent credibility in the charges of the Samaritans.

In a letter sent to Rome on behalf of Pilate, he was complaining about the smug insolence of Caiaphas and the High priests. Pilate had complained to Rome that these priests were totally untrustworthy, insolent, arrogant, greedy, and self-serving. They had even refused to attend a banquet given in their honor by Pilate. By the time of the crucifixion, Rome was already aware that anything involving Caiaphas and these High Priests was to be regarded with suspicion. Thus, it was soon after the crucifixion that, according to *Antiquities* 18.95, Vittelius '*removed* from his sacred office the high priest Joseph surnamed Caiaphas.'

And now the real crucifixion plot begins to unfold, and was even discussed in far-away India.

Assuming that Jesus survived the crucifixion, then he was obvi-ously never harassed or openly 'hunted down' after the crucifixion, even though many were aware of his survival and recovery, including the Romans. However, we read about a true rebel who *was* hunted down, someone who was about to steal relics of Moses. Following fast and hard on that event, we next discover that soon after the crucifixion, Caiaphas lost his position as High Priest, a decision supported by the Romans themselves.

The *Bible* says of Pilate: *'For he knew that for envy they had delivered him (Jesus.)'* Pilate was well aware of the larger plot underway, a plot instigated by the jealous and greedy Caiaphas himself.

A group of Samaritans were attempting to steal something of Moses, something they obviously had no rights to. Why? Recall that Moses told the Israelites to wait for the next prophet, the next Messiah who would be known to them because he would possess holy relics that were once owned by Moses himself. With Jesus well and truly out of the way, they rushed to steal these relics, thinking this would then establish the credentials they needed to support their own false messiah, and perhaps to place an illegal usurper on a remote throne in Kashmir.

Interestingly, there are three references outside of the Bible that provide us with details about events very similar to this. The first, taken from the *Book of the Bee* describes an incident where Judas did actually steal the 'Rod of Moses' from Jesus. The *Rajatarangini* also describes how a king of Kashmir, an usurper named Jayendra, had stolen the wealth of the rightful king, Sandimatti, and had him either jailed or exiled. Eventually, in a jealous rage, Jayendra had him crucified. This is the *only* crucifixion story ever to appear in Indian literature, and it is a most compelling parallel to the events of the crucifixion of Jesus. Obviously, both accounts were based upon the same historical individual, Jesus.

The *Rajatarangini* then goes on to mention the next king, Megha-vahana, who had acquired a magic 'parasol.' the Indian equivalent of a rod of kingship. The premise about parasols is to infer a halo or aura of protection around auspicious individuals, something that conferred high rank and even enabled magic. He had obtained this most valu-able relic through Amri-ta prabha (Mary, the first queen or Mother Queen). Both of these stories took place about the time of the crucifix-ion, and are connected to auspicious relics. The Rod of Moses had been with Jesus since his birth and was therefore his hereditary property.

During the crucifixion, it was Pilate who steadfastly believed in the innocence of Jesus. It was Pilate who realized that the claims of Jesus were legitimate. Pilate liked and respected Jesus. Some have gone so far as to suggest that Jesus and Pilate attended the same Druid College and had known and befriended each other years before. It was Pilate who offered Jesus shelter and safety inside the Pretorium. It was Pilate who told the guards to 'go lightly' on the scouring and crucifixion of Jesus. The *Gospels of Nicodemus* tells us that Pilate had instructed his soldiers,

> *Let Jesus be brought with gentleness* (presumably throughout his trial)

The reports about nails driven into Jesus' hands do not all agree. Some say that his hands *bore scars*. These could well have been scars from the ropes that held him to the cross. Nails may _not_ have been used in his hands. Any Roman guard who had performed several crucifixions would know exactly how to use the ropes and nails. By applying just the right degree of tightness, or by changing the thickness of the ropes or the nails used, and the angle at which they penetrated the skin, he could worsen, or lighten, the pain and suffering he inflicted. The legs of Jesus were not broken. He was taken down from the cross in only three hours, unconscious and either in a coma or a state of shock.

It is probable that Jesus survived the crucifixion without ever realizing what heroic efforts were taking place around him to save his life. He would never have realized just how far Pilate, his guards, Joseph of Arimathea, and others who believed in his innocence would go to insure his survival. Jesus *did* survive a great trauma, one that few men could have survived under any circumstances. There is no doubt about that. However, without the direct *human* intervention of others, including perhaps a few good centurions, Jesus would surely have perished that day. How much help came from 'divine intervention' remains to be determined. No doubt there was an element of the miraculous to his survival too.

Pontius Pilate sent an account of the trial of Jesus to Rome. So impressed was Tiberius with the event and all he heard about Jesus, that he asked the Roman Senate to enroll Jesus among the Roman gods.

Conspiracy Theorists

Some authors have come up with several conspiracy theories that seem to imply that Pilate and Jesus collaborated together to insure the survival of Jesus. They think that the whole crucifixion was a staged hoax that had been worked out between Pilate and Jesus, or Jesus and his disciples. Such books include *The Passover Plot* by Hugh J. Schonfield, *The Jesus Papers* by Michael Baigent, and *The Jesus Dynasty* by James Tabor. **(5, 66)** There are additional books of this genre that suggest there was active fraud on the part of Jesus. They put forth the premise that Jesus was being manipulative, and trying to convince us (and himself) that he was, in fact, the expected messiah. Such theorists believe that he survived through a carefully worked-out and preconceived plan of deceit to make it appear as though he had fulfilled all the prophecies for the expected messiah. Even the Qur'an claims Jesus did not die on the cross.

One theorist about such a crucifixion 'plot' is author Barbara Theiring, who has based her theories on her discovery of the so-called Bible Pesher Codes. Pesher is a Hebrew word that means to 'interpret' or 'provide a solution.' This often takes the form of citing a biblical passage or quotation out of context, sometimes even slightly altered, followed by the words, *'Peshero'* or *'Pesher-ha-davar'*, meaning 'its interpretation' or 'the interpretation of the passage is....' Theiring's work is based on some very controversial assumptions about the meanings of certain stories and words that appear in the *Bible*, the *Dead Sea Scrolls*, and other documents. The primary problem with this is that the meanings and interpretations are apparent *only* to her.

In interpreting these secret meanings, Theiring and others have come up with the following assumptions- there never was a virgin birth, or a crucifixion, or a resurrection. She believes that these are deliberately manufactured myths that never happened. She also believes that the Gospel authors, the apostles, knew this, and yet every one went along with the fraud. These views are not accepted by most religious scholars.

James Tabor, author of *The Jesus Dynasty,* describes how it was Annas, father-in-law of Caiaphas, who wielded the real power behind the scenes.

'Five of his sons were officially appointed to the position of High Priest. Next to Herod Antipas, Joseph Annas was the most wealthy and powerful Jewish leader of the time. This would not be the last time the Annas dynasty attacked the Jesus dynasty. In 62 CE, Annas 2nd had James, brother of Jesus killed.'

Pilate seems to have been willing to risk everything for the sake of Jesus and his family. By keeping Jesus under the care of his own soldiers, and on his orders alone, he knew there would be a chance to control the outcome. This is why Jesus was handed over to one of Pilate's most trusted centurions. Had Jesus been given entirely back into the custody of the priests, his fate would have been very different. It was Pilate who made sure that he and his closest soldiers remained in control of Jesus at all times, and thus helped determine the outcome. Jesus had no part in their decisions on his behalf because Jesus put his faith in God, not in his fellow man, and seemed quite prepared to accept that death would be his final outcome.

The Ethiopian and Abyssinian (Coptic) Churches canonized Pilate for his help during the crucifixion. He is now one of their official saints. There are two mountains in France named after him, with the town of Avalon not far from Mount Pilatus. Some say that Pilate eventually committed suicide. Some accounts even suggest that he was murdered, but the truth is not really known about where, when, or how he died. He could have died peacefully as an old retired country gentleman for all we know. Certainly he died with the knowledge that Jesus survived because of his direct intervention. Like Jesus, Pilate has become an enigma.

Let's look at what other eye witnesses have to say about seeing Jesus even years *after* the crucifixion, and how these statements support the claims that he did indeed survive (no one claimed they were seeing the ghost or spirit of Jesus):

Jewish Wars 6; 2:2(August 70 CE.)Flight to Pella

As Josephus spoke these words, with groans and tears in his eyes, his voice was intercepted by sobs. However, the Romans could not but pity the affliction he was under, and wonder at his conduct. But for John, and those that were with him, they were but the more exasperated against the Romans on this account...they and the city were doomed to destruction. Some also there were... watching a proper opportunity when they might quietly get away... fled to the Romans, of whom were the high priests Joseph and Jesus, and...the sons of high priests....

The Bible (c.40-70 CE)

There are written accounts in both Luke and Mark that they witnessed the ascension of Jesus into heaven after the crucifixion, as for example in *Luke 24:50-53*

Jesus *'was carried up into heaven'*

This is very specific and it eliminates any possibility of this being a spiritual, self-generated ascension. This clearly indicates that Jesus had help, that he was *carried..* These ascensions were not described as though a man were appearing as an apparition, a ghost, or a spirit separating from his body. The broken body of Jesus, in his weakened condition and unconscious state of mind, was *carried* to heaven.

The two angels in shining garments who appeared at the empty tomb assured everyone that Jesus was in a safe place where he would recover. In the *Synoptic Gospel* Magdalene is asked (in some accounts by the angels, in other accounts by Jesus himself, who appeared as a gardener) *'Why weepest thou?'* There was no need for sadness, for, in truth, they already knew that Jesus was alive. He was going to recover.

The story that Magdalene saw Jesus momentarily as a gardener after the crucifixion can be taken an incredible story of love and of Jesus' concern for others. In his terrible and weakened state, his body still swollen from traumas and racked with pain, Jesus somehow managed to be carried to the side of the road just long enough to see her and reassure her of his survival. The next brief appearance of Jesus came eight days later. Jesus said to the apostles:

"Look at my hands and my feet; see that it is I myself. Touch me and see; for a ghost does not have flesh and bones as you see that I have" *(Luke 24:39).*

After he said this, he was taken up before their very eyes, and a cloud hid him from their sight.

They were looking intently up into the sky as he was going, when suddenly two men dressed in white stood beside them. "Men of Galilee," they said, "why do you stand here looking into the sky? This same Jesus, who has been taken (Greek *analambano*) from you into heaven, will come back in the same way you have seen him go into heaven." *Acts 1:9-11*

The apostles did not understand the ascension to mean that Jesus was no longer with them. They did not express grief or fear or disappointment. Instead they "returned to Jerusalem with great joy" *(Luke 24:52)*. That's not the emotion you feel when you lose your best friend. The ascension did not mean they lost something. They gained something wonderful and miraculous and they knew it, because they witnessed it themselves.

There is nothing in the *Old Testament* that spoke of a *resurrected* messiah because this was not a Hebrew concept, but one that began appearing only in the *New Testament*. Because Jesus survived the crucifixion and returned from a 'near-death' experience, this has led to the Christian idea that *all* bodies would be physically resurrected again. The lines between the Christian concept and the Buddhist concept of Ascended Masters, rebirths, and resurrections become hopelessly blurred here. Let's examine more claims for the appearance of a physical Jesus after the crucifixion. These are presented roughly in chronological order as they appear *outside* Biblical references from the apostles:

Ignatius of Antioch (c.35-100 CE)

Ignatius is generally considered to be one of the Apostolic Fathers (the earliest authoritative group of the Church Fathers) and is a saint in the Catholic Church. He is also responsible for the first known use of the Greek word katholikos meaning 'universal,' from which we derive the word Catholic. He has left us several letters that are among the earliest surviving church documents written during the time that Jesus actually lived. In his *Epistle to the Church at Smyrna* he wrote:

I know and believe that he was in the flesh even after the Resurrection, and when he came to those with Peter he said:

"Take, handle me and see that I am not a bodiless phantom."
Origen quoted a similar passage from *The Gospel of Peter*
(Jesus said to them) "The son of man has risen from the sleep
(sleep as in either coma or shock.)

The Pillars at the Temple of Solomon in Kashmir

Can we find additional evidence outside the Bible that Jesus
survived the crucifixion? Yes, we can. Earlier, we discussed the pillars
at the Temple of Solomon in Kashmir that were carved by Jesus and
Thomas in 45 CE. These inscriptions were in the Persian *Sulus* script.
One inscription read;

> 'In these times (of Gondopharnes) Yuz Asaf was here to pro-
> claim his prophethood, year fifty-four.' (Yuz-Asaf, Jesus, son of
> Joseph)

> *(note:* the year fifty-four is a translation. The inscription gives
> the year 3154 of the Lukaka era.) The other pillar is inscribed:
> 'He is Yasu (Issa) prophet of the children of Israel.' (*Dareen
> waqt Hazrati Yuz Asaf da' wa-i-Paighambari mikund. Sal pinjah
> wa char).* The next inscription reads;

> 'Son of Marjan erected this pillar. The mason of this pillar is Bi-
> hishti Zargar' (Thomas) (see also *Illustrations of Ancient Build-
> ings* by A.A. Coli that shows additional photographs taken of
> these inscriptions.) The book *Jesus in Heaven on Earth* also
> contains photographs of the same inscriptions that were taken
> by Major H.H. Cole. **(1, 21, 24, 27, 36, 37)**

The Bhavishya Mahapurana (c. 115 CE)

Written in 115 CE, this account recalls the sojourn of Jesus to
India and his meeting with King Shalivahana in the year 78 CE. From
the 'Tomb of Jesus' website, we are offered this information:

The main text that supports the theory that Jesus was buried in Kashmir is the *Bhavishya Maha Purana*, the ninth book of the eighteen texts
considered holy by Hindus; this text records the encounter between
King Shalivahan and Jesus Christ, long after the crucifixion. In this
passage, Jesus describes himself as being born of a virgin and as the
Son of God. The description of Jesus in the *Bhavishya Maha Purana*

records him as being fair skinned and wearing a white garment. Historians contend that this document has great value because, unlike the Gospels, this can be traced to be a specific date, the year 115 CE, which according to the account that Jesus lived 120 years, would have taken place five years prior to Jesus' death.

Irenaeus (c.130-202 CE)

Irenaeus was a Church Bishop in Gaul (Lyon, France). Today, both the Catholic Church and the Eastern Orthodox Church consider him a saint and a father of the early Church. He was a disciple of Polycarp, who was a disciple of John the Evangelist. Irenaeus wrote a book called *Against Heresies* in which he claimed that Jesus lived to be an old man, remaining in Asia with his disciple John, and others, up to the time that Emperor Trajan's reign began in 98 CE. Although this assertion of Saint Irenaeus has puzzled Christian scholars for centuries, Basilides of Alexandria, Mani of Persia, and Emperor Julian, all have stated that Jesus went to India after his crucifixion.

Clement of Alexandria (c150-c215) History of the Church 2:1

In the sixth book of Hypotyposes…"The Lord, after his resurrection, imparted knowledge to James the Just, John, and Peter, and they imparted it to the rest of the apostles, and they imparted it to the seventy.

In this case, above, 'imparted' is used to denote 'direct contact' down an ordinary chain of command. The apostles never communicated as spirits, or from the clouds, or any ways other than ordinary communications. Communications from Jesus and from the apostles are here lumped together as 'imparted' in ordinary ways.

Gospel of Philip (c.180-350 CE)

Those who say that the Lord died first and (then) rose up are in error, for he rose up first and (then) died… Flesh and blood shall not inherit the kingdom of God *(1 Co 15:50)*… Jesus took them all by stealth, for he did not appear as he was, but in the manner in which they would be able to see him.

Eusebius of Caesarea (c.263–339 CE)

When he wrote his *Ecclesiastical History* the primary concern of Eusebius was to accurately record historical records before they disappeared, before eyewitnesses might be killed, before libraries might be burned down during the next persecution. He faithfully transcribed the most important existing documents of his day, thus enabling later generations to have a collection of factual history about the first three centuries of Christianity. Eusebius' *Ecclesiastical History* is one of the classics of early Christianity, and stands in equal stature with the historical works of Josephus. One thing that Eusebius mentions, from the writings of Hegisippus, is how the royal Jews prided themselves on their well-kept genealogies and their illustrious ancestry.

Askew Codex (Pistis Sophia) (c.250-300 CE)

This text describes events between Jesus, the Marys, and his disciples, in 44 CE. This is clearly 11 years after the crucifixion. Jesus promises to take his disciples to see 'Heaven' and the spheres. After training his disciples, he sent them on to their missions to build churches and gain followers, while Jesus himself was witnessed 'ascending' in something 'giving off a very bright light.'

The Court of Gondopharnes at Taxila records Thomas and possibly Jesus with him in 45 CE, just a year later. Two independent and quite remote sources now confirm the survival of Jesus and his whereabouts in 44 and 45 CE.

Clearly, Jesus, Mary and the disciples are still all together long after the crucifixion, and planning travels and long periods of separation. In due time, they spread out and travel in completely different directions. There is no mention of Magdalene being pregnant at this time. Certainly there is no mention of a divorce at any time, and it would be strange to think that they would divorce if Magdalene was expecting 'their' child. Finally, there is no mention that Magdalene ever moved to France. The Eastern Orthodox Church maintains that Magdalene retired to Ephesus with Mother Mary and died there, that her relics were transferred to Constantinople in 886 and are preserved there. How a cult of Mary Magdalene first arose in Provence is not clear, but it obviously had much to do with relocation of her bones. As we have seen throughout, bones were often moved, and this has resulted in historical misinformation and baseless legends. Yes, the Marys could have traveled to France, perhaps to accompany priestesses who were establishing new churches. The Church of the East Holy Scriptures include the Gospels of Thomas that spoke of Magdalene as a priestess who assisted Jesus by training female priests and helping them establishing ashrams (convents, places for religious orders to run schools and medical centers)

There was a change of kings in Kashmir, and a coronation, approximately 40 CE and again at around 60 CE. Jesus was said to have 'increased in stature.' (Laurence Gardner, *Bloodline of the Holy Grail,* **24**). In addition, there is ample evidence along the Old Silk Road that Mother Mary accompanied Jesus on this 45 CE journey to Kashmir. This may be the journey when Jesus, still a prince in waiting, received the title 'Shresta-rasena.' This would explain why he 'increased' in stature. The title simply means the brightest or best light, one of numerous titles awarded to princes as they matured and assumed new responsibilities.

When strung together, these events present quite a striking picture, one of a vibrant, busy, active family. They were still training disciples, and still traveling great distances to establish new churches.

Panarion (c.374-376 CE.)

Bishop of Salamis, Panarion 29:7:7-8
The Nazoraean sect exists in Beroea near Coele Syria, in the Decapolis near the region of Pella, and in Bashan in the place called Cocaba, which in Hebrew is called Chochabe…all the disciples were living in Pella after they moved from Jerusalem, since Christ told them to leave Jerusalem and withdraw because it was about to be besieged. For this reason they settled in Peraea and there, as I said, they lived. This is where the Nazoraean sect began.

The Second Jewish War and fall of Jerusalem was in 135 CE. It is hard to imagine Jesus still alive at this advanced age. It is more realistic that he spoke with them around 70 CE, during the First Jewish War and destruction of Jerusalem.

8. Crucifixion

The Rajatarangini (c.1147-1149 CE)

The excerpt below depicts the only crucifixion ever to be described in India. It has been taken from the Sanskrit translation notes of the *Rajatarangini* by Jogesh Chunder Dutt:

'Sandimatti was taken illegally in the middle of the night. He died impaled by orders of Jayendra. His religious instructor, named Ishana, went to that place of death to perform the last ceremonies. He found the body fixed to a stake and reduced to a skeleton. He carried the corpse away from there. On the corpse' forehead words (titulus) proclaimed that he was a king who would return again to rule. As Ishana guarded the corpse and wondered how this could be, he then saw yoginis coming in a bright light. They took the skeleton away with them. Ishana tried to run after them with a sword in his hands, afraid they were stealing the skeleton and depriving him of a proper burial.

He found them restoring the corpse. He smelled strong perfumes and burning incense... Then, when Sandimatti recovered, he was dressed in radiant new clothes. When the people heard of this, many gathered to see Sandimatti but his appearance was so altered that they suspected it was someone else. They asked him personal questions and soon realized he knew the most intimate details and was the same man who spoke with them prior to his hanging on the stake.'

This crucified man, Sandimatti, was also known as the 'white raja' or 'King of the Aryans.' He was a member of the senate (much like the Sanhedrin) where he served as a Chief Minister. Upon his hanging, the sign on his head (titulus) predicted that one day he would be coronated as king. The titulus over the head of Jesus also proclaimed him king of the Jews. This was always taken as mockery, when in fact it may have been intended as the highest honor, recognition of his real position in life, one that Caiaphas tried to snuff out.

Book of the Bee (c. 1222 CE)

This is a historical compilation of Bible legends, written 98 years after the *Rajatarangini*. They were written on different continents and seem to have been based upon separate and independent resources. *Book of the Bee* was written by Solomon, Bishop of Bassora in Syriac, and is regarded by the Nestorian Christians as 'sacred history'. From chapter 30 we get the impression that there was a much bigger plot afoot when Judas Iscariot betrayed Jesus. As we have examined earlier, Judas was apparently helping a group of Samaritans led by Taheb, who wanted to be the new messiah. By producing the relics of Moses, especially the Rod of Moses, he thought he would fulfill the prophecy of Moses. Could Taheb have been Judas Iscariot? Yes, it is probable that he was, or that they were somehow connected with Caiaphas in their plot against Jesus.

Judas has also been described as the 'failed messiah'. Another interesting note here is that Judas was of the tribe of Gad, and Gad was also the name of a brother of Gondopharnes, a king who Thomas would soon visit at Taxila.

The rod that was mentioned in this quote will be discussed again, because it becomes the most vital clue linking Jesus to the tomb found in Kashmir. *The Book of the Bee* **(105)** states:

After all the children of Israel were dead, save Joshua the son of Nun and Caleb the son of Yôphannâ (Jephunneh), they went into the Promised Land, and took the rod with them, on account of the wars with the Philistines and Amalekites. And Phineas hid the rod in the desert, in the dust at the gate of Jerusalem, where it remained until our Lord Christ was born. And He, by the will of His divinity, showed the rod to Joseph the husband of Mary, and it was in his hand when he fled to Egypt with our Lord and Mary, until he returned to Nazareth. From Joseph his son Jacob, who was surnamed the brother of our Lord, took it; and from Jacob, Judas Iscariot, who was a thief, stole it. When the Jews crucified our Lord, they lacked wood for the arms of our Lord; and Judas in his wickedness gave them the rod, which became a judgment and a fall unto them, but an uprising unto many.

Re-Evaluating Salvation

The whole concept upon which Christianity is based is that Jesus died for our sins. Through this act, he redeemed our souls for us. This entire concept has been based upon just one subtle mistranslation of *Isaiah* 53:5. It does NOT say 'He was wounded *'for'* our transgressions, crushed *'for'* our iniquities. Rather, the proper translation is: 'He was wounded *'from'* our transgressions, crushed *'from'* our iniquities.'

8. Crucifixion

The correct meaning of the crucifixion is not that he suffered to *'atone'* for the sins of others, but that he suffered *'because'* of the sins of others. This difference is ever so subtle, yet crucial. It means that we, alone, are totally responsible to ourselves for ourselves. We are accountable for our own actions when we stand before God.

What of baptism? Baptism was once known as 'photismos,' which means illumination and enlightenment. Clearly then, Baptism represents the 'opening of our eyes to the light,' to a willingness to look for God and to act within the law. It's a form of 'pledge of allegiance,' a sworn oath, an initiation ceremony into a religious concept. It is really about the *willingness* within each of us to at least be 'God-conscious.' But it is not an 'exclusive' club initiation that keeps all 'non-members' out of heaven. It is a symbolic religious act, similar to those that exist in all religions.

If Jesus survived the crucifixion and went to India, then Jesus was there during the seventeen years after the crucifixion that Thomas also spent in India. And in fact their paths crossed many times and their relationship was one of very close and continued friendship for their entire lives. We can examine the life of Thomas in India, and the extent and influence of his teachings, and gain a whole new respect for the great accomplishments of both men in India. Theirs continues to be an amazing story of two amazing lives. But as we go over the past history of these men and India, it also becomes pertinent to understand modern India and Pakistan. The graves we have examined thus far, all but Solomon are known to be specifically in either India or Pakistan. The fate of these relics and graves may in part be determined by which country has possession of them now.

Wahabi and The Future of The Rod and Graves

In India, a democratic form of government rules, one that allows religious freedom to all. All of upper India was once regarded as part of Kashmir. This gradually shrunk and when Pakistan was newly formed by Partition, there went the remaining half of Kashmir. It is now an Islamic majority state that currently borders on strict fundamentalism. One aspect of that strict fundamentalism is called 'Wahabi' or Salafi School (Muwahhidun or unitarians). Almost all people in Mecca and Medina, almost all residents of Saudi Arabia belong to this school and try to propagate their fundamentalist Islamic beliefs around the world. Under Al Saud rule, governments have shown readiness to enforce compliance with Islamic laws and interpretations of fifteenth century Islamic values on themselves and on others. Democracy is neither admired nor a goal for them. Their interpretations of Islam forbid (among other things) listening to any music that is not about God; forbidding the drawing or any replication of human beings or any other living things; harsh restrictions upon women, even dictating the burkha they are required to wear and forbidding them to drive a car; also forbidden is praying while visiting tombs (they prefer to destroy all tombs, such as the 3,000 year old tomb of Joseph and even Mohammed's tomb). The oil-rich Saudis, who are all practicing Wahabis, have not spread hospitals, schools, or equality and enlightenment across Islamic nations, but mosques, madrassas, and propaganda backed by endless oil dollars meant to convert everyone in the world to Islam, and especially every Muslim to their Wahabi Islam. The Taliban are an example of their success and view of the world.

Theirs is the influence that seeps into Pakistan and Kashmir, destroying once vibrant economies and threatening the sites visited in this book. They do not believe in preserving any part of the past that could be used as a focal of worship. Even the act of praying at such places is sinful although they are willing to overlook these edicts when it suites them, such as at the Cave of Machpelah where Abraham and Sarah are buried.

Whether it's the Bamiyan Buddha, the rod of Moses, or Michelangelo's *David*, they must eventually be destroyed. We will talk about this again later because it has a direct impact on the tomb of Jesus, but next we will follow the path of Thomas in India, for no one since Buddha had more profound positive influence on religion and politics in India than the presence of Jesus and Thomas there.

9. Thomas

National Stamp of India, date of issue unknown

Was Thomas a brother to Jesus, or his twin? No. He was Judas Thomas, of the Herod family. The earliest church fathers believed he was the twin brother of Lysius, whose parents were Diophanes and Rhoa of Antioch (Syria). In the *Clementine Homolies* Thomas was believed to be the twin of Eleezer. Thus it becomes understandable why he is called 'the twin.' However, he was never the biological twin of Jesus.

Many writings attributed to and about Thomas have survived (*Acts of Thomas, Infancy Gospels,* et al), yet not once does Thomas call Jesus 'my brother,' or refer to Mary as his mother or 'our' mother. In fact of all the apostles who have left us writings, none of them has claimed that Mary is their mother, even though they are called 'brothers' of Jesus in the Bible. **(18)**

Origen mentions that the *Book of James* and the *Gospel of Peter* stated that the 'brethren of the Lord' were actually elder sons of Joseph by a former wife. This is the first mention that we have saying that these sons were not born of Mary, and this was declared in a book no older than the early second century.

Taxila

Taxila, as we saw earlier, was a great city of learning that attracted Roman and Greek students. After leaving the Holy Land in 44 CE, Thomas went with Haban to the court of Gondopharnes. A year later, in 45 CE, Jesus, John Mark, and Julian of Nisibis were also there. John Mark had been the official 'Chief of the Proselytes' of the Egyptian head of the Therapeutae at Qumran, but here he was known as Moroko (or Malaka), the Chief Minister to Jesus. Eutychus was the Greek name for Bartholomew, another name identified with John Mark.

In excavations at the Jaulian Monastery at Taxila, a series of sculptures has been recovered showing a man who looks like Jesus. They are dressed as travelers and their fine horses appear with them on several plaques. The edict that identifies this group dates to circa 49 CE, and reads *'The man with the peaked cap is the donor of the group.'*

How the Jaulian Monastery got its name is uncertain, but according to Sir John Marshall (the archaeologist who headed twenty years of excavations at Taxila) it was probably named for Julian of Nisibis (old Iraq city) who accompanied Thomas to Taxila, and may have been in charge of the construction and engineering for the entire village. As we saw earlier with Magdalene, the building of ashrams, convents, and monasteries was, and still is, an integral part of most all religious groups. The Aramaic inscription there reads that the 'foreigner' (peredisia -priyadarsia) was a carpenter-master builder (naggaruda) who was accompanied by a sun-god (rudradeva -romadota).

In one of the depictions, there is a young man standing next to Jesus. He wears similar clothes, except that he also has a 'mukhat' (like a bishop's hat or a small crown) to indicate he held an important rank.

After their plans were made, Thomas and Haban went in advance to make the preparations for the arriving caravan. Jesus and Mary were not expected to arrive until many months later. On this journey, Jesus was leading a small caravan of family members and refugees. According to the various accounts found along the Old Silk Road (and manuscripts located at the Farsi Library in Islamabad), there were more than twenty family members in this group, mostly women and children, and they traveled slowly. It took nearly nine months to make the journey that normally only took several weeks.

The Essenes wrote of the last visit Jesus made to see them before his departure: "His soul was greatly moved, and his heart was filled with sadness, for he knew this would be his last walk in Judea."

Nearly a year later, in 45 CE, Jesus, Thomas, Julian, and John Mark would all be reunited at the court of Gondopharnes. Some of those in the caravan with Jesus may have been the wives and children of the apostles. In the cities of Mylapor and Malabar, Thomas had also made similar arrangements for the emigration of an entire Jewish community.

Khwaja Nazir Ahmed cited accounts along the Old Silk Road that chronicled the travels of Jesus, and were written in Persian (Farsi), Arabic, Latin, Greek, and Aramaic. Many of these have not yet been translated into English. He clearly mentions that Jesus had the rod with him at all times. At each place that they stopped to rest for a few days, either an oral tradition or a written account was left about them. Although there are dozens of places known as 'the resting place of

Mother Mary' there is only one that is known as the 'final' resting place of Mother Mary, and that is on the Queen's mountain in Murree.

Gondopharnes provided the additional land for the building of the Jaulian town and monastery. This was a far more practical solution for all because it meant having year-round residences near to, but not actually in Kashmir, which could be inaccessible during long, hard, winter months. Most of the kings who lodged in the valley of Kashmir only went there in the summer months, and some kings rarely went there at all for years at a time because of its remoteness. They left ministers in place to manage the affairs of the country and keep them informed. No elaborate palaces were ever built in Kashmir. Kings usually reigned from large, comfortable wood and stone homes. These were always regarded as family property, and so with every new king, a new location, and often an entire new city had to be established for h8imself and his retinue. In most circumstances it was unthinkable to demand the departure of the current families from their homes. Every ruler had to start over with new residences.

The Carpenters

Thomas and Jesus were both known as carpenters, which doesn't mean this is how they made their living. It denotes just one of many skills that an accomplished man of their day would possess. Thus Thomas was regarded as having the required skills to repair the crack in the dome at the Temple of Solomon. Although local Brahmins objected that a 'foreigner' had been chosen to repair the temple, they were assured by Gondopharnes and Jesus to allow Thomas to complete the work. The entire story sounds strangely suspicious. Anyone could repair a cracked dome. Why was the assistance of Thomas required for this particular endeavor?

First, it seems like the same ruse that had been used by Menelik when he visited the Temple of Solomon to do 'repairs.' It seemed to be an excuse for many men to be present around the temple with digging tools, donkeys, carts and supplies needed for a stay of at least a few days on the mountain. Menelik then left Kashmir with a huge golden 'bench.' It must have been hidden somewhere under or near the temple, because something as valuable as a huge golden-clad throne would not have been left unattended in plain site.

9. Thomas

The word carpenter has been historically misleading. Jesus, and his father, Joseph, have always been portrayed as 'humble' carpenters with meager skills. However, the word terton, as applied to them, was used to signify a special kind of builder, usually a master in stone cutting, one who understood the complexities of laying temples out geometrically, based on astronomical alignments. In Tibet, the word terton suggests 'secret wisdom' and is still used by Buddhist monks to denote those who have memorized the secret wisdom. James Barclay says in the *Mind of Jesus* that a tekton was a construction engineer or architect.

As tertons (special knowledge-the 'architects') and tektons (special skills-the 'builders') they would apply their knowledge of 'sacred geometry' to create intricate labyrinths and false passages, places to hide the real treasures of the tombs and temples.

Somewhere in, or near, the temple was a safe hiding place, an 'ark' (archival) where the Rod of Moses and other relics could safely be hidden. This was the real reason they came here, not to make repairs, but to covertly make sure the vault was secure, and perhaps even to make some withdrawals and deposits of their own.

Remember, Jesus carried the rod with him all the way from Judea, and there would certainly have been other family valuables they would carry on this journey. We know that historically many family heirlooms were kept at Glastonbury, and these were lost in the great fire of 1184 CE. It is worth considering that as Jesus and Mother Mary brought half the family valuables to Kashmir, Magdalene, possibly accompanied by Joseph of Arimathea and a daughter of Magdalene may have been bringing sacred family relics to Glastonbury. She may have been managing the relocation of other apostles, their families, and women who were ordained as priests to establish new convents, monasteries, and churches in the family name. But this does not suggest that she remained there permanently.

Among the many records once stored at Glastonbury was the *Kolbrin*, (30) a book about creation that, according to legend, Jesus himself read from, because there are several coincidences in the spoken words of Jesus and the written words of the Kolbrin. At first it was presumed to be lost in the fire along with many other documents and relics, but a copy was found years later, and has recently become widely available around the world.

The Church in India

Thomas had successfully established churches in Palestine, Mesopotamia, Parthia and Ethiopia, before coming to India.

Following the death of Mother Mary, Thomas left northern India with seven other religious leaders and their families. Among them was Prince Kepha (Peter), who had also become a Bishop. He assisted Thomas for several years. They established seven new churches, and trained hundreds of new priests and bishops. This information was provided to me by members of the Church of Thomas at Kerala.

Thomas used the city of Kodungallur as his home base. This location proved to be highly rewarding. This was a prosperous sea port, a place from which contacts could be maintained with countries in many directions. Near the port of Muziris (Muchiti) on the Malabar Coast, this was the great commercial center for spices that were in great demand in the Roman territories. Rome spared no effort to make these ports fast and safe. It took less than forty days for a spice-laden ship to leave here and deliver its goods to Rome. This became known as the southern route or 'Spice route.' Jews, Arabs, African and oriental merchants shared their lives on a daily basis here, and these ports were bristling with their vibrancy.

From the very beginning, Thomas was warmly received. Within eight days of his arrival, Thomas had already ordained two bishops, Kepha and Paul, for the cities of Malabar (presently known as Kerala) and Coromandal (Mylapor).

Prince Kepha's father, Prince Anthrayos (Andrew), the King of Tiruvanchikkulam (Kodungallur), and the entire royal family had become Christians. These kings were Hebrews. As the result of Thomas having the support of such prominent and wealthy families, Christianity was warmly received here and spread rapidly. The

Thomasian arrivals and converts were granted many exceptional privileges and honors. This is attested to by the number of documents and copper plates that have survived. These have become known as the '*Magna Carta*' of the Thomasine Christians.

These Christians were respectfully addressed as the *Nazarini mappilas,* or the 'sons of kings.' They were regarded as people of high and noble birth, greatly reputed for their fairness and good behavior, and well-formed (handsome) good looks. All of the churches in India that are associated with Thomas were known as Saivite temples (not the same as temples to Shiva). The Saivite temples were first used as the original Christian churches of India.

The Malankara Church of Syria recorded that, among the converts that flocked to Thomas, several were of the high caste 'Nambuthiri Brahmins.' They included families from the Kalli, Kalikavu, Pagalomat-tom, and Shankarapuri of Paylayoor. According to Antony de Gouvea, no other caste was held in such high esteem among the Malabarians as these Syrian Christians. They were even allowed to have their own military force because they were also regarded as the protectors of certain low-caste groups. They were allowed try legal cases, and even inflict capitol punishment if necessary.

Goueva said that these Christians had even supplied the Raja of Cochin with an army of fifty thousand men. The success of a king in times of war would often depend upon the number of Thomasian Christians that would support him. This actually led to a competition to gain the favor of these Christians in India, and many non-Christian kings rushed to endow them with tax-free lands, and appoint them as ministers and councilors.

Cochin has been significant to both Jewish and Christian history in India, at least since the days of Solomon, for it is Solomon who is credited with first developing and improving the seaports. His warships brought back merchandise from Muziris, the Cranganore-Egyptian settlements along the India coastline. While discussing the dealings of the Phoenicians with Muziris, Pliny, the Roman historian (23-79 CE), complained that every year they were sending large sums of money to India for silk, spices, pearls, and gems.

The *Book of Esther* cites decrees that were enacted by Ahasu-erus, which related to the Jews who had dispersed in his empire from

Hodu to Cush (India to Ethiopia). There are two copper plates in Cochin's main synagogue that detail the privileges that the Jews of Anjuvannam were granted to them, *'so long as the world and the moon exist.'*

No 'Hindu' temples exist that can be dated before the first century. However, after the first century all Hindu temples were built followed the plans of Hebrew temples. This temple concept later extended to the Watts (temples) of Buddhism and the churches of Christianity. Visitors would often mistake a Hindu or Buddhist temple for a church because the appearances were so similar and the interior designs almost identical.

All over India, the ancient signs of the Star of David and of the cross appeared with the symbol 'Ohm' (amen). This symbol remains in every Christian church in India, and om (pra-Nava mantra) appears with almost all objects of worship in all religions in India.

M.M. Ninan (45) points out that the impact of Jesus and Thomas on India was huge. Their influence rippled through all of India and into every religion on India soil. Thomas transformed India totally the way that John transformed the western world.

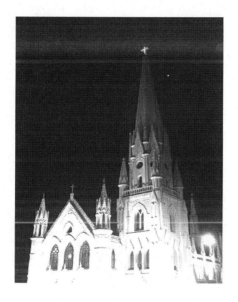

Saint Thomas Church, Chennai India, built over his tomb

Amen in Arabic   **Amen in Hebrew**

Sanskrit Om

Jain Om

Tamil Om

Sikh (Ek Onkar)

Vedic Om

There were three broad classes of religions when Jesus and Thomas entered India; Aryan Vedic (nature-sun-star worship) Buddhism (anti-theistic) and Jainism (non-theistic). Of all the sacred Hindu scriptures, only one Veda tradition existed at the time, and it was written in the same Persian script as the Zend Avestas of Zoroastrians.

The symbol of the fish in early Christianity (Pisciculi) also appears in India. The fish symbol has been used for millennia worldwide as a religious symbol associated with the Great Mother Goddess. However, in Christianity it is believed to be an acronym used by Christians. The Greek word for fish is ichthus. **Ι Χ Θ Υ Σ**

Each letter translates to represent the beginning of the words 'Jesus Christ of God Son Savior."

India and Rome remained intricately interactive not only through trade but also through marriage. At the Council of Nicaea in 323 CE, there were 318 Bishops who attended, and India was represented by a Persian named Bishop Johannes.

Death of Thomas

After having spent 17 years in India, Thomas had been successful beyond all expectations. However, the Brahmins were still a force to be reckoned with. It was primarily because of the rejection of Brahmin caste systems and the priests unrelenting and superstitious demands for rituals that enabled the Hebrews, Buddhists, and Christians to thrive in India. The King of Mylapor had fallen under the influence of Brahmin priests who wanted to declare war on all other faiths in India. They wanted to outlaw them and seize their temples and their riches.

The wife of this king fled from him and became a Christian. She asked Thomas to baptize her. When the Brahmins told the king what his wife had done, he became enraged and ordered the death of Thomas. The soldiers seized him at his church and quietly led him away so as not to raise any suspicions that might lead to a riot in the city.

When they were in a secluded place, Thomas realized that his death was imminent. He asked the four soldiers to allow him to say his final prayers. The soldiers became afraid and began weeping because none wanted to kill a holy man. After he finished praying, he told the soldiers that they should obey their king, and he outstretched his arms. Two men then held him while another pierced his heart with a sword. Thomas slumped to the ground and bled to death while he was still praying. The grieving soldiers then carried his body back to his church. When the community found out what the king had done, there were bitter riots that lasted for months. The grieving congregation dressed the body of Thomas in the finest garments of royalty and gave him a royal burial, placing his stone sarcophagus inside the Church.

> *When we go, we should be able to say to Nature, take back a spirit that I've made better than when you gave it.* (Seneca, contemporary of Jesus)

Thomas died in 72 CE. Jesus was still alive at this time and living north of Mylapor, in Kashmir. The news of the death of Thomas spread quickly. Some of the older church traditions claim that it was through the efforts of Haban the Merchant that the body of Thomas was secretly taken out of India, and brought to Edessa. We know this was done in secret because several years later the son of King Mahadevan fell ill. He thought if he could obtain a bone from the saint, that this relic would cure him. When he sent his men to get a bone from the corpse of Thomas, they discovered that the tomb was empty, and his body was gone. Later church historians were able to trace the route of Thomas' bones.

In 1144 CE, the Turks began destroying churches in Edessa. The bone relics of Thomas were then taken to the Island of Chios to prevent their loss or desecration. In 1258 CE, they were then transferred to Ortona, on the Adriatic coast of Italy, taken there in a ship called the *Leo Acciaiuoli*. Eventually, most of his bone relics were acquired by the Church of Edessa, and several of his bones were then distributed to the various churches in India, Hungary, and on the island of Athos. Athos is a place that Mother Mary had once stopped and admired while she was on a visit to see Lazarus at Cyprus. A temple was built there in her memory. Thomas, who had been so reluctant to go to India, had finally come home to rest.

'The famous cross on the tomb of St. Thomas near Madras, India, Known as the Nestorian Cross. Marco Polo's interesting account can be found in his well-known travel book.' This cross still remains the symbol for eastern Christianity today. (Courtesy nestorian.org)

Thomasine Christians

Since those very first days when Thomas had appointed the first two Bishops of India, the Christians of India have been called 'Thomas Christians.' Dr. Berchmans Kodackal, the current Catholic priest of the Syro-Malabar Church in Kerala, India, gives this history of the Thomasine Churches:

'The Church of the Thomas Christians was one of the four great 'Thomite Churches' of the East. The three others were

the Edessan, the Chaldean (of Mesopotamia or Iraq) with Se-
leucia-Ctesiphon as its center, and the Persian (of Persia
proper or Iran). Among these Churches the Church of Seleucia-
Ctesiphon emerged as the organizational centre, mainly owing
to the political importance of this place as the capital of the
Persian Empire. The Indian Church had close contact with
these Churches. A connection to the East Syrian Church
(Chaldean) was established after the arrival of another Thomas
(Knai Thomman) and several families from Cana in the year
345 A.D. This infused new blood to the sagging old church established by St. Thomas. Later, we cannot say when but certainly in or before 7th century, it became hierarchically
subordinated to the Chaldean Church, and the succession of
indigenous prelates came to an end. In their place the East
Syrian prelates started to rule. The apostolic Church of India
was thus reduced to a dependent status. This dependence,
which lasted until the end of the 16th century, prevented it from
developing an Indian theology and liturgy with an Indian culture. During this long period, not a single indigenous bishop
ruled over the Thomas Christians. Until the rise of Islam, Aramaic (Syriac) was the commercial language throughout the
East, including India. The Jews who spoke this language were
very powerful in India. Aramaic was also the vehicle of evange-
lization. It came to be called Syriac, after Syrus who ruled over
Mesopotamia, and had became the official language of the
Persian Empire around 550 B.C. When the East-Syrian Church
began to exercise control over the Indian Christians, the Malabar Church became Syrian in rite with Syriac as the ecclesiastical language. '

Many Indians are still told to regard St. Thomas as a myth who
never lived in India. To them, Thomas represents a story brought in
with the Portuguese centuries later as a way to denigrate local Shiva
temples. There are an estimated 30 to 50 million Christians in India
today. Many are still persecuted and killed yearly by fundamentalists of
one sort or another.

The goddess Quan Yin, intelligent and beautiful, the Sarasvati of S.E. Asia & China.

Asian Bathtub Toys; time to relax on the Old Silk Road.
Since ancient times milk from water buffalo is still added to
sweeten cups of tea.

The Q Gospels

The *Q Gospels* are believed to be the main source from which the
canonical *Gospels* are based. It is the 'master' document that was
written much earlier than the four *New Testament Gospels*. This theory
began with German researchers searching for such a missing document. They termed it 'quell,' which means 'the source.' This was later
shortened to 'Q'.

This theory resulted from the realization that that 'Parallel Gospels'
appeared in *Mathew, Mark,* and *Luke*. About 225 verses of *Luke* and
Mathew came from this source.

The author of *The Gospel of Thomas* seems also to have quoted from Q.

The same sayings and the same events lined up in all three *Synoptic Gospels* when they were shown side by side on the page, even though they were written years apart, and in three different languages. They had all obviously referred back to the same source. They continued to be written down that way for another 35 years.

It seems that Q was written at the beginning of circa 50 CE. It is regarded as a 'missing link' between the Jewish world of Jesus and the early Christians. Christ was still regarded more as a great philoso-pher-teacher, than as a messiah-god. Christians believed that he was preparing them for how they should live on earth:

Thy will be done, thy kingdom come, on earth as it is in heaven.

Scholars have divided Q into three sections known as Q1, Q2, and Q3. Of these, Q1 is centered totally on concerns relating to man's relationship with God, and how to live on earth while anticipating the return of God. Jesus was regarded as a great teacher for the people of earth. In Q2 the status of Jesus increases to one more like that of Abraham and Moses. By Q3, Jesus, like Abraham and Moses, has been conversing directly with God.

It was long suspected that a document such as Q once existed, but that it has been lost. With the discovery of *The Sayings Gospel of Thomas* found at Nag Hammadi in 1945, the theory of Q becomes much more realistic.

There is no reference to the death of Jesus, even though the Gospels were compiled between 40-50 CE, and up to 100 CE. Additional sayings seem to have been added around 70 CE, when the Roman-Jewish wars were finished, and the Jews were being driven out from Palestine. It was then that the book of *Mark* was written. If Jesus were actually alive until around 100 CE, then this all makes sense.

There is still hope that a copy of Q will be found some day, perhaps among those ancient documents yet to be discovered, or perhaps they are still hidden in Kashmir.

We go now to Kashmir and examine the kings who ruled there, hoping to find Jesus among them. Why would we seek a Jewish king in Kashmir? That's an interesting question and it has interesting answers. We have been studying all the prior Jewish connections with Kashmir. The question is not "why was Jesus a King in Kashmir?'

After such an extensive family background in Kashmir, the answer becomes 'Why not!"

10. Kings

The Rajatarangini

The *Rajatarangini* is also known as *'The River of Kings'* or *'Kings of Kashmir'* **(16,51)** It represents the records of the kings of Kashmir that were gathered by the scholar Kalhana. They were recorded in Sanskrit between 1147 and 1149 CE. In the 19th century, several translations of the *Rajatarangini* came to light. Notable among these are the translations by Jogesh Chunder Dutt, R.S. Pandit, and Marc Auriel Stein. Each version is rich with footnotes that are like stories within the story.

Stein, an archaeologist, was a Hungarian Jew who became a British citizen. He lived in Gulmarg (Meadow of Roses) which was near to both Srinagar and the tomb of Jesus. He collected manuscripts and art objects that are now in museums around the world. The search for further proof of Jesus in India may lie on dusty museum shelves in St. Petersburg or London, not in Himalayan monasteries. Some of his collections represent important contributions to the study of Buddhism in central Asia. However, he is often condoned for his methods and seeming lack of concern for local heritage **(64)**

Stein said of Kalhana's book that, owing to the unreliable records of past chroniclers, hardly a page of Kalhana is without error, yet hardly a page is without its truths as well. Kalhana read ancient poems and songs for information. He also looked at rock inscriptions, the *Nila Puranas*, the consecrations of temples, grants given by former kings, and other written works that were already ancient, and in fragmented condition, in his time. This led to errors and guesswork about the earliest kings.

Kalhana wrote in the prose style that was popular in his era, richly embellishing his stories. Thus, a man might have 'dozens of wives' and 'hundreds of children,' and make '1,000 shiva lingams' a day. This is how Kalhana explained wealth, status, good health, and 'signs of righteousness'. And all good men, of course, 'must' have been good Shivites and good Brahmins in order to be sympathetic to, and understood by, the readers of his day.

Events are left out simply due to lack of knowledge when kings were far away, often for years at a time. These extended journeys were often described as places of 'wilderness' or deserts, meaning places unknown to the author. A king may have had several sons and many daughters, but unless they were notable in some way, there was no reason to mention their existence. His reports about children and heirs were never meant to be a complete genealogy. This book was not meant to preserve a complete record of all brothers and sisters, just a succession of those who actually became Kashmir kings.

According to the translation by Jogesh Chunder Dutt, the calculated dates of his king list, just like Pharaoh lists and Biblical dates, can be off by as little as a year or two in one place, yet as much as fifty or even hundreds of years in another. Kalhana seemed to favor 'rounding out' the corona-tion dates. Without an exact undisputed date, he simply guessed and rounded out the dates so a coronation that might have happened in 46 B.C., was rounded out to either 45 or 50 B.C. As new edicts and coins are uncovered, new information appears that will continue to change the dates in the future.

Like the power struggles in the Bible, the *Rajatarangini* is also a catalogue about priestly supremacy. Hebrews against Brahmins, Brahmins against Buddhists and Christians. They jostled with each other again and again, and in every genera-tion, until all ended with the Brahmins in full control of India, that is until the arrival of Islam.

Josher Chunder Dutt **(16)** said:

> In this period (during the compilation of the *Mahab-harata*, *Ramayana*, and *Upanishads*) the Brahmins once again succeeded in monopolizing the supremacy in thought and learning that the Kashtriyas had tried so hard in vain to share with them. Not only were philosophy, astronomy, rhetoric, and cognate sciences cultivated by Brahmins, but social laws were laid down that forbade anyone else from having access to this knowledge.
>
> The people under the Brahmins labored in superstitious ignorance. This invested Brahmins with a halo of unapproachable sanctity and glory. They used this power to their own advantage, creating one set of laws for themselves, and another set for others. They alone performed all religious services and received gifts and support from all other castes. They reserved the best positions of government and education for themselves.
>
> However we may admire their six schools of philosophy, their astronomy, their sciences, their genius of this period, we must deplore the loss of equality between men and women, the rights of humanity that were sacrificed (compulsory sati, caste prejudices, et cetera) in order to increase the privileges and control of the priests.

Like the *Bible*, the *Rajatarangini* has certain significant lines of kings, especially descendents from Yudhithistira (comparable with King David in the Bible), for these kings have always been the hereditary rulers of India.

In spite of the shortcomings of the *Rajatarangini*, Kalhana's chronicles *have* survived against tremendous odds, and without them even less would be known about the history of Kashmir. Through Kalhana's efforts, we have an excellent starting place from which to continue further research and discovery.

Kalhana told us that Kashmir was restricted to Hebrews since ancient times, that its borders were guarded diligently, and no one was allowed permanent residency, nor even a temporary safe haven, without consent from the king or his ministers. In the twelfth century, El Bironi, the Arab historian, wrote;

> *Permission to enter Kashmir was given only to Jews.* The priest, Monstrat, in the fifteenth century, said: *All inhabitants of this area have been living here since ancient times and trace themselves to Hebrews.*

The Secrets of the Ark, the Tertons, Sacred Geometry

Why would Kashmir be so carefully guarded? There have been obvious clues leading us to the solution in the previous chapters. Solomon and Hiram Abiff came to India to trade, but they also came to build and repair temples. Soon after Solomon's death his son Menelik traveled the great distance from Ethiopia to Kashmir to repair the temple that bore his father's Hebrew name. Menelik carried away a great golden 'bench' that once belonged to his father. This may have represented the famous throne of Solomon, but it could also suggest that the Ark of the Covenant had been hidden in Kashmir

This explains how the hill acquired the legendary name, 'Throne of Solomon' hill. It appears to be based upon actual, historical fact. It also explains the legends of Menelik taking the Ark away without Solomon's knowledge, as suggested by Graham Hancock **(26).** This led to a version of how the Ark came to rest in Ethiopia. There was something hidden in Kashmir, something important enough that Menelik was willing to travel great distances to retrieve it, knowing exactly where to look for it.

The small temple at the summit of Solomon's hill faces east, out across the lakes and mountains that stretch far below. The view is spectacular. Understandably, this has been the site of a shrine or a temple for thousands of years. The first recorded permanent temple mentioned in the *Rajatarangini* was built there by Sandiman (Sandeepan-Solomon, a Pandava prince) circa 2629-2664 B.C.

The hill also bore the ancient name of *Jayesthevara* (or Jyetha-Rudra) hill, meaning the hill of light, a place used for either star or sun-based worship. There was once a shrine to Durga on the summit, and at another time it was called Gopaditiya or Gipradi Hill (after the Kushan king Gopaditiya, who did some repairs c. 426-364 B.C.) Adi Shankara is said to have rebuilt the temple again roughly one thousand years ago. Then the hill also acquired his name, Shankacharaya hill.

The simple little rotunda, resting on a massive stone platform, seems hardly a fitting place to hide anything. Solomon and Hiram Abiff were masters at building secret chambers like those built inside the pyramids and at the tombs of the pharaohs in the Valley of the Kings, and under the structure known as the stables of Solomon. It is logical to assume they also replicated *secret* chambers. Away from the main temple rotunda is a small underground room. It appears that there was once a passageway leading underground and back toward the temple. The room is small, about ten by ten feet, supported by beautiful stone columns and beams. Each is hewn from one long rock that extends the entire length of the room.

There are ancient inscriptions carved into the stones that can only be seen with a light shined up and under from a cramped angle. It appears to be an early Phoenician, Brahmi, or Hebrew script **(52)**. Was it possible to keep secrets here? Could things have been so well hidden that people would come daily and walk right over secret labyrinths and rooms without ever figuring out their existence? As we know from other locations being discovered regularly around the world, this in fact happens all the time.

The caves of Qumran held their secrets for over 2,000 years. Near Qumran is the sacred hill of Gerazim, still dotted with ancient temple sites. It too was once used as a hiding place for holy relics. Today Gerazim is still one of the Samaritans most holy of places. The Essenes and Samaritans were sects both waiting for the return of the prophet predicted by Moses. This prophet would recover the hidden relics of Moses. Revelations predicts that at the end times, when the messiah appears, he will have the rod of Moses in his possession. It seems apparent that Jesus has been the hereditary heir of this rod. It had been in a direct line in his family for generations.

To unlock the secrets, one would have to know the secret hiding places, or the sacred geometry used to build them. Jesus had that kind of knowledge. He was not a simple carpenter. He was a terton, a master of 'the secrets of the interior parts of the earth.' And Jesus had possession of the rod on previous occasions. He knew exactly where it was to be hidden when he left this earth. It was placed in his tomb with him.

Identifying Kings

Kalhana's *Kings of Kashmir* names several kings who are difficult to identify. They served under many titles. Some were foreign. Aramaic, Greek, Latin, Ethiopic, Phoenician, Pali, and other languages are all represented in the inscriptions found at Taxila. One king might appear in several languages, making his true identity difficult to pinpoint. An example would be the names of the three magi who visited Jesus at his birth, from a sixth-century Syrian source, cited by Zoroastrian scholar Dariush Jahanian.

The numerous rajas and kings of India, those who had ruled for over 2,000 years, actually represented just eight prominent families. These were Lava (Levi, founders of the village of Kapilavastu, home of Buddha) Yudhisthira (David) Megava-hana, Pravarasena (same family as Parshva, Parbhat, Haris-ena and Rasena), Abhimanyu (or Abdigases, 'abdi' or 'abhi' being a prefix title for a priest from the family of Aaron), Ashoka (Greek Ptolemy), and Tungjina. These families were all related to one another through dynastic marriages. Vik-ramaditiya, Ravenna, Ashoka, Kanishka, Tungjina, and most well-known founding rajas and kings of India come from these families. The dynastic roots of Gautama Buddha and Jesus lay with these families.

The Hebrew kings were *elected* monarchs. If one happened to be a strong ruler and loved as King David was, then he might establish a rule for his family that would last another three or four generations. However, the choice of kings was *always* limited to members from within these eight families.

Egyptian chronologists like author-researchers Ahmed Osman (*Out of Egypt* **47, 48**) and Ralph Ellis (*Jesus, Last of the Pharaohs* **19**) have attempted to slide the Biblical and Egyptian rulers up and down a time scale until they *seem* to line up. This has upset traditional dating for the Pharaohs and caused the dates for famous men, and even for some histori- cal events, to change dramatically. Of course this has led to rebuttals from the world of archaeology and history. Many will disagree with some of the conclusions, but not all. Every generation rewrites history as new facts become available and old facts are re-interpreted. This is inevitable. So it is probable that Jesus may indeed have been considered a Hebrew king, *and* prophet, *and* a pharaoh through his family line, *and* a king of India through the same family dynasty. Each of these premises may be valid through the complex labyrinth of genealogies that always leads back to same small group of founding families.

The *Rajatarangini* describes two rulers in Kashmir both called Sandimatti. K.N. Ahmad and others have interpreted this as Sulayman, (or Suleiman, the Arabic name for Solo- mon). However, Sandimatti could also mean Sanhedrin. An alternate translation has been Sandhiman (one who merges). The meanings are similar.

From 2629 to 2564 B.C, Kashmir was ruled by another Sandiman. The second time the name appeared in the king lists was for a king who reigned from 22 B.C. to 20 CE. It becomes impossible to know which interpretation to apply. We have the same name for two men separated by over two thousand years. The same name may not, in fact, have the same meaning each time.

Joseph, the father of Jesus, was a member of the San- hedrin during the years that Jesus was in India. Could the Chief Minister referred to as Sandimatti be Joseph the San- hedrin member? Names are very problematic, but when we can get through this, the rewards are surprising and historically important.

Hari (lord) Rasenas (light) were a ruling family of Kashmir during the lifetime of Jesus. The name indicates that he was of the family of Ra-senas. A Pharaoh who was named Harsiese (King Hedjkheperre Setepenamun Harsiese or Harsiese A) indicates a member of the same family that would include the Harisenas of India. The Sanskrit name Rasena is originally derived from the Ramesses Pharaohs and Pharaoh Ra-sena.

If the family of Jesus was descended from Egyptian Pharaohs, then this becomes very important to know when looking for the purpose of Jesus in India. For example, if Jesus were indeed the '*Last Pharaoh*' as author Ralph Ellis suggests, *and* a potential duly-elected king of Kashmir, then the events of the crucifixion becomes quite a different matter. The titulus nailed to the cross that identified Jesus as a king becomes a statement of *fact*, not of ridicule or of condemnation. Linking the pharaohs of Egypt to the kings of Kashmir indicate that Jesus was indeed not only a member of the Herod family, but akin to Cleopatra and the Ptolymies, and was expected to serve as a king. We just never realized until now all the ways these genealogies connect these Herodian and Hasmonean families with Indian dynasties.

Following the Jesus Trail on the Old Silk Road

The Hari-senas and Prava-Ra-senas were supporters of the monks at the Ajanta Caves. **(46)** The Ajanta Caves are located on a main branch of the Old Silk Road near the seaports of Solomon at Ophir (Biblical Sofir, or Abhira). Inside these caves are the paintings of the important Buddhist patrons. Two of these definitely appear to be Jesus. One of them is of a young Jesus. Another depiction is of a much older, more mature Jesus. It becomes apparent that these are meant to be the same man because the monks made sure to show him wearing the same clothes, in the same colors, and even down to the same unique belt. In the hundreds of icons, paintings and coins that exist, there is a commonality that has enabled us to identify Jesus in works of art across the ages and around the globe. The depictions of Jesus all seem to be remembered from a single source.

Large Jewish communities sprang up all along India's coast-line around ports such as this one near Ajanta. The most famous among these are the Ophir, Cochin, and Malabar Jewish communities. These ancient Jewish communities have survived intact down into modern times, and they still occasionally make news when they apply for resettlement back to Israel. Jews were well established in India, especially along the seaports established by Solomon, and trade routes going between Ajanta and the Old Silk Roads.

Ajanta Caves lay undiscovered for 2,000 years; Construction began around third century BC; the monastic complex includes several viharas (monastic residence) among its 29 caves. According to Chinese scholar Hsuan Tsang, Ajanta also served as a college monastery.

Fig 75   *Fig 76*

'God' (Brahma) bringing donations to the monks.
Statue found near Bamiyan, Afghanistan and dated to
circa 100-200 A.D. originally in the Kabul Museum, now
in an unknown private collection.

Numerous such 'Brahmas' and 'Buddhas' may be
mistakenly identified by archaeologists. These
depictions suddenly flourished in the first and second
centuries and all looked remarkably like depictions of
one man, Jesus. Were they all intended to represent
the presence of Jesus in Central Asia? Were they
mistakenly identified by twentieth century archaeologists who presumed Jesus had died on the cross and
never ventured to India?

Jesus (?) and youth (son?) at Taxila; this man appears in several carvings retrieved from Jaulian Monastery near Taxila. The unique belt also appears in paintings at Ajanta Caves with yellow hair and wide-eyed gaze of excited wonder. From Taxila Museum, Pakistan

Rock carving circa 2,000 CE, found by author in the
dirt at Pahlgam, Kashmir, at a ruined temple site:
Man with rod of kingship and a cross, youth at his
side, ascension of same man is depicted as he
appears 'above' himself. The famous 'ka' rock that
levitated was once located here (now missing)
Photo by author.

Ajanta Caves; a young Jesus: In the hundreds of icons, paintings and coins that exist, there is a commonality that has enabled us to identify Jesus in works of art across the ages and around the globe. The depictions of Jesus all seem to be remembered from a single source.

Ajanta Caves: 2,000 year old paintings mature Jesus with alms bowl (giving donations to the monks): The paintings are in full color; he had long white hair and pale blue-grey eyes. The visible black is a form of mold attacking the paint and destroying the images. Paint is now falling off in huge flakes. In all the depictions along the Old Silk Road, the belt and clothing are identical; exact same *color* clothes in all the paintings identify this man at Ajanta, Taxila, and Pahalgam (Kashmir) leaving no doubt they all represent the same man. Ajanta photos are by Jean Louis Nou, with permission from India Archaeology Survey Department

First century coin dated 55 A.D. from Taxila, declare in Greek that this represents Abdigasses, nephew of King Gondopharnes; reverse refers to a savior (private collection).

Gold coin; in Greek says 'Osho' (Issa) first century, Taxila; private collection. Hundreds of such coins have been recovered that mention Jesus as Parshva, Ieousus-, and Isha. Presuming Jesus perished on the cross causes many to overlook obvious clues to his later destiny as king of Kashmir.

Fig 75

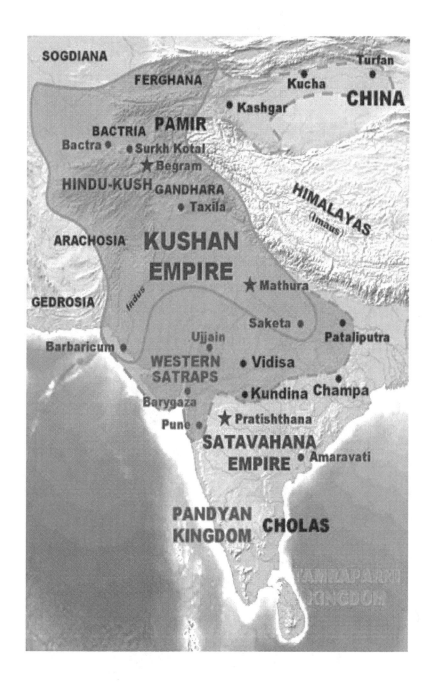

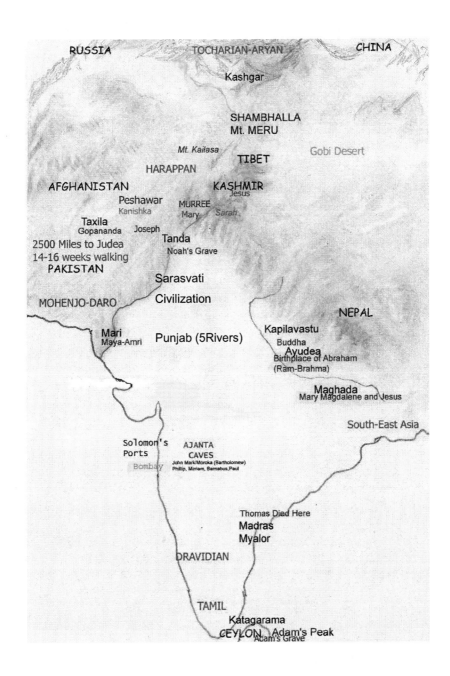

Disappearing Evidence

The *Apocrypha* texts tell us something about the apostle Thomas in Kashmir. In Judaism the *Apocryphia* are texts that can be useful to read as additional commentaries, but are not accepted as 'the word of God.' These writings were included in the early Greek translations of the Bible (the *Septuagint*) but not in the original Hebrew Bible. Roman Catholics, but not most Protestants, regard these books as part of their canon. So how one interprets such writing is strictly a subjective choice.

From *The Acts of Judas Thomas*:

> At that time a merchant named Habban, an emissary from Gundaphorus, a great king of India, arrived on the scene. He was looking for someone to build a palace for his ruler. Jesus pointed Thomas out to him as a skilled carpenter and a 'slave' whom he was willing to sell. The price was agreed upon and paid in silver. Thomas then set sail with Haban for India.

Fida Hassnain picks up the story in his book, *The Fifth Gospel* **(27)**

> Thomas met the king of Taxila (Gondopharnes) and was introduced by Abdigases. (The source cited for this is *John Reland's Library Bulletin*).

Thomas then attended a wedding of the king's daughter (possibly to Abdigases). A famous relic, unearthed at Taxila, describes this event in some detail, even suggesting that Jesus was there and attended the wedding with Thomas. Soon after, Jesus and Thomas went to the Temple of Solomon to 'repair' the dome. They left several inscriptions at the temple as confirmation of this visit.

What quickly becomes apparent is that the entire story about Jesus 'selling' Thomas to Habband may have been a ruse to get Thomas in to the court of Gondopharnes on official business without arousing the ilk of those nearby. He would make the way clear to openly work at 'restoring' Solomon's Temple without arousing suspicions. Thomas' story and the excuse for the visit all seemed prearranged and agreed upon.

Circa 45 CE, Thomas and Jesus left two inscriptions, in the Persian 'Sulus' script, on the pillars at the Temple of Solomon hill;

> 'In these times Yuz Asaf (son of Joseph) proclaimed his prophethood;' and on the other pillar: 'He is Yasu (Jesus), prophet of the children of Israel.'

Several historians, who were scholars in these ancient scripts, had visited the temple and recorded their translations. The above translations appeared in the book, *Tarikh-i-Kashmir,* by Khwaja Hassan Malik (from the Srinagar Research Library). In his book, *Jesus in Heaven on Earth,* Khwaja Nazir Ahmad published photographs of the inscriptions before they disappeared **(1, 27, and 36)**

Sikhs in Kashmir

During the period when Afghans ruled the Punjab, the inscriptions left by Jesus and Thomas were deliberately mutilated; the temples were once again the targets of racial and religious intolerances. Fortunately modern records of these inscriptions do exist for us.

The presence of the Sikh religion in Kashmir has also affected the fate of these historic sites. It is the youngest religion in the world, founded by Guru Nanak (1469-1539 CE) as an alternative to the senseless and unjust religious dogmas of both Hindus and Muslims. It has always been regarded as a progressive religion well ahead of its time since it was founded over 500 years ago, The Sikh religion today has a following of over 20 million people worldwide and is ranked as the worlds 5th largest religion. Guru Nanak preached a doctrine very similar to Christianity, one of tolerance for others, equality for all, and a rejection of excessive priestly rituals and idol worship. Guru Nanak and his successors gave woman a status equal to that of man.

Guru Nanak lived for a time at Mecca, where he challenged the fanaticism and intolerance of the Muslims of his time. During his visit to Mecca, he taught that God's house is everywhere and not in the direction of the Kaaba. Similarly, Guru Nanak exposed the meaningless ritual and caste prejudices prevalent among the Hindus. So many Muslims flocked to join him that had he remained just a year longer at Mecca, it probably would have altered the course of world history forever. Instead, at the height of his success at Mecca, he had to return to the Punjab, where the largest populations of Sikhs still live today

During the Muslim-Afghan rule in the early 1800's, Kashmir and parts of India were ruled over by cruel Afghan tribal warlords. During this period, Kashmir again suffered heavy losses. Temples were ravaged and leveled; Sikhs and Hindus were butchered and murdered; no one was permitted to worship outside of Islam, and the young women were abducted for export to Kabul.

The Sikhs of the Punjab, appalled at what was happening in India, came to the aid of their brethren in Kashmir by forming a large army in what amounted to the Sikh version of the First Crusade. The Sikhs secured Kashmir, restored religious freedoms, rescued what ancient texts and relics they could salvage, and got schools, temples, and even churches rebuilt for worship.

Since no Christians or Hebrews were around who would 'claim' the Throne of Solomon Temple as part of their heritage, it was then put to use as a temple to Shiva, and so it remains to this day. Inside is a huge shiva lingam that fills the interior rotunda, guarded by a large hooded cobra and a small representation of 'Nandi' the bull. It is a forlorn place now, seldom visited by tourists or pilgrims, especially since the Indian Army has ensconced itself in barracks next to the temple and erected a satellite antenna. Seeing the idols and symbols of a different religion inside the rotunda is somewhat unnerving, and not what is expected. It is like going into a church and seeing a replication of Nandi the bull on the church alter or a cross dominating a Jewish temple.

The pillars and inscriptions on the hill of Solomon that were left by Jesus and Thomas have since disappeared and can only be verified through old photographs and previously written history books like those of Aziz Kashmiri and Fida Hassnain. But it was due in large part to the efforts of the Sikhs that the temple has survived yet another onslaught in modern times. Now that we better understand the tenuous challenges for the survival of these temples, and their frequent name changes, we can return to the history of Kashmir that affected Jesus and affects us today. Sikhs played a major role in shaping the future of Kashmir.

*In 1699, all Sikhs took the last name 'Singh'
to eliminate high and low caste names*

Picture by RM Singh, Tribune

**Sri Guru Nanak Dev Ji, founder of the Sikhs, a man far
ahead of his time. On right; Turban of Sikh Soldier in the
Indian President's personal guard. In ancient Egyptian
civilization, turban was an ornamental head dress. They
called it pjr from which is perhaps derived the word
'pugree' commonly used in India and other Asian
countries.**

'Turban' is derived from the ancient Persian word dulband through the Turkish tarbush, is a long scarf wrapped around the head. It is a common head-dress for men in Middle Eastern and South-Asian countries. As a form of head-dress, it is of Semitic origin and was an essential part of the Israeli High Priest's uniform in Moses' day, 1300 BC, as stated in the Old Testament (Exodus, 28: 4). In India, it is to be seen depicted in the Ajanta caves (200 BC) and on the Sanchi Gateway (150 BC).

There are several unique features in Sikhism that are unequalled in world religions. Sikh males hold women in the highest regard. Women are regarded as man's companion in every walk of life. The Gurus thought this equality worked to their mutual benefits. For example, woman is the *first* teacher of man as his mother. Her function is to mould children and discipline them. She has to be educated so that her children may develop their potential to the fullest. She was allowed to join holy congregations, participate and conduct them. They were appointed missionaries. They were called 'the conscience of man'. The practice of Sati, (the custom of burning a woman with the dead husband on the funeral pyre), was prohibited and widow-remarriage was encouraged. Women soldiers fought side by side with male soldiers in one of the battles which the tenth Guru fought.

In the Sikh way of life, women have equal rights with men. There is absolutely no discrimination against women. Women are entitled to baptism. They have equal rights to participate in social, political and religious activities. Women are allowed to lead religious congregations, to take part in recitation of the Holy Scriptures, to fight as soldiers in the war, to elect representatives to the Gurdwara (temple) committees and Indian Parliament and Provincial Assembly. Sikh women have played a glorious part in history, and examples of their moral dignity, service, and upholding of Sikh values are a great source of inspiration. Sikh women never flinched from their duty, never allowed their faith and ardor to be dampened, and have always upheld the honor and glory of the Khalsa. (One famous example is that of Mai Bhago (Mata Bhaag Kaur) who bravely fought in a war for Guru Gobind Singh, when some soldiers deserted him and returned home).

The Tomb

There are three kings of Kashmir who lived during the era of Jesus. King Gondopharnes (Gopadatta-Gopananda) should also be included as a fourth king, although he was the ruler of Taxila at the time, and not of Kashmir.

One of these Kashmir kings was crucified in a manner that strongly resembles the crucifixion of Jesus. Taken away to jail in the middle of the night, he was fastened to a tree, impaled, and left for dead. A titulus (sign) appeared on his head proclaiming him the rightful king. He was rescued by the rishis (magi or angels) who had been summoned by his loyal companion Issana. He was revived from death and all of his wounds and broken bones were restored. Years later, he fulfilled the prophecy of the titulus and became the rightful king.

In all of India there is not another record of a crucifixion and certainly none that mimics so many details from the crucifixion of Jesus. Crucifixion was unheard of on Indian soil. Sandimatti, the 'crucified' Kashmir king, began his reign in 22 B.C. and he served for 47 years, until 25 CE. Obviously, the reign of Sandimatti began well before Jesus was born, so we have some riddles to solve. The years for Sandimatti don't represent Jesus, but they could represent his father, Joseph.

In the tomb of Roza Bal is buried a prophet known as the prince Yuz Asaf (son of Joseph), who left us clues to his identity. In his tomb is the stone carving of a man's feet that clearly indicate crucifixion wounds. Now we know that a king of Kashmir was crucified, and that he is in the tomb known as Roza Bal, and that he chose to be remembered as 'the son of Joseph.' Another clue found in the tomb is the rod called 'The Rod of Moses.' This even came with an ancient manuscript, a sort of 'pedigree.' This had begun to crumble apart so a group of historical chroniclers, the rishis, copied the ancient manuscript into the Sharda script in order to preserve the historical information. It said the rod had been known as the rod of

Jesse, then the rod of David, the rod of Moses, and finally it became the rod of Issa. That seems like absolute proof that the man buried in Roza Bal tomb is Jesus.

ROZA BAL TOMB
Srinagar

Casket, once inside Roza Bal tomb, has been removed and replaced with a flimsy substitute. The
actual burial is in the cellar under this room. This
casket is just over eight feet long to hold the Rod of
Moses, artifacts, and scrolls once stored inside.
(*Photo courtesy 'Tomb of Jesus' website*)

The old interior of Roza Bal tomb. Inside this ancient wooden 'cage' was the ancient casket that housed the Rod of Moses, the genealogy of Yuz Asaf, and other artifacts. The carved stone feet with crucifixion wounds were also inside this room. In this photo, it still contained its original blue color trim of its Hebrew tradition.*Photo courtesy of Tomb of Jesus website*

Old wooden structure, sword, candlestick, shrine,
ancient casket, old carved wooden entry doors, and
brass shield are gone. Now there is a glass
enclosure around a fake casket, doors and trim
stripped of their original blue are painted green.
There were stairs underneath that led to cellar and
real tombs. These have been blocked off. The tomb
of Yuz Asaf is now seriously destroyed by local
'remodeling,' representing Wahabism. Total
destruction is the ultimate goal if left unnoticed.
*Photo courtesy of Ken Lee at eleven shadows
website, where there are additional views of the
tomb.*

2,000 year old footprints carved in solid black rock at Roza Bal tomb show how crucifixion wounds would appear asymmetrical. This would only be obvious to those who actually witnessed the crucifixion or saw the unusual scar pattern after the event. *(Photo courtesy Tomb of Jesus website)*

After the crucifixion, footprints began appearing of Buddha showed 'wheels of dharma' identical to actual wounds on feet of Yuz Asaph. This First Century Buddha foot was found in Gandhara, near Taxila, and is now in the Taxila Museum. Compare Buddha foot with Tomb foot.

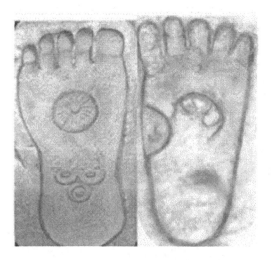

Buddha foot from Gandhara (near Taxila) on the left, Yuz Asaph foot from Roza Bal tomb on the right. No such 'dharma' wheels appeared on Buddha hands or feet before the First Century AD.

Kalhana mentioned that the king, Pravarasena, possessed a jeweled sword that was deeply sentimental to him, and he often carried it around with him. In the tomb was a strange piece of wood, now stripped of any jewels and decorations, which had been described as a crucifix or cross. However, looking at it in old photos, it is obviously not a cross but a sword, because the top and short cross piece clearly appears to be a handle, not the top of a cross. This must have been the ceremonial sword of Pravarasena that was placed in his tomb with him. Through the centuries, looters and opportunists have gradually picked away at the embellishments on the sword, until nothing is left now except a deteriorating piece of wood. When science has the opportunity to properly date and document this relic, it may prove to be one of the most valuable relics in all Christendom.

10. Kings

By connecting the legend of the sword with a specific king, and a sword prominent in Roza Bal tomb from the first century, we can now determine that it is definitely Pravarasena buried in the tomb. Pravarasena must have been both the crucified prophet *and* the crucified king. Pravarasena and Jesus must be the same man. They have been identified through many titles and knicknames: Isha, Yeshua, Oesha, Issa, Porous-Poro (same title as the king who Alexander the Great met and admired-possible great grandfather of Jesus?) simha, Shresta-rasena, Prava-rasena, and Parshva to name a few. Now we can continue examine the stories of the kings to look for more clues about Jesus.

Who is buried in Roza Bal and why is it important that we find out?

Sandimatti: ruled 47 years

from 22 B.C. to 25 CE.

Suggestions for the meaning of the title Sandimatti are varied: Hindu-Sandiman; Hebrew-Solomon; Arabic-Suleiman; Aramaic-Sanhedrin. Sandimatti was also known as Ariya-Raja, Chief of the Aryans. He was serving as a Chief Minister (or Senator) under the king, Jayendra. The name Jayendra might have been a Sanskrit equivalent for the name James. Because Sandimatti was born long before Jesus, we can assume he might represent Joseph, father of Jesus.

The Story from Kalhana

Jayendra was an usurper to the throne. He was not legally elected, and not of the royal bloodline from Yudhisthira (King David). The people wanted Sandimatti to rule in his stead, partly because Sandimatti was of the bloodline entitled to the throne. Jayendra's ministers, eager to keep their own positions, kept suspicions foremost in Jayendra's mind, always plotting for ways to prevent Sandimatti from gaining the throne. Jayendra managed to seize Sandimatti's wealth, and then tried to have him imprisoned. After several years, as Jayendra neared death, his ministers inflamed him with more stories about the success of Sandimatti. Jayendra was still seething with jealousy, and ordered that Sandimatti be killed. Sandimatti was then taken away illegally in the middle of the night to be crucified.

Miraculously he survived. His guru, Issana, watched carefully over him as the angels restored his limbs. Issana and Issa are both names of Jesus in India. In all probability, Issanas were followers or apostles of Issa. Issa lived at Ishabar, on the shores of Dal Lake. How could Jesus be Issana, and witness a crucifixion, instead of *being* the one who was crucified? It is clear at this point that Kalhana wasn't sure either, and applied names to events as best he could understand them.

One suggestion would be that Sandimatti was actually Joseph, father of Jesus. At the time Sandimatti was Chief

Minister, Joseph was a member of the Sanhedrin. The names suggest that both men were ministers in a similar capacity at about the same time. Earlier, we realized that Jesus attended schools at Taxila, and visited the court of Gondopharnes with Thomas. This places Jesus and his father in the area together.

Joseph must have been the 'Sandimatti' serving as minister at Jayendra's court. We have another clue that there were actually two men, Joseph and Jesus, in this quote from *'Ferozul Lughat'* (Urdu Jamia, as appears in *Christ in Kashmir*)

'The name of Solomon's Minister-Gatherer was Asaf.'

In this case, the author has interpreted the name 'Solomon' to be understood as 'Sandiman'- a minister or Sanhedrin member, thus Joseph. 'Yuz Asaf' is properly translated as 'son of Joseph.' A magi who visited at the birth of Jesus was Gushy-nasaph...asaph=son of *Gu-shy*=? (Could be Gad or Gondopharnes before his coronation? We have Joseph the father as a 'Senator,' Chief Minister, or Sanhedrin, and his son Jesus as *his* aid, or administrator.

Jayendra was not about to give up the throne. He stole his minister's wealth and had him imprisoned. Could this have been done to Joseph? Had Jayendra somehow acquired the Rod of Moses from Joseph's family? When Jesus returned to the Holy Land, was it to gain supporters to help free his father, and to recover the family wealth and their rightful claims to the throne of Kashmir?

Could Joseph have been persecuted and perhaps even killed by Jayendra? Could Jesus have been the rightful ruler of Kashmir, but Jayendra blocked both the father and the son? In fact, Sandimatti was probably Joseph, and Issana was his son, Jesus.

Meghavahana: ruled 34 years: from 25 CE to 59 CE.

Meghavahana became the next king after Sandimatti. Meghavahana also bore the title 'Abdigasses,' as indicated on coins found at Taxila. This is our first clue to his real identity. James was the Bishop of Jerusalem during this period

The descriptive word often applied to priests began with Abi-as in Abimanyu, Abdigasses, and Abiathar; these words indicate a *great* priest, a *renowned* priest, although not necessarily the *high* priest. At the time of King David, in the *Old Testament*, this was not a titular title, but the proper name of the priest who served David for forty years. Abihu, a priest, was also the title of the second son of Aaron. A somewhat similar word, Ashvagosha, is applied to all Buddhist monks descended from Buddha. Ashvagosha was also the name of an assistant priest-monk at the nearby court of Kanishka (circa 70 CE). The word Meghavahana may be a derivative of the word Meghananda, a son of Ravenna, and one of the kings of Lanka. Meghananda means 'sound of thunder' or 'sound of clouds.'

James was the Bishop of Jerusalem who was killed by Ananias 2nd in 62 CE. If this James were an actual full-blood brother to Jesus, then he would have to be *younger* than Jesus, because Jesus was the first-born son of Mary. But James was recognized as one of the elders of the early Church. It is estimated that he died at about age 78. If he was age 78 in 62 CE, then he must have been born in 16 B.C. He must have been an older *half*-brother to Jesus by Joseph's first marriage. Our only alternative would be if Meghavahana was *not* a brother of Jesus, but either a cousin, a step-father, a brother of Joseph and Gondopharnes.

However, this leads us to the next problem, why would a senior Queen identified with Mother Mary and the magic parasol that she brought with her (translate as the rod of Moses) be at court and presumed to be the *wife* of Meghavahana? Because she was regarded as the senior queen.

Mary may have remarried a brother of Joseph and/or Gondopharnes. This is more in keeping with traditional Jewish practices of the era. Furthermore, the 'son' of Meghavahana and Amritaprabha would rule next. If their son, Pravarasena, proves to be Jesus, then Meghavahana could represent a step-father of Jesus, someone Mary married after the death of Joseph. An alternative explanation would be that Kalhana got it 'half-right.' The *son* of Mary *did* rule next, and Meghavahana reigned over a home filled with queens and princesses, friends and apostles and family members, many who bore the title 'Mari' or 'Mara.' He was the head of the household and the king, but he was *not* the official or natural father of Pravarasena. When the records from the tomb are finally made public, the truth should become apparent. Until then, we can only speculate on the possibilities.

Laurence Gardner states, in *Bloodline of the Holy Grail* *(24)* that after the great fire of Nero's Rome (July 18-19, 64 CE) and the stepped up persecution of the Christians, it was Paul who, just before his death, got a message to Timothy stating that Jesus was 'in a safe place,' believed to be Kashmir. Large numbers of Nazarenes and Christians had to flee, and no doubt Jesus led many to safety in India. This would be around 62 CE, the date associated with the death of Magdalene, the death of James, the end of the reign of Meghavahana, and the coronation of Pravarasena as king of Kashmir.

Gondopharnes was related to the Ptolemy dynasty of rulers from Egypt and Greece. Apparently he was an uncle to Jesus through Joseph. According to the *Rajatarangini*, a prince in exile had got into some difficulty and Gondopharnes gave him shelter. Could this have been his brother Joseph and one or both sons, Jesus and James? Yes, and we can certainly place Jesus at the court of Gondopharnes several times.

Returning to the *Rajatarangini*, this exiled prince had a son, Meghavahana, who wanted to rule. As a descendent of Yudhithistira (King David) he had a legal claim to the throne. Gondopharnes anticipated that by helping this young prince, he might be able to enrich his own coffers and annex the entire kingdom of Kashmir. And so, with the help of Gondopharnes, Meghavahana became the next ruler of Kashmir.

However, before his coronation, Gondopharnes sent Meghavahana to Assam (then a part of the kingdom of Magadha) to bring back a new bride in what appears to be a political arrangement. The name of the woman that Meghavahana had to bring to the court of Gondopharnes was Amri. She brought a certain powerful 'parasol' (a rod or scepter of authority). With this magic relic, Meghavahana was able to perform many wonders, and even experience flight with the gods.

One of the powers of the rod was to enable Meghavahana to 'cross over water,' comparable with the story of Jesus walking on water (*Matthew* 14: 22 -*Mark* 8: 31 -*Luke* 9: 22).

There are several parallels between Jesus and Meghavahana; the wife named Amri could be Mary Magdalene. The magic parasol could be the Rod of Moses that was stolen in Judea. Jesus was a priest who could have been the Abdigasses. Jesus and Meghavahana both walked on water and 'ascended' with the gods, and we can definitely place Jesus at the court of Gondopharnes. The circumstantial evidence certainly does favor Meghavahana as Jesus. If Meghavahana was not Jesus, but his stepfather, or his brother James, then we move forward to the next king, Pravarasena, and look for Jesus there, but first let's look closer at the queens of the era.

Mary, Maya, and the Queens

According to the relics and rock edifices found in Kashmir, several queens and princesses were associated with the reign of Meghava-hana. They were *not* all his wives, as Kalhana supposed when he lumped them all together. Meghavahana was described as a religious Buddhist, a vegetarian, a gentle and quiet man who ruled well. This does not preclude any Jewish roots he may have had for as we discussed earlier practicing aspects of Buddhism did not require a full 'conversion' from one's religion. The numerous queens and princesses that he gave shelter to in his home were probably apostles, their wives, and assorted relatives. However, there seems to be nothing that links Magdalene with this king, although Magdalene is linked with Kashmir in two other very important sources.

Magadha and Magdalene

We are told of cities or places named Magadha without knowing a specific location. There were several places called Magadha in Biblical times. Attempts to place Magdalene at Magadha in Judea are useless, especially because that town of Magadha did not even exist while

Magdalene lived in the Holy Land. However it existed in India long before.

   Her name is associated with towers or ziggurats associated with temples. Sumerians were the first great builders of ziggurats, and these were an established part of religious ceremonies. They represent the first monasteries and convents of a particular religious order. According to Herodotus at the top of each ziggurat was a shrine. The building of ziggurats eventually led to the building of pyramids, and soon both forms appeared around the world. These in turn led to the concept of church steeples and minarets.

   The name Magdalene may stem from her association with a particular religious order associated with towers or her association with an entire kingdom known as Magadha.

In Ethiopia, the ancient tower of Makada still exists. The Queen of Ethiopia, Makeda, had a palace nearby. It is probable that her name is a variation of Magdha or Magadha (**100**) Thus we have two powerful Biblical women, both associated with powerful Biblical men, and both women associated with the same suggested religious order upon which the name Magadha was founded upon.

   In India, Magadha represented an entire empire, one of the sixteen great regions of India. Two of the greatest empires, the Maurya and the Gupta, originated in Magadha 500 years before Christianity began. Magadha was founded by eighteen magi families who were invited to settle there and create a good educational and religious environment for the benefit of the local Brahmins (religious leaders) who wanted to have this knowledge available at a local level. It was from Magadha that India then acquired the greatest advancements in science, mathematics, astronomy, philosophy and religion. Magadha was ruled primarily by Greeks, as we shall see later. Brahmins were predominantly Mediterranean Phoenicians. Historically the Brahmins were always a little resentful of the Magadhans, who were the last to become Hindus. From the Magadha kingdoms came forth several great religious figures. Mahavir, founder of the Jains, and Siddhartha Gautama who was born a prince of Kapilavastu in Magadha and was the founder of Buddhism. These men acquired their fame as philosophers at a time when the tradition of the great philosophers was in full blossom. Plato and Aristotle represent to the west the great philosophies of Mahavir and Buddha in the east. They all addressed the question of "what is life" and used logic and reason, not mythology and superstition, to answer.

The Eastern Orthodox Churches of India, known as Thomasine churches, have several branches. All claim to have original writings of the apostle Thomas in India. The Church of The East had a location in Kashmir for centuries, and was driven out in recent times due to militancy. They regard their "Eastern Bible' as Gospel. The Eastern Bible is divided into three sections. In one section called 'The Acts of Thomas' are many interesting stories about Jesus and Magdalene in India, before Jesus left for his ministry and brief three year sojourn in the Holy Land.

According to the Eastern Acts of Thomas, Mary Magdalene and Jesus began their journey together as priests. After they completed their educations at Magadha they set out together to work as High Priests, building schools, ashrams, temples and training locals to become priests. Long before they arrived in the Holy Land, they had built a religious ministry and a career together. There is no mention of their marriage while in India. However, there is enough information in 'Acts of Thomas' to ascertain that Magdalene indeed did acquire that title while in India.

Professor Fida Hassnain learned of a grave in nearby Kashgar called the grave of Marjan Bibi Anjeela. Roughly translated, this means 'Lady Marjan from the Bible.' Marjan might be Miriam, but it could not mean Mother Mary. There are several Mariams in the Bible; however none can be associated with Kashmir. In the Rajatarangini, Marjan was the wife of Pravarasena (Jesus). Could this grave in Kashgar actually be the grave of Magdalene?

Returning to King Meghavahana, one of the queens whose name appeared frequently during the reign of Meghavahana was Queen Amri-ta-prabha, or Mari Gibira; Mother Mary, the Queen Mother. As mentioned earlier, 'Queen Mother' may not have been the *wife* of Meghavahana, but his *mother* (or step-mother). Confusion is easy because several queens in Kashmir were called Mari and Marjan leaving Kalhana to guess their relationships with the kings.

Amri means Mary and *Prabha* or *Grabha* means 'first' or 'senior queen.' The name of Buddha's mother was Maya (taken to mean *illusion* or *enchantment*) leading many to compare that name to Mary.

Scholars say that the name Maya seems completely unrelated to
Maria or Mary. And yet the Greek goddess Maia *literally* means mother
(in this case, mother of Hermes).What scholars fail to take into consid-
eration is the very close relationship the Greeks had with the rulers of
India, many of whom were, in fact, Greek themselves. It would not be
unreasonable to presume that Maya also meant Queen Mother or
Mary.

Amri-ta-prabha's son was Pravarasena: *Prava* is the same as
Prabha - Parbha meaning the first or best; *Ra-Sena,* as we saw earlier,
is from the Egyptian sun god Ra, and *sena* is 'of light.' Prava Rasena
was also called Parshva which means Joshua or Yesua. Thus we have
a mother named Mary and her son named Joshua, another name for
Jesus. The Rasenas were a ruling dynasty in India related to the
HariSenas and Vakatakas. Most of the ruling families in India were
connected through just a few founding names that kept dividing to start
new family groups **(25, 46, 50, 60, 67, 73, 86, 87, 94, 104, 106)**

Witnesses spoke of Amri-ta-prabha ascending to the heavens with
the gods. They also witnessed Meghavahana and Pravarasena
ascending. This is very rare in the *Rajatarangini.* Few kings or queens
ever 'ascended.'

There is one interesting story during the reign of Meghavahana
concerning flight. Local farmers feared that so many ascensions were
damaging their crops. They captured a group of nagas who had been
flying in machines and landed in their fields and confined them. Their
wives, described as 'celestial beauties,' then pleaded before Meghavahana for the freedom of their husbands, assuring that no crops
would be harmed after their release. Meghavahana released them with
instructions that they avoid the farmer's fields. Meghavahana 'could'
have been Jesus, but we have one more king to examine, the king
who had the jeweled sword, Pravarasena.

Pravarasena: ruled 30 years, from 59 CE, to 89 CE.

Pravarasena ('*prabhava*' means first, best, of glorious birth-'*ra*'
god-'*sena*' of light) was presumed to be the *son* of Meghavahana and
Mari (Amri-ta-prabha). However, this may be a great historical error
made by Kalhana. The Queen Mother in this case could have been

mother (or step-mother) to one or *both* kings, Meghavahana and Pravarasena. So which is it? Was Pravarasena the stepson of Megha-vahana, or his brother?

Pravarasena also had the titles 'Shreshta-rasena' (Great Mountain Lord-Lord of Light; he may have acquired this title during his visit to Taxila in A.D. 45 with Moroka, or John Mark as mentioned by Gardner **(24)** Tunjina 2nd, Parshva (for Yesua or Joshua), and Ra-Sena, also the name of a great-grandfather of Buddha. Pravarasena was distinguished for his shining white hair and beard. Jesus would have been approximately 60 years old when Pravarasena was coronated. If this is Jesus, then why had it taken so long for him to be coronated king of Kashmir? The answer may simply be that he was content to let James or others rule, just as he was content to delegate the management of the churches and the affairs of the apostles to James in Jerusalem and to Peter in Rome while he and Thomas managed the Churches in India.

As noted previously, Pravarasena had a jeweled sword that he was very fond of, something of great sentimental value to him. He had a chief minister named Moroka, and a wife named Marjan. He had among his children two sons who would rule after him. He was known to have direct contact with the gods and make ascensions from Hari Parbat hill (Hari means *lord*, and prava or parbat means *first* or *best*). Near this hill is the location of the tomb of Jesus.

The final and most convincing clue to the identity of Pravarasena is what we have just discussed, that he was also known as Prabha or Parshva. Parshva is simply a version of the name Joshua, Yeshua, or Issa. (M.M. Ninan *'The Emergence of Hinduism from Christianity* **45***).*

The entire Hari Parbat hill is littered with a dozen sacred little shrines, each representing a different deity. Years ago the Brahmins labored endlessly to maintain these little shrines and extensive gardens and almond groves ·

Har-Naum, the birthday festival of the Goddess Sharika (the Divine Mother, Mahashakti) is celebrated here at the Chakrishwas Shrine with night long singing of hymns (bhajans) to the goddess. She is believed to be the deity who protects Srinagar and its Kashmiri Pandits. The entire hill has been one of the most sacred places in all

Kashmir since ancient times and today the few remaining Pandits of Kashmir still maintain portions of the hill and hold festivals there.

Unraveling the Story

Aziz Kashmiri, in *Christ in Kashmir* states:

> Sandimatti was killed at the <u>age of 37</u> by putting him on a stake. On learning of this event, his guru Issana went to the funeral ground and saw the body and said: 'Alas, my <u>son</u>, I am alive and come to see you in such a plight

Sandimatti could not have ruled for forty-seven years, and then be crucified at age 37. Issana could not also be Issa (Jesus) because it was Issa being crucified in the western version. Issana *could* have been Issa (Jesus) trying to rescue his father Joseph from the maliciousness of the jealous Jayendra.

Jesus left with a caravan for India at around age 13 or 14. Then the record goes completely silent about what happened to the entire family during the fifteen years that Jesus was absent from Judea. Realistically, the entire family may have been together in India while Jesus attended schools and Joseph acted as Chief Minister at the court of Jayendra.

Recall that the magi had made an exceptional journey at the birth of Jesus to bring him gifts and acknowledge that he was a future king. *The Book of the Bee* **(105)** carries the story forward by noting that Joseph went to Egypt with the rod of Moses. It would appear that the magi kings had brought the rod with them, and included it among the gifts given to Joseph and Mary. Was it a 'gift,' or was it a hereditary legacy meant specifically for Jesus? Jesus now possessed the scepter of a future king, and the relic of Moses, sign of the expected messiah.

Recall also that Jesus left the Holy Land at about the age when it was customary to begin school at Taxila. Gondopharnes had a brother named Gad. In the *Acts of Thomas* we learn that when this brother died, Gondopharnes grieved because he loved Gad very much. Joseph also had a brother named Gad (through Leah's maid, Zilpah) Therefore, Gondopharnes and Joseph may have been brothers, and Gondopharnes, king of Taxila, would then be an uncle of Jesus. But the story takes an unusual twist here.

At the beginning of this century, Ernst Herzfeld, in his research into the history of Persia, discovered that one of the three kings who visited at the birth of Jesus was Caspar or Gaspar, whose real existence was confirmed by the substantial amount of coins recovered with his name. He further identified Gathaspa by his Greek name, Gondopharnes. He ruled from 46-19 BC. The kingdom ruled by Gaspar was called in Greek 'Arachosia,' or Harawatia, whose residents were Harawats. This is modern Kandahar in Afghanistan.

And in fact there *were* two kings named Gondopharnes ruling almost simultaneously between Taxila and Kandahar. The two cities are within a few days journey of each other by foot. Could Gad have been the brother of Joseph and Gondopharnes, *and* the king Gasper from nearby Kandahar? This simply means that rulers of adjoining kingdoms were members of the same family.

Greeks had more power in India than did Rome. Clearly then, there was no reason for Romans to order the death of Jesus merely over some squabble between petty kings of kingdoms outside their reach. Pilate would not have ordered the death of Jesus solely over the squabble of a small kingdom in Kashmir, but Caiaphas might, especially if he was in any way connected with Jayendra. If this proves true, then they apparently had the help of Judas Iscariot in carrying out their plans. They may even have anticipated putting Judas on the throne of some minor kingdom in Asia if he had succeeded in helping them.

Joseph died mysteriously in India, and Jayendra may have been responsible for his death. There is no proof of how, or where, or when Joseph died. However Pakistan TV did a mini-documentary some years ago about a grave on the Old Silk Road, very near Kashmir. Historically, this has always been regarded as the grave of Joseph, father of Jesus. It is not far from Pindi Point, the Queen's Mountain, where Mother Mary spent her last days. It is now up to science to do the hard-core investigations into these graves to determine the truth.

Ethiopians, Unraveling Magadha and the Marys

The Church of the East claims to be founded upon the original writings of Thomas, dating back to 45 CE. In these very books, Thomas speaks of Jesus and Magdalene together in school at Magadha.

Thomas wrote that Magdalene had joined the religious order begun by Jesus, and that she had become an ordained priestess. Later in Judea she would advance to the position of Bishop in the new church. Thomas went on to say that Jesus depended heavily upon Magdalene for training women. She and Jesus traveled with a small group, training others and founding communities similar to the communities of the Essenes at Qumran and the Nazarenes.

The Queen of Sheba was an Ethiopian sovereign named Makeda, or Magda. Migdal means 'tower' in four languages; Egyptian, Hebrew, Greek, and Sanskrit. The word 'Magadha' does not, however, signify just a 'tower,' but a specific star-based religious system associated with towers, just as we might associate Episcopalian or Baptist churches today with church steeples, and mosques with Sunni or Shia minarets. Obviously these temple names somehow connect Makeda in Ethiopia and Magdalene in India.

Lion of Judah
symbol of Ethiopia

Ethiopia was well known to the ancient Greeks. They regarded the Ethiopians as a sacred people that were 'most loved' by the gods. Memnon was regarded as one of the noblest heroes in the Trojan Wars, and was so handsome that the gods could not bear to see him destroyed and face a mortal death, so they made him immortal. To this day one can still recognize a true Ethiopian in a crowd, so unique are their finely chiseled features, aquiline noses, high cheekbones, and tall stature. They look regal and distinctive wherever they are in the world. Many Falasha Jews of Ethiopia have resettled in Israel to continue practicing their religion.

Thus, it would not be the 'son' of Meghavahana who ruled next, but his brother, the *son* of Mary, the Queen Mother. Kalhana had it 'half-right.' It was Jesus who took the title Pravarasena for his coronation. Pravarasena also had a wife called Mari, and this was

Mary Magdalene. In the *Rajatarangini*, many of the kings' wives were chosen from among women who had roots in Kashmir, including the Assam and Magadha princesses like Magdalene and the mother of Buddha. They were held in high esteem as naga (magi) princesses.

The stupas and edifices that have survived at Kashmir and Taxila say that Amri-ta-Prabha and Marjan supported many churches, temples, ashrams, and convents. Some were called 'Meghas' as mentioned in the *Rajatarangini.* The author Graham Hancock believes the name 'Magdala' represented temples associated specifically with dragon worship. However, we have already seen that the original association of snakes with nagas was incorrect. The word Magdala and the word Magdha are obviously meant to have the same meaning. David Wood, author of *Genesis,* believes she was the High Priestess of the Temple of Ishtar at Magdala. If Ishtar was associated with *all* Magadha temples, this remains to be determined from future research.

Marjan, wife of Pravarasena, bore two sons, Toraman and Hiranya, who were to rule jointly (she may have had other children, but only those necessary to follow the bloodline in India were recorded by Kalhana). It has become fashionable lately to support the theory that Mary Magdalene divorced Jesus (a Barbara Theiring theory) , fled to France while she was pregnant, and there gave birth to a girl named Sarah (or Tamar). This theory was made popular with the book based, in part, on the use of 'Pesher Codes', *Bloodline of the Holy Grail* by Laurence Gardner. The theory has also been investigated in popular books like; *Woman with the Alabaster Jar,* Holy *Blood- Holy Grail, The DaVinci Code,* and others. Every one raised the question, where was Jesus when Magdalene supposedly 'fled' to France? Was he already dead? If he was not and he and Magdalene were still together eleven years after the crucifixion, then obviously none of these meanderings of modern scared feminists can be correct.

What they have missed is because very one of them fails to address the writings from India, or the history of Jesus in India. Without this background, it becomes impossible to grasp the full understanding of the life and times of the family of Jesus. It seems they have missed the historical Jesus completely and filled in the gaps with a lot of impossible and unreal speculation, including everything from church conspiracies to Tarot cards, secret societies, and missing holy grails presumed to be anything from the womb of Magdalene to a decorative chalice painted by DaVinci. Without much new research, they continue to build on the errors of each other. One example concerns the death of Magdalene.

The first mention of any travels or relics of Magdalene in France did not actually appear until after 745 CE, and it was not until 1052 CE that Abbot Geoffrey 'rediscovered' the bone relics of Magdalene at Vezelay. A different Eastern Orthodox tradition maintains that Mary Magdalene retired to Ephesus with the 'Theotokos' (Mother of God) and died there. In this tradition, her bones were transferred to Constantinople in 886 CE.

According to the discovery of Professor Fida Hassnain, Marjan has a grave in Kashgar, China. Kashgar is on the Old Silk Road going north from Kashmir. It is a huge bustling center of trade that can absorb as many as ten thousand visitors and traders a day. This grave, known as the grave of 'Bibi anjeela' (Marjan bibi-lady/anjeel-Bible, or, 'the *lady Mariamne from the Bible'*) is located in the Tarim Basin, the heart of the ancient home of the Tocharians and Sogdians of Kashmir.

The recovered Tocharian mummies can average six feet 1.82 meters) in length and even the women were this tall and stately. We have been following them on a long, winding, and complicated journey from Africa to India to Judea for a specific reason. The DNA trail established by geneticists like Dr. Victor H. Mair (University of Pennsylvania, who does archaeological work in China every year) proves that they made the journey again and again. They came down from the north during the end of the last Ice Age and settled vacant Himalayan hills and valleys that were still too cool for most of mankind **(6, 20, 32, 41, 54, 56, 65, 68, 93, 96, 106)**

This explains why Mary Magdalene could have been a Magadhan princess from India (Assam or Magadha) yet still had red hair, or flaxen hair and blue eyes as she is most often depicted in ancient art. The eye color is most interesting because here we find the rarest colors in the world, like the topaz color of cat eyes, and the deep greens and bright golden eyes; the rarest eye colors in the world are found here among the Tocharian mummies and their descendents in the area.

Dr. Mair found through his DNA studies **(41, 65, 68, 93)** there was almost *no* blending with present day East Asians until they arrived much later. A strong presence of Sogdians and Tocharians, nearly forty percent of the population, are the Europeans of today. He went on to say (South-East Asian Conference on Mankind, San Francisco, 2005) that the original families from the Himalayas, those families we have been following here since Adam, are now extinct. Their once unique DNA has long since been passed into the general populations of Europe and rarely appears at all in India.

It seems more probable that Jesus and Magdalene never divorced. Magdalene, as a High Priestess and Bishop of the Church, may have made the journey to France several times. Churches and monasteries have been dedicated to her in France just as they were in Kashmir. It was a way of acknowledging rich benefactors, not a presumption for unsubstantiated family problems, death, or divorce.

Regarding a possible bloodline of Jesus, it is alluded to in the *Gospel of Philip*, written sometime after 180 CE and found among the *Nag Hammadi* manuscripts:

> There is the Son of Man and there is the *son* of the Son of Man. The Lord is the Son of Man, and the son of the Son of Man is he who creates through the Son of Man. The Son of Man received from God the capacity to create. He also has the ability to beget... He who has received the ability to beget is an offspring. He who creates cannot beget. He who begets also has power to create. Now they say, "He who creates begets". But his so-called "offspring" is merely a creature. Because of [...] of birth, they are not his offspring but [...]. He who creates works openly, and he himself is visible. He who begets, begets in private, and he himself is hidden, since [...] image. Also, he who creates creates openly. But one who begets, begets children in private.

Hiranya and Toraman (ruled circa 90-120 CE) sons of Pravarasena

Hiranya

This is not a proper name but a descriptive name. The word has two meanings in Sanskrit Hira-Nya means 'something golden' (a golden flower, or a golden child) Hir-anya can also mean 'a potter's wheel' referring to the potter's family that raised this child. A third Sanskrit scholar thought the 'Hiri-Hiran' could be the name 'Erre-Erin'. (Most of these Sanskrit to English translations are based upon *Co-*

logne Digital Sanskrit Lexicon (from Monier-Williams' *Sanskrit-English Dictionary*).

Hybernia (derived from Ivernia) was the name for the British Isles at the time of the Romans. In Sanskrit, the word Hiranya also mean 'wintry' places and it appears on the old Vedic maps of the British Isles. India had exact maps of the British Isles by this time. In the *Ramayana*, Ravana was using descriptive titles like 'The White Island' and 'Suvarna-dwipi' or 'Island of the Sun' when referring to England and even to Iceland, with which he was very familiar. So the best we can translate Hiranya from its Sanskrit is 'a fair child born, in a wintry place, somewhere in the British Isles.'

Toraman

This name is derived from a Buddhist-Turkish name, and is also a descriptive title, not a proper name. It resembles the title Turamaya, who was Ptolemy 2nd, also known as Philadelphos of Egypt, from 285 to 247 B.C., one of the dynasties of twenty or so Greek Ptolemys who ruled Egypt and Rome. This represented the height of the Greco-Buddhist and Indo-Greek cultural and religious exchanges that spanned nearly 800 years.

Toraman also relates to a 'teacher-scholar of the law' referring to the Torah, the first five books of the 'Tanakh.' Aziz Kashmir mentioned in his book, *Christ in Kashmir,* that just outside Srinagar was a legendary grave for 'Tanook,' a descendent of King David who was versed in the law. The words Tanakh and Tanook are very similar. Could this be the grave of Toraman? Tanakh and Toraman (Torah) are both names based on the Hebrew Old Testament. It will have to be decided after further research in the years ahead.

Pravarasena and Marjan expected their two sons, Toraman and Hiranya to rule jointly. However, there was an altercation between the brothers over how their coins should be minted, and in whose likeness. The will of Toraman prevailed. All of the coins were minted with his name and image on them. As the result of their continued disagreements he had Hiranya either imprisoned or banished, or he may have fled to some 'far-away' place. A secluded monastery might be regarded as imprisonment by some. As this name implies, it was somewhere in the 'cold wintry' Anglo-Saxon lands, where his son Pravarasena 2nd was born.**(76)**

Saul wrote that in 64 CE, he met a son of Jesus called 'Elymas.' However, this name also means 'of Eli', or the Sumerian god Enlil. Nothing further is known about Saul's claim.

The Grandchild, Pravarasena 2nd - The Grail Child

There are no records left for any probable children of Toraman. The *Rajatarangini* goes on to tell us about the fate of Hiranya and his family. Hiranya's impoverished wife accompanied him into exile. There she bore him a son. They named him after his grandfather, Prava-rasena 2nd. Laurence Gardner, in *Bloodline of the Holy Grail* identified a grandson of Jesus by the name Galains or Alain, born about this same time.

This child was raised secretly by a potter's family because of the mother's poverty, and for her fear of Toraman, that he might have any heirs killed. This grandson was an 'auspicious child', with unusual features that stood out from the potter's children. An uncle, Jayendra, (no relation to the former king of Kashmir) heard a rumor about this grandchild and searched for him. When he found the family he imme-diately recognized the child as the true grandson of the king. The young man hadn't known who his real father was, or about his father's imprisonment, or what his royal heritage was.

Jayendra explained his family history to him, and the banishment and poverty of his parents. This young grandson possessed many of the gifts of his grandfather, including the ability to animate clay figures, and the ability to communicate with the gods. Kalhana said he ac-quired the 'secrets of the underground treasures' from the naga gods who followed him.

When his uncle Toraman and his father Hiranya both died, this grandson did not return to Kashmir. *The Magna Glastoniensis Tabula* and other manuscripts cited by Laurence Gardner, say Joseph of Arimathea was accompanied by his nephew Josephus on several trips to Gaul. Joseph of Arimathea died in 82 CE. He would have been old enough to know both the son, *and* the grandson of Jesus.

Following the death of Toraman, no one appeared to claim the throne, so the poet Magragupta ruled Kashmir for four years (120-124

CE) When this news reached the grandson, the fact that someone had taken over the throne and family heritage illegally, he immediately returned to Kashmir (from an unknown land) and was coronated as King Pravarasena 2nd in 124 CE.

His name officially remained on the record of kings for 60 years, until 185 CE. His son (also named Yudhithistira 2^{nd,} who actually would be the 3rd or 4th) ruled 185-206 CE, followed by his son, Lahkhana Narendradatiya (Lahkhana-Lakshmana-206-220 CE) and then the brother of Narendradatiya, Ramaditiya (Tunjina 2nd 220-300 CE) then his son Vikramaditiya who ruled in 519 CE, for forty years, until 561 CE. Here the direct line of kings from Pravarasena in India ended. Their descendents are dispersed all over the world.

If Pravarasena 1st was Jesus, and if Hiranya was his son, then any claims to a European bloodline through Jesus, would have to come through this grandson, Pravarasena 2nd. Can any of this be proven? Yes. There are still family genealogies in Kashmir purportedly stretching back to the first century. All that is required now is to link them with the European branch of their families and the descendents of Jesus will be traceable.

Mother Mary has a grave very near the tomb of Jesus in Kashmir. We will review the legends of her grave and her death next.

2,000 year old Buddhist stupas hold sacred bones, scrolls and relics, similar in purpose to 'arks' or baris and even to the ossuaries of the Hebrews; this one is located at Jaulian Monastery, Taxila

Gondopharnes palace compound at Kandahar, large enough to keep people, horses, goats and sheep safe when under siege.   Were these kings uncles of Jesus? Reconstructed by Afghanistan Archaeology Department

Scythians enjoying music at court of Gondopharnes;

courtesy Kabul Museum

Author's photo of Mother Mary's grave, all that remains are these stones piled under a satellite antenna on Pindi Point. Author placed yellow silk roses there.

'When dust rises to heaven, it is still dust. When a jewel falls into the dust, it is still a jewel.'

(Jalal Rumi; philosopher, 1207-1273)

Kashmir Point on left, Pindi Point on right, author's home lower right (by the tree). This is Murree, Pakistan, Queen's Mountain, the final resting place of Mother Mary.

Murree

About 45 miles from Taxila, in the forested hills above the hot plains of Rawalpindi, is the summer resort town of Murree (Mari). It is a jumbled chaotic spread of buildings clinging around the perimeter of the steep mountain.

This mountain is unremarkable, positioned among many such mountains in the 'Middle Himalayan' range. It consists of forest-covered ranges and fertile valleys that are sparsely populated, isolated from each other and from the plains of the Indus and Ganges rivers in northern India and Pakistan. The major centers have always been built in the valleys, centers like Srinagar, Katmandu, and Kangra. A few hill towns exist that are similar to Murree, such as Darjeeling and Simla. The numerous gorges and rugged mountains make surface travel difficult in any direction.

Few roads or transport routes exist between towns, partly because it is expensive to build them over the high, rough terrain. Only major population centers are linked by air and roads with principal cities in India and Pakistan. The climate around Murree, at an elevation of 2,286 meters (7,600 feet) can be comfortable and pleasant, even through the chilly winters and occasional severe storm. From the center of the Islamabad-Rawalpindi area, Murree is reachable by a main road in a scenic journey of about two hours through densely wooded hills. During the clear spring and autumn, the snow-capped mountains of Kashmir can be seen. Dazzling twilight and cloud effects are seen from the summits. Until the British arrived in the last century, there was nothing here but faint trails leading to the simple shrine on the summit. It was the British who first began developing the area into the sprawling, overcrowded hill town of today.

The entire mountain is called 'The Queen's Mountain' after Mother Mary, or Queen Mother. Its name, Mari, was changed to Murree by the British. It has also been called the 'mountain of bulbuls' (*bulbuls, in Urdu, are 'nightingales', however, the word is often used for birds in general*) because of the huge number of song birds that flock here. The top of the mountain is divided into two separate hillocks. One is called Kashmir Point, the other is Pindi Point. On Pindi Point we find the tomb of '*Mi Mari de Asthan*', '*the final resting place of Mari*'. Along the Old Silk Road are many places that have been called 'a resting place of Mother Mary'. However, this is the one and only *'final'* resting place.

Catholics believe in the 'Dormition (Assumption) of the Theotokos' which is celebrated on August 15th. They believe that Mother Mary went into a deep, sleep-like state and was then buried in Gethsemane. When the apostles arrived at her grave, her body was gone. Catholics believe that she was taken directly to Heaven. Is it also possible that she was buried at Gethsemane, and later her body was moved? As we have seen with Aaron, Moses, and Thomas, where one dies is not necessarily the 'final resting place.' According to Eastern Orthodox tradition, between three and fifteen years after the crucifixion, in Jerusalem or Ephesus, Mary died while surrounded by the apostles. Later, when the apostles opened her tomb, they found it empty, and concluded that she had been bodily carried into Heaven. "Mary's Tomb," a tomb in Jerusalem, is attributed to Mary, but it was unknown until the 6th century. The 'House of the Virgin Mary' near Ephesus, Turkey, is believed by some to be the place where Mary lived until her assumption into Heaven. The *Gospel of John* states that Mary went to live with 'the Disciple whom Jesus loved most' *(John 19;27)* who is traditionally identified as John the Apostle, and early writers stated that John went later to Ephesus, which may provide the basis for the early belief that Mary lived also in Ephesus with John. However, as we shall see, John spent a good deal of time in and around Taxila and Kashmir. Since we do have records of an older Mother Mary traveling the Old Silk Road with Jesus and the apostles, we can safely assume this is correct, except they didn't understand the intended location.

Mary would have been in her mid-fifties during the crucifixion, and eleven years later she would have been in her mid-sixties. By some accounts she died during the fifth year of the reign of Emperor Claudius, who assumed the throne in 49 CE. Five years later would have been 54 CE, well after the time that Jesus and Thomas had made their appearances at the court of Gondopharnes and left their inscriptions at the Temple of Solomon. Thus she lived about ten years in Kashmir before she died there.

On this journey, Mother Mary had acquired the status of a super star. She gained attention for healing many whom she had met along the way. Jesus, by comparison, was relegated to 'honorable mention' in most of these accounts.

Jesus went to Central Asia around 44-45 CE, where he later met up with John Mark (Bartholomew-Moroka), Julian, and the apostle Thomas. Laurence Gardner stated that during this trip Jesus 'increased' in stature, which implies that either a son was born to him, or he was coronated (increased in stature) with a new title.

Mir Muhammed bin Kwawand Shah Ibn-i-Muhammed wrote *The Gardens of Purity, Biography of Prophets, Kings, and Caliphs (Rauza-tus-Safa fi Sirat-ul-Ambia wal Muluk wal Khulafa)*. The travels of Jesus and Mary appear under two headings, *The Migration of Jesus from Jerusalem* and *The Journey of Jesus to Nasibian* (Nisibis). After mention of Jesus at *Nisibis* in *Acts Thomas* the research of Khwaja Nazir Ahmad surmised that Jesus is not mentioned again in Occidental literature, but he begins appearing again in Oriental literature. *The Gardens of Purity* mentioned that Jesus had the rod with him and he visited the grave of Shem (Sam, son of Noah) on this journey (from David Fraser, *Short Cut to India*).

The Magi

Mother Mary was born about 26-20 B.C. (author's arbitrary conclusion) and she gave birth to Jesus at about age nineteen. *The Oxford Bible Commentary* regards the magi as the 'spiritual' Hebrews who brought great wisdom to the Gentiles. This may be closest to the truth, for indeed the magi were Hebrews, *and* priest-kings. The *Book of the Bee* states it was the 'Sarman Brotherhood' of Magi who first sought out Jesus at his birth. Zoroastrians are proud to declare that *they* were the first who recognized the birth of Christ. If they delve deeper into their own history they will recall that Judaism and Zoroastrianism were simply branches of the same faith that flourished together in the Persian Empire, and the magi kings were none other than uncles and relatives of Jesus. (10, 28, 57, 90, 106)

Book of the Bee states that one of the magi kings was the son of Gandaphar (Gondopharnes), and indeed one of the magi was called 'Gushynasaph'…asaph =s on of Gus-hyn (Gush-hyn/Gu-shyn) or Gondopharnes.

'Lion of Judah' an
Ethiopian Magi Prince

It would appear, as mentioned previously, that among these kings and young princes, some, if not all, were uncles and cousins to Jesus.

Book of the Bee Chapter 39: *The Coming of the Magi from Persia*;

When Jesus was born in Bethlehem of Judah, and the star appeared to the Magi in the east, twelve Persian kings took offerings--gold and myrrh and frankincense--and came to worship Him. Their names are these: Zarwândâd the son of Artabân, and Hôrmîzdâd the son of Sîtârûk (Santarôk), Gûshnâsâph (Gushnasp) the son of Gûndaphar (Gondopharnes), and Arshakh the son of Mîhârôk; these four brought gold. Zarwândâd the son of Warzwâd, Îryâhô the son of Kesrô (Khosrau), Artahshisht the son of Holîtî, Ashtôn`âbôdan the son of Shîshrôn; these four brought myrrh. Mêhârôk the son of Hûhâm, Ahshîresh the son of Hasbân, Sardâlâh the son of Baladân, Merôdâch the son of Beldarân; these four brought frankincense. Some say that the offerings which the Magi brought and offered to our Lord had been laid in the Cave of Treasures by Adam, and Adam commanded Seth to hand them down from one to another until our Lord rose, and they brought (them), and offered (them) to Him. When the Magi came to Jerusalem, the whole city was moved; and Herod the king heard it and was moved. And he gathered together the chief priests and the scribes of the people, and enquired about the place in which Christ should be born; and they told him, in Bethlehem of

Judah, for so it is written in the prophet. Then Herod called the Magi, and flattered them, and commanded them to seek out the Child diligently, and when they had found Him to tell Herod, that he also might go and worship Him. When the Magi went forth from Herod, and journeyed along the road, the star rose again suddenly, and guided them until it came and stood over (the place) where the Child was. And when they entered the cave, and saw the Child with Mary His mother, they straightway fell down and worshipped Him, and opened their treasures, and offered unto Him offerings, gold and myrrh and frankincense. Gold for His kingship, and myrrh for His burial, and frankincense for His Godhead. And it was revealed to them in a dream that they should not return to Herod, and they went to their land by another way. The name Casper appears in the Acts of Thomas as Gondopharnes (ruled 27 CE to 47 CE) Casper is derived from Ghudapharsa-Gasper. This Gondopharnes was also a Suren, and declared independence from Parthia to become the first Indo-Parthian king; he is thus likely to be descended from Rustaham-Gondofarr, who was visited by the Apostle Thomas.' (Source: Wikipedia)

Latin	Greek	Hebrew	Persian	Ethiopia
Caspar	Apellius	Galgalat	Hormizdh	Hor
Balthazar	Amerius	Malgalat	Yazdegerd	Basanater
Melchior	Damascus	Sarachin	Perozadh	Karsudan

Alternate Hebrew Names: Galgalath, Malgalath, and Sarrachim.
Courtesy of Catholic Encyclopedia) (Gushyn-'asaph' is 'son of' Gondopharnes like Yuz Asaph is 'son of Joseph')

The names of the kings who led the caravan were Balthazar, Casper, and Melchior. Balthazar had the title 'King of Arabia'. Gaspar/Casper was a European magi king (Farsinet.com explains that, translated from Farsi, the word Caspar mean 'keeper of the treasures' and that he was indeed a European king). The name Casper is also associated with King Gondopharnes, who, as we saw earlier, may have been an uncle of Jesus. This means that one of the visiting magi was his own cousin acting as 'keeper of the treasures'. Could the Rod of Moses have been one of the treasures he brought them?

When trying to link Gad as the Gondopharnes of Kabul, and as brother to Gondopharnes of Taxila, and as brother of Joseph, we come across another version of the name for Gad, which is Giliad, the same as the name of the 7th son of Jacob.

Melchior had the title 'King of Persia' and yet his title can also be found in Scotland among the Druids, and recent research has even attempted to link this title with the family of Pilate.

Thus the magi who visited Jesus at his birth were, in fact, all Greco-Roman kings ruling many small satraps along the Old Silk Road, who were probably family members of Joseph, or Mary, or both.

Immaculate Conceptions

In recent times, as we've entered the Space Age, it has become fashionable to re-examine *Genesis*, and ask if the Elohim stories of *Genesis* can be comparable to the Immaculate Conception of Mary and the Virgin Birth of Jesus. Again, if we source outside the Bible, we get quite a different picture of the world that Mary lived in, verification that her story could have been shared by many hundreds, or even thousands of others who lived at the time. And that is precisely what Genesis states:

*Gen.*6:1, 2.

When men began to increase in numbers on the earth and daughters were born to them, the sons of God saw that the daughters of men were beautiful and they married any of them they chose.

11. Mary

The sons of the gods produced children who would become the mighty men of renown. (Genesis)

In keeping with this Biblical precedence already established in *Genesis*, we will presume that the experience of Mother Mary was no different from Genesis encounters with Elohim. Why would we accept one explanation for Genesis, and then try to devise a completely different interpretation for Gabriel? Could he simply have been another Elohim? The major difference was the keeping of careful genealogy records. The family records of Mary and Joseph survived where others did not. In attempts to define who these gods were, theories have suggested they were fallen angels or mortal kings who were defined as gods. If the experiences had simply ended with the closing of *Genesis,* that places events in a different perspective. However from *Genesis* to Mary, such sightings and direct experiences with the gods was continual and ongoing, not only within the Bible, but even well *outside* and apart from Biblical sources.

Mary lived during an era when 'sightings' and encounters with these gods had almost become a public nuisance. Recall the farmers of Kashmir who complained that numerous ascensions from their fields were ruining their crops.

When Mary gave birth to Jesus, the light that the magi followed, as described in the *Book of the Bee,* could *not* have been a star. It was closest in description to the Biblical light that the Israelites followed on their Exodus out of Egypt. It rested when they rested. It shone at night to light their path. It waited for them, and moved with them during the day.

It was the light described in *Exodus* 13.21;

'The presence of God was in a pillar, a cloud of fire that led the assembly. It went before them by day in the pillar of cloud, and by night as a pillar of fire to give them light, so they could go by day or by night. '

323

The star, or light, the magi followed was *not* an astronomical event.

In *Genesis* there are 362 verses that describe flying objects as vehicles. There are 162 verses that describe specific flight patterns. *The Vedas* described similar objects. Let's look over what has been said by witnesses:

> • In 593 B.C. Ezekiel had his famous encounter with the great 'wheel' in the sky.

> • In 332 B.C. in Phoenicia the Greeks saw a fleet of 'flying shields.'

> • In 392 B.C. Alexander the Great saw two great silver shields in the sky. They came so close it frightened his horses and men.

> • In 200 B.C. Emperor Ashoka started a secret society called the 'Nine Unknown Men' who were the greatest Indian scientists of the day. Each wrote a section for a catalogue of all known sciences. One of the books produced was titled *The Secrets of Gravitation.*

> • In 214 B.C. Julius Obsequens (*Prodigiorum Libellus*) described how at Hadria an 'altar' was seen in the sky, and soon men in white vestures appeared.

• In 122 B.C. roughly one hundred years later, the *Obsequens Prodigiorum* makes a similar report about '3 suns and a moon' seen crossing the sky.

• 85 B.C. Pliny, *Natural History* book 11, Ch.34: "In the consulship of Lucius Valerius and Caius Marius a burning shield was scattering sparks along the sky as it traveled."

• In 81 B.C. It was also written in *Obsequens Prodigiorum* Ch.114: 'Near Spoletium a gold-colored ball rolled across the sky and came to the ground. '

• In 42 B.C. From the Roman Prodigia of Julius Obsequens "Something like a sort of weapon or missile rose with great noise from the earth and lifted to the sky."

• In 20 A.D. When Apollonius left Kashmir (1st Century CE.) he wrote a farewell letter to the sages that said,*" Iarchus and the other sages, greetings from Apollonius. I came to you by land and with your aid I return by sea, and might even return by air, such is the wisdom you have imparted to me."* According to his traveling companion Damis, Apollonius had indeed ascended with the sages of India at least once.

• In 50 A.D. Meghavahana was asked to free 'sons of the gods' who had been captured and held as prisoners by some local farmers who complained that their flying machines were ruining their crops.

• 70 A.D. Josephus wrote in *The Jewish Wars* "On the 21st of May, 'a phantom of incredible size appeared in the air just before sunset 'and was seen by the whole countryside."

• 98 A.D. Rome: Conrad Wolfhart, Lycothenes, a medieval writer reports "At sunset a burning shield passed over the sky. It came from the west and passed over to the east."

All the above leads us to some very interesting speculation about the experiences of Mary, and of her son Jesus. For centuries the Bible has spoken of ascensions, and we did not believe this meant a strictly physical and normal experience, although we ourselves have now mastered flight. For centuries we sought a natural, even if he was an illicit father for Jesus, assuming that her immaculate conception was 'impossible,' although our physicians now routinely perform 'in vitreo' fertilizations.

In fact, if the Biblical traditions are correct, then Mary came from a long line of mothers who were traditionally chosen for this experience. This may be the reason this Hebrew family were 'The Chosen People' who follow their bloodlines only through Jewish mothers. It's about following a dedicated and unique bloodline with 'designer genes' that would eventually be passed to all mankind. (**24, 63, 70**)It's speculation of course, but it represents another way to interpret their Biblical experiences that began in *Genesis* with the Elohim. Since we are never told their departure date, can we assume they were still actively involved with affairs of this world when Mary met Gabriel? Mary may have had the help and support of all those around her. After all, to be chosen by the gods would have been an outstanding and joyous responsibility. It's even possible the visit from Gabriel was anticipated, if we take into account what had just happened to Mary's cousin Elizabeth. Mathew 11:11 tells us that John the Baptist was the greatest man who ever lived up until his time. Luke says, "He (John) shall be filled with the Holy Spirit, even from his mother's womb" (Luke 1:15). Both John the Baptist's mother, Elisabeth, and father, Zacharias, were 'filled with the Holy Spirit' (Luke 1:41).

What is meant when they are 'filled with the Holy Spirit' even in the womb? It sounds like some kind of direct and purposeful intervention. Paul Von Ward *(Gods, Genes, and Consciousness)* left us his interesting study dealing specifically with the historical 'proofs' for this theory. It is available for anyone interested in pursuing this idea further. It is a concept well worth considering when we try to understand the words and the experiences of Mother Mary and her son Jesus. Suddenly, yet without changing the Bible, we become aware of wondrous new possibilities for mankind and for our place with God and in a larger community. The message Jesus left for us was about our place among the stars with an extended family of intelligent beings, and yet all believing in one God.

11. Mary

Elizabeth was aware that she had conceived a son through divine intervention and told this to her cousin Mary. Since the days of the Elohim women have born children of the gods, and we've been struggling, usually with disbelief, to understand their experiences. Now that we have finally caught up with them scientifically, we can reconsider their experiences in light of modern science.

Waiting for Gabriel: *'The Wait'"* with permission by artist
Christophe Vacher.

Did Mother Mary later conceive more children the natural way? That too has become a debated issue. Everyone called Jesus a brother and he responded to them in a like manner. And yet, just when we thought we had this matter all sorted out, we have this to contend with:

> We have forsaken our fathers and mothers and villages to follow you, Jesus said to James, for it is not without reason that I have called you my brothers, even though you are not. (*First Apocalypse of James*).

In all the writings, both within the Bible and without, that refer to Jesus as a brother, even among the prolific writings of Thomas, John and James, there is not one mention by anyone, not one line, nor even one word, that says "And *my* mother, Mary….." or, 'And *our* mother, Mary.' Not once, and that seems most odd if indeed they were all children of Mary and many were such prolific writers.

Unless new evidence proves otherwise in the future, it is this author's opinion that Mary did *not* have additional children after Jesus.

In Pakistan, Afghanistan and Kashmir men and women frequently introduced me to twenty or thirty of their closest 'brothers' and sisters' over the course of several weeks or months. Traditionally this means either a close relative or someone from the same village.

The Death of Mother Mary-Going Home

According to Catholic traditions, Mary's frail body was taken physically to heaven. Catholics call this the '*Assumption*' (they do not use the word 'ascension' for Mother Mary's death). Hers is the only 'Assumption' in the Bible, but there are many 'ascensions'. Enoch, Elijah, and Moses all made ascensions, that is, physical visits to heaven. Moses returned each time. So did Enoch, until finally he decided not to return again. Solomon was certainly a 'frequent flyer' by all accounts.

There is an amusing legend about the death of King Solomon. He was sitting, as if in sleep, and leaning over on a wooden staff. He was in that position for such a long time that no one realized he had actually died in that very position. It was not until the wooden staff had started to fall apart, that anyone realized Solomon was deceased. Of course it is just a myth, but it suggests a death that Buddhists would quickly recognize as an 'Ascended Master.' A smile might appear as they wonder when western minds will ever catch up to the knowledge of the ancients.

The 'sleep' described for Mother Mary is very similar to Ascended Masters, especially those in Buddhist literature. The belief about Ascended Masters is that they can abandon a body 'at will' and 'ascend into the light.' In Chapter One we realized that science has now embraced the concept that *light* can also be 'intelligent.' Everything in the world is made up of energy, and for humans this energy can be controlled by thoughts and feelings. This energy can travel long distances, yet still follow natural laws of the universe. The microcosm we see around is but a mirror of the macrocosm that is the universe, even intelligence and travel by light generated energy.

The Journey Home

When Jesus brought Mother Mary up the mountain to her final place of rest, it would have taken considerable effort and several days, especially if she was old and frail. I lived on that very mountain, in the town of Murree, and visited the site of Marie de Asthan numerous times. It is easy for me to imagine their journey.

It's highly unlikely that Jesus would attempt to reach the summit alone, with only a donkey pulling Mary in a cart. There would have been a group of people and several donkeys for pack animals. It's probable that even Thomas was with them, because tradition says that Thomas was the last of the apostles to see Mary and be with her when she ascended. For our purposes, we will take this to mean her ascension 'up' this specific mountain.

Carts can break down, especially on bumpy, stony ground; people can slip and get hurt. Firewood needs to be gathered. Animals need to be tended. In modern days, we even had to carry guns for protection against packs of wild dogs, and, of course, encounters with marauders on the trails. It is highly probable that an entire group accompanied

Jesus and Mother Mary. Even in Central Asian culture today, families maintain very strong ties and respect for the elderly. It is unthinkable that Jesus would have been expected to make this difficult journey all alone with Mother Mary. No one else in the family would have allowed it, and be cut off from what they regarded as their devotional duty. Mary would be surrounded by those with whom she had spent most of her life, those she loved most, and who loved her most in return.

If Mary died in August (Catholic tradition) the weather up there would just be starting to get chilly and wet as winter approached. This mountain is a very steep climb, with dangerous vertical drop-offs along the trails. Some areas are dark because of the thick old pine trees that block out the sunlight, and the thick pine needles make the forest an eerie, silent place, where every slight noise like the wings of a bird feels like a loud intrusion. There are slippery, gravelly areas where one can slip and fall great distances if not careful. Fallen logs and rocks, rushing rivulets of water from the mountain streams, make it a hard strain for any pack animal, especially pulling a cart. It would be a long, slow climb for man and beast.

A cart filled with straw and covered with thick kilims woven of the finest and warmest threads would be toasty warm and comfortable. There would be rolls of canvas accessible for quick cover during rainfalls. If they were lucky to have found a farmer who had a water buffalo on the road below, they could have brought a pot full of fresh crème. These water buffalo produce a crème that is incredibly rich and sweet. When added to a hot cup of tea, it's like drinking ambrosia from the gods.

There would be dry kindling, grains and flour to make roti (bread) tea, herbs, dried nuts and fruits, and a few basic pots and utensils for cooking, all loaded onto the pack animals. They most certainly knew why they were making this journey, so there would also be a discreet bundle of shovels, hammers, and stone chisels tied to the sides of the baggage. Teams of relays could run provisions up to them from the farms and villages in the valley below. They could remain on the mountain for days, or even weeks if necessary.

'Kangris' are small clay pots that get filled with the embers from the cook fires. Each person would sleep under the blanket curled around his little kangri at night. They are still the only form of heat available to most Kashmiris today. One can get on any bus in Srinagar, on any cold winter day, and see the little coal pots bulging from underneath their warm woolen farins (huge flowing outer-coats).

A journey up any one of these mountains can still be difficult today, even in a car traveling on a modern road. Averages of one or two busloads of people a month still perish on the mountain of Mari, as drivers fail to negotiate a hair-pin turn on a steep, washed-out section of road. Everyone in the vehicle plummets down the scraggy cliffs to their death.

The journey could have taken several days through the dark, silent forest, depending on where their starting point was. However, when they reached the summit and stepped onto the meadow, the sunshine would dazzle them with sudden brilliant light. The sounds of the songbirds in their hundreds fill the air. The clearing is on a grassy knoll where thick carpets of wild flowers once grew with wild abandon. There was once a 360 degree view of the Himalayas in all directions. The horizon is very far away, and the view seems to stretch to eternity. When I stood there, I could see two or three rainbows at one time in the sky, so vast is the panorama.

Wild herbs grew up there, and local legend says that they found some sweet herbs and made Mother Mary a cup of tea. Another legend tells of the spirit of a huge mountain lion who would visit the grave and use his tail to sweep leaves and twigs off of her grave. At night, from the small villages scattered far below, sometimes the mountain glowed with eerie lights.

To find our way home, we must remember where we came from.

Mother Mary knew the way home. This would have been the scene of a very different kind of pieta; one that was unmatched and unimagined by any Michelangelo. It was the place of the last farewell between two extraordinary people, this mother and her son.

It could take several days to prepare a proper grave and to make a proper stone marker for the location. From the few surviving films and photos that remain, one could see that the small stone monument was still reasonably intact, as it may had been for nearly two thousand years, at least until the British arrived. The British mocked the legend, and then set out to destroy the site.

In the nearby town of Muzzaffarebad, a few mountains away, there is still the lingering legend about the grave of Jesus' donkey. This legend states that the donkey that had pulled the cart for Mother Mary died of exhaustion soon after, and Jesus buried that donkey with full honors, and with ancient Egyptian rites otherwise unknown in this part of the world. I went in search of that grave for the donkey, with the help of old timers and villagers who thought they remembered where it was from the descriptions from their grandparents. Try as we could for many days on horseback in the mountains, we could not locate the grave again.

Until a few years ago villagers still made weekly moonlight pilgrimages to light candles there and quietly sit beside her grave in respect of her memory. I had the privilege, while living in Murree, to see a rare film taken well before the buildings and the satellite TV antenna blocked the view. Even then, as the buildings started to encroach on the summit and animals had grazed off most of the flowers, there were still a few surviving flowers clinging to the ancient rock alter, and wind horses were fluttering in the breezes. The small shrine was covered with candle wax, and the snow-capped peaks of Kashmir could still be seen in the distance. It was a beautiful place.

The huge satellite TV antenna was built right to edge of the grave, and there is a barbed-wire fence all around the steel legs of the antenna. Propped up against the rusting steel legs is just one left-over gravestone, all that remains of the grave of Mother Mary. Nearby are the minarets of a mosque and the steeples of a church. They turn their backs and look to heaven to make prayers and supplications to honor someone who may be in the dust and dirt right there at their feet.

I have spent an occasional moonlit night beside the broken rock remnants that once marked her grave, but no one else goes there anymore and new local buildings press in ever closer. There is almost nothing left of the old site now except these legends and the hopes that one day science will settle these issues correctly because religion has failed to do so.

We still don't seem to understand the core questions that we need to be asking. Is the Biblical tale of creation about faith? Is it about science, or science-fiction? Theology or Mythology? We cannot be sure. That's why we cannot stop asking the questions.

11. Mary

R.S. Pandit, translator of the *Rajatarangini*; Srinagar, Kashmir July 18, 1934;

'The heritage of India which has come to us through the medium of Sanskrit is a living one. The great and stirring words 'of the language of the gods' finds a ready echo in our hearts; we have known them from childhood and their subtle music expresses to us the thoughts of men whose lives, in the remote past, must have been unimaginably different from our own. Sanskrit, like ancient Greek and Latin and indeed every other language, paints a picture of the world, and though there may have been only one world, the pictures are different. In this translation (of the *Rajatarangini)* an attempt has been made to use English words so they may produce Indian experiences. '

Goddess Lakshmi; prosperity, purity, chastity and generosity, favored of the gods. One palm is always open to bestow blessings on all who need her help. Is she based upon the legends of Mother Mary?

333

12. Tomb

Srinagar, near author's home and tomb of Jesus;

Hari Parbat Fort is on the hilltop.

As we approach the end of this search for Jews and Jesus in India, I trust it has now become apparent that Kashmir could be regarded as a Hebrew private sanctuary, their private family estate. Kashmir, in fact, was at the very heart, the very center of their lives and traditions. Looking back historically it appears that many have come to this realization before now. Let's review the presence of Jews in India, and especially the Jews of Kashmir. This sense of 'exclusivity' was realized since long ago.

Jews in Kashmir

John Noel wrote in *The Heavenly High Peaks of Kashmir;*

> One thing about these people strikes you with enormous force. They seem more perfectly Jewish than the purest Jews you have ever seen. It's not because they wear flowing cloak-like garments, but because their faces have the Jewish caste of features.

Aziz Kashmiri states in *Christ in Kashmir;*

> They call this land 'Heaven on Earth' and the 'Gardens of Solomon'. The Temple of Solomon is a perfect example of Israeli art and is just like the tomb of Ezra situated in Palestine. The many temples and ruins of Kashmir are examples of Babylonian art, quite contrary to that of Hindu or Buddhist art.

Sir Francis Younghusband said:

> Here, especially in the upland villages, we find the old patriarchal types just as we have always pictured the Israelites of long ago. Here the Israelite shepherds tending their flocks and herds may be seen any day.

336

G.T. Vigne, in Travels *in Kashmir said;*

> I was struck with the great resemblance which the temples bore to the recorded disposition of the Ark and its surrounding curtains, in imitation of which the temple at Jerusalem was built, and it became a question whether the Kashmiri temples had not been built by Jewish architects. It is a curious fact that ancient Ethiopia was also called 'Kush' after Kashmir. The ancient Christian churches are not unlike those of Kashmir and they were originally built in imitation of the temple by Israelites who followed the Queen of Sheba to Aksum. She had a son of Solomon named Menelik who became ruler of Kush.

The *Bhavishya Maha Purana* (Sholok 30)*:*

> The entire land belongs to the followers of Moses.

E.F. Knight, author of *Where Three Empires Meet:*

> They are bearded and fine looking in their white robes. Some have the features of Hibernian Celts, and pass for an anomalous creature, the Irish Jew.

Aaron Revisited

In Sri Lanka we found ancient six-pointed stars carved on rocks and used as the main theme for mandalas, and as a symbol of worship. We followed the trail from Adam's Peak in Sri Lanka to Noah's grave near Sialkot, where he was remembered as the god Manu. From there, we explored the presence of Abraham and Sarah in India, where they are remembered as the gods Brahma and Sarasvati, then on to David and Solomon, followed by Moses and Aaron, the ancestral grandfather of Mother Mary. The grave of Aaron in Harwan (Haroon-Aaron) is near the grave of Moses in Bandipore (Beth Peor). It isn't simply the graves that are so significant. What is extraordinary is knowing that the graves *and* the rod of Moses are in the same general area.

The Rod of Moses may be regarded as among the most significant relics of the entire Old and New Testaments, along with the Ark of the Covenant and the Ten Commandments. 'The Rod of Moses' is mentioned in the *Book of the Bee* as something that seems to be relevant to the crucifixion plot against Jesus. To find an actual rod in Kashmir called The Rod of Moses so near to the graves of Moses and Jesus has to be more than mere coincidence or deliberate fabrications.

Sarah was 'considered' a great Biblical prophetess, but there is only one woman in the Bible who has ever been *called* a prophetess, and that was Miriam, sister of Aaron. There is a grave in Kashgar for 'Marjan, or 'Bibi Anjeela' as she is known locally, the lady from the Bible.' This can only be either Mary Magdalene or Miriam, sister of Aaron, because history has already placed Mother Mary's death either in Ephesus or on Queen's Mountain in a place formerly part of Kashmir, and the traditions about Magdalene dying in France are still highly disputed. The Kashgar Marjan could represent a second wife for Jesus, but that would need a lot more supporting evidence, and to date there is none. Proof may exist within her tomb.

The Fourth Buddhist Council was one of the greatest events in Buddhism. It took place at the homestead of Aaron and this is duly noted on a plaque placed there by the India Government. But was this mere coincidence or was there some greater significance to this decision to bring together this event and a homestead directly associated with Jesus and Mary?

The Fourth Buddhist Council

The Fourth Buddhist Council was equal in importance to the Nicene Council of Christianity. Since the death of Siddhartha Gautama Buddha between 483 and 380 B.C., everything remembered about his life and teachings was passed between the monks and members of the sanghas (viharas-temples and religious communities) verbally, just as it was at first in Christianity.

Emperor Ashoka was coronated 116 years after the death of Buddha, and later in his reign he pledged his entire kingdom to Buddhism. Emperor Ashoka, being Greek himself, had both Greek and Persian architects and sculptors at his court. The Ashoka monolithic columns were the works of these Greek sculptors, and their depictions of Buddha show a robust man with curly hair and sometimes a moustache. He wore long flowing robes in the Greek style. Ashoka also dedicated Kashmir to Buddhism, and he gave large grants to the monks for monasteries, schools, and housing. Opportunities for schooling were available for a modest fee to all who could keep up with their studies, regardless of their country or religion. As these monks completed their studies, they carried Buddhism to the far corners of the globe. (**25, 35, 42, 50, 54, 57, 60, 61, 67, 81, 88, 106)**

Kashmir was a Hebrew sanctuary, fiercely guarded by its Jewish inhabitants. How could Buddhism, a religion seemingly so radically different from Judaism, be welcomed by the Hebrews there? Had all those Hebrews 'converted' to Buddhism before the arrival of Jesus? Ashoka was remembered as a Persian-magi king, even though he was Greek. However, this is where the confusion enters. Ashoka was also a grandson of Gupta, founder of the Maurya Empire (found in the *Kings of Lanka* genealogy of Gautama Buddha **77, 99**). Ashoka still maintained very strong family ties with Greece. Therefore, was Ashoka more Greek or European than Asian?

Amri-ta-Prabha was descended from a king of Assam (a division of Magadha) and they too were Kushans, Greeks, and Persians. Mother Mary was connected through her mother, Anna (Hebrew Hanna) with Greece (although these legends now seem to have disputed origins). To have a father who had been appointed a king of Assam would be in keeping with a Greek family tradition.

Even further, the Songsten dynasty of Buddhist kings ruling China, Tibet, and Nepal were related to the ruling families of Magadha, who had many Greek families and intermarriages among them. The Songsten Dynasty was also known as 'The Kingdoms of the Oasis of the Western Lands.' (XiYu or Xingjian means 'western.') This is the area from Kashgar and the Tarim Basin south To Nepal. The Kashmiri monks worked with the Tibetan ministers to create a new script. It was so successful that variations of it are still in use in China today.

Ashoka was also regarded as a Sakya prince from the tribe of Gad. Judas was also from the tribe of Gad. Gondo-pharnes and Joseph both had a brother named Gad. It appears most of these kings were related to one another. Since it was the custom of most kings to acquire young princesses as wives from surrounding territories to insure peace, then it comes as no surprise to find the young prin-cesses had common bloodlines criss-crossing repeatedly in their past, bloodlines connected with Europe and India.

After Ashoka, Kanishka was the next great supporter of Buddhism. He was one of three kings who ruled jointly (Hushka, Jushka, and Kanishka) from his capitol city at Peshawar. His summer capital was at Kapisa, north of Kabul and north on the road from Kandahar. The Russians paved over his old court there, in order to build a landing strip for their airplanes during their invasion of Afghanistan. This city is located near Khyber Pass, which gave Kanishka enormous control over trade on the Old Silk Road when it was the meeting place of four great civilizations, Greco-Roman, Persian, Indian, and Chinese.

In more recent times, when Afghans were given metal detectors to locate and destroy land mines, they began uncovering thousands of coins and relics here and created a lucrative side business. Many of the ancient coins they find are displayed on blankets spread out in street markets all around Afghanistan and Pakistan. It was not at all unusual for me to meet shepherd girls in the high mountain passes who deco-rated their hats with incredible rare coins they found along the goat trails.

Kanishka was a Kushan-Pahlavi ruler, and Greek was the primary language used on his coins and edifices. His empire reached into Kashgar and the Tarim Basin, where his coins have also been found. The image on the coins shows him with the typical flowing beard, shirt and trousers, and a cloak hung over the shoulders. This is the same style worn by the bene-factors at the Ajanta Caves. This style was worn primarily by men who were excellent horsemen, who were accustomed to dressing for traveling great distances. Thoroughbred horse breeding began on the Arabian Peninsula with Solomon., and was well established when these kings ruled. It would not be improbable that Jesus was also an avid horseman.

Buddhism gradually split into eighteen different sects and no one could agree on the correct teachings. The dates for the life and death of Kanishka have varied widely, and some have placed him half-way into the second century. It may well be that he was alive when the Fourth Buddhist Council was conceived, but did not have as important a role as his historians gave him.

However this may prove to be, Kanishka is historically credited with suggesting that over 600 Buddhist sanghas from Sri Lanka to Kashgar should convene a grand council to agree on standardization of Buddhist teachings and organization. They would work under the direction of Pravarasena or Parshva, the King of Kashmir who we have tentatively identified as Jesus.

The Fourth Buddhist Council was convened in 79 CE. Before this, in 49 CE, James held a similar council called *The First Council of Churches* in Jerusalem. Among the main issues to be decided upon were new guidelines for circumcision and baptism. These were problems for the earliest followers of James, who were called the *Jewish Christians*. They believed that circumcision should be continued. However most converts were abhorred at the prospect of circumcision and disagreed that it should be required in their new faith. The hierarchy of leadership for the churches was also established at this Council. Thomas then followed the *Council of Churches* guidelines for the seventeen churches that he later established in India.

Jesus, as Parshva (Prava-Poros-Yeshua-Joshua), welcomed the Buddhists to Aaron's ancestral home, and even went so far as to have additional new cottages built for many of them. I have walked among the remains of those cottages behind Aaron's home. The Government of India has erected a signboard there commemorating the event of the Buddhist Council, but no mention of Aaron. He would most assuredly be positively identified through the head stone that the Government of India has since removed from his grave there.

How did Jesus acquire this property? Had it been a family homestead for generations, passed down until finally reaching Mary (Aaron was her ancestral grandfather) and then Jesus?

The Buddhist Council lasted for a year. When it was over, Buddhism and Christianity were identical in virtually all ways, even to the structure of their churches, the rules for nuns and bikhus, and the hierarchy of priests and bishops. It cannot be doubted that the guidelines set by James at the *First Council of Churches* were the same guidelines adopted by the Buddhist monks. These similarities have been pointed out by Buddhist and Christian scholars alike over the years. Buddha even began appearing with the wheels of dharma on his hands and feet late in the first century. This must have been a direct result of their first-hand witnessing of the scars on Jesus, or of their visits to the tomb of Jesus, where the carved stone depiction was once on prominent display. And finally we must consider that these images were mistakenly labeled as 'Brahma' or 'Buddha" because traditionally Jesus died on the cross. Why expect to see him after that?

There are 'Ten Commandments' in Christianity and eight of them are identical in Buddhism. Brahmins also had commandments, but divided theirs into five 'Principals' and ten 'Disciplines.' After the Council, the Brahmins thought many of the decisions were too radical, such as obliterating caste and eliminating idols, so the split between the religions remained. (There is nothing in Islam comparable to 'commandments'). After the Council, Buddhist women did not fair as well as Christian women. Women who had full rights as Romans and Christians lost these rights as Buddhists. The topic of Buddhism and its early discrimination against women has been widely analyzed by modern scholars.

Buddha's physical description was recorded in Pali as *'The Physical Characteristics of the Buddha' and 'The 32 Signs of a Great Man'*. These are still one of the central texts of the traditional Pali Canon. Buddha had long, flowing curly brown hair, a tall muscular body, long graceful fingers, an elongated face, sharp, well-defined nose, and bright blue eyes. His skin was light golden color.

Marcus Borg, author of Jesus and Buddha, The Parallel Sayings (9) *found* over a hundred identical sayings between Jesus and Buddha. Even the conspicuous exaggeration of the supernatural elements crept into both religions simultaneously after the first century, and continued to mirror each other for centuries later. Buddha, however, just like all the great philosophers (like Plato, Socrates) always remained focused on man, whereas Jesus always remained focused on God. As we touched upon earlier, Buddha never made any claims to see or speak with God. Jesus did so on a regular basis. Each man spoke from very different experiences.

Buddhism and Hinduism blended even further after the Fourth Council decided to allow their Pali texts to be translated into Sanskrit. Buddhism in India then became indistinguishable from Hinduism in India. To this day, they share many of the same myths, beliefs, temples, rituals, and holy days. Kanishka descendents were kings of Kabul for seven centuries, and they shared a mixture of Christianity and Buddhism, which took a very different course of development outside India. Although they were finally forced out with the arrival of Islam, they often took refuge in Kashmir and continued to marry Kashmir women.

The Himalayas are impassible; this limited the contact between races, cultures, and countries

Influence of Jesus in India and China

There is a belief in the Church of the East, supported by their Gospels, that the Brahmins approached Jesus and asked for his help in finalizing the composition of the *Bhagavad-Gita*. Scholars agree that it did not achieve its final form until the first century. This was an era when Brahmin scholars regularly visited Kashmir to study. Naturally the Gitas were well known in Kashmir.

The *Gita* is now regarded as sacred text, especially to the followers of Krishna. It is a both guide to Hindu philosophy and a guide to life, much like the *Sermon on the Mount* for Christians, and it's no wonder they bear such similarities, since the philosophy of Jesus had an unpredicted influence upon their final version. Since Abraham had become the god Brahma in India, and since Jesus was a direct descendent of Abraham, the Brahmins must have felt it was divine providence to have Jesus so close at hand. They availed themselves of his help with Holy Scriptures just as Abraham had helped them centuries before.

Technically, the *Gita* is considered a 'smriti' but its status is comparable to 'revealed' knowledge (Holy Scripture). Smriti-Smerdis-Smritic –sabha-samiti- Manu-Smriti (Laws of Manu) and in Latin, Shem; these Sanskrit words translate to 'Semitic" associated with teacher, knowledge, or wisdom.

India has modeled its modern democratic government on the law established by Yudhithistira in the *Mahabharata, and* this was based upon the final revision that Jesus and the Brahmins worked on together in the first century. These are even strikingly similar to the foundations that would later be laid down in the Constitution of the United States. Thus the influence of these great ideas has helped build the civilizations that still govern much of the world today.

'Some realize the Self within them through the practice of meditation, some by the path of wisdom, and others by self-less service. Others may not know these paths; but hearing and following the instructions of an illumined teacher, they too go beyond death.' The Gita (250 BC-250 AD)

Chinese scholars who attended schools in Kashmir then carried both Buddhism and Christianity back to China with them. This explains how we can now find traces of the same 'Jesus' influences in Taoism and *The Way*. Martin Aronson wrote *Jesus and Lao-Tzu: The Parallel Sayings*.(4) He found over ninety parallel sayings between Tao-ism and Christianity. *The Jesus Sutras* or the *Lost Sutras of Jesus* are early Chinese manuscripts of Christian teachings. Similar to the discovery of the Dead Sea scrolls, they were found sealed and hidden in the Mogao Cave near Dunhuang. Their language and content reflect Buddhist and Tao influences, but they reflect much Christian canon too.

Christians in China are shown on cave paintings and rock carvings. Thousands exist along the Old Silk Road. Many show Christians riding their fine steeds and wearing the same royal traveling clothes found depicted at Taxila. Good horsemanship was simply taken for granted, much like good motor drivers today. Even Jesus may have been an accomplished horseman. It would have been a standard part of every traveler's basic skills.

Dr. John Young, in By *Foot to China(75)* found evidence that Christianity in China had even surpassed Buddhism for centuries. Christians, especially Nestorians, thrived in Asia until the advent of Islam. Marco Polo and the Roman Catholic missionaries of later centuries found huge Christian communities well established throughout China. Buddhism had begun to fade. In recent times however, Buddhism has experienced a large revival in China as the deeply spiritual Chinese people seek the wisdom of their ancestors in their modern world.

India and Pakistan today continue to be charged with intellectual energies that reflect an intellectually amazing people from an amazingly rich and stimulating background.

The Survivor

Now, when we think of Jesus as a survivor of the crucifixion, this changes everything about the Christian faith, and yet it changes nothing about the information he left for the world. The Scriptures remain unchanged, but the realization of God in the lives of the patriarchs and in our own lives is now understood with refreshing new clarity.

Immediately after the crucifixion, Jesus appeared almost exuberant. He was ready to join his disciples and resume his teachings. However, at the urging of Caiaphas, Joseph of Arimathea was arrested on charges of 'complicity. 'Could it be that Caiaphas, upon realizing he had been duped and that Jesus survived, was trying to lash out in anger at all who aided in Jesus' survival? We know that Joseph was released almost immediately, an indication that Caiaphas had already pushed his power to the limit and was now in disfavor.

Jesus quickly realized that his every move and every word would now endanger everyone around him, everyone he loved. With quiet determination, and right under the nose of his enemies, Jesus just seemed to 'disappear.' That was not an easy thing to accomplish in a small community, to hide a man who had received such wide-spread notoriety and had, by most estimation, at least over 5,000 followers in Jerusalem alone. And yet he and the apostles succeeded.

The behavior of Caiaphas toward Joseph and his family was one of long-standing jealousy and animosity. It was Caiaphas who challenged the legitimacy of Mary's pregnancy. It was Caiaphas who demanded the arrest and death of Jesus. It was Caiaphas who went to the Roman authorities and accused Pilate of complicity, hoping to get rid of Pilate. It was Caiaphas who had Joseph of Arimathea arrested after the crucifixion. Joseph was of royal Hebrew lineage and one of the richest and most powerful and respected men in Judea. His dynasty had been deposed by the Herod family. Perhaps Caiaphas viewed them as a potential threat to his own position of power, one that he was determined to keep a tight grip on to benefit his own family. Whatever motivated Caiaphas, whether jealousy, greed, lust, or fear, he was a formidable enemy.

Looking down from the cross and seeing the pain and despair on the faces of those he loved most, he realized that surviving was not just about being brave and stoic through pain and suffering. Surviving was also about outwitting a relentless enemy, one who would continue to destroy every-thing that he loved long after he was gone. He must have had a huge will to live, a huge concern for those he loved. It was a heroic struggle to overcome the pain and injury from his wounds and remain alive.

Image courtesy of biblia.com

Most religions teach us to accept death as part of God's plan for our lives. If you truly believe this, then you must also accept that the *survival* of Jesus was part of God's plan too, or it couldn't have happened.

There were three men who witnessed the Ascension of Jesus, and they seemed to form an elite core within the group of twelve apostles. The three men were Peter, James, and John.

It was Peter (d.64 CE), the Bishop of Rome, that the succession of Popes regarded as the founder of the Church. But it was James (d. 62 CE) the Bishop of Jerusalem, who was regarded as the real power in the early Church, especially by the Jewish coverts to Christianity.

> 'No matter where you come, it is to James the Just that you shall go, for whose sake Heaven and earth came have come to exist.' *Gospel of Thomas.*

James Tabor wrote that Caiaphas and his family were relentless in their hatred of Jesus' family. For thirty more years James would remain safe. He outwardly led the Church while Jesus worked quietly in the background. It was Ananas 2nd (Ananus ben Ananus) who finally succeeded in getting James killed in 62 CE.

However, it was the Romans who would avenge the deaths of both Jesus and James, for it was the Romans who killed Caiaphas in 36 CE, three years after the crucifixion. It was the Romans who later killed Ananus, and threw his remains outside the city gates *'as food for the dogs.'*

John was the only apostle who lived to an old age and died of natural causes. It was John who spent many years in India with Jesus, and it was John who would deliver the *Book of Revelations* and 'the seven letters to the seven churches.' It looks more probable now that Jesus could have heavily influenced the composing of the *Book of Revelations* and the seven letters to the seven churches.

It was forty to seventy years after the crucifixion that the *Gospels of Mathew, Luke,* and *John* were compiled, and they followed the standardized *Q Gospels.* If Jesus was still alive during these years, it then becomes obvious why no mention was ever made about the 'death' of Jesus.

Oriental sources that discuss the death of Jesus mention that Ba'bad was with him **(27)** The word in Persian means 'old friend of long standing' or 'an ancient one.' Ba'bad has often been associated with the apostle Thomas but we know that Thomas died in 72 CE, at least twenty to thirty years *before* the death of Jesus. It is this author's opinion that Ba'bad is translated as friend or companion and this is a direct reference to the apostle John, or Anjuna, who had been at the Taxila monastery for a number of years. The famous Oriental scholar-historian Shaikh Al Said-us Sadiq wrote about Jesus, and had traced his steps all across Central Asia, translating accounts left in Iran, Afghanistan, and India. From these translations, he compiled *Ikmal-ud-Din*, a detailed account of events in the life of Jesus during his journey to India to meet with Thomas at the court of Gondopharnes.

He determined that the wedding held at Gondopharnes court was for Meghavahana, or Abdigasses, who was a son of Gad, the beloved brother who died. However, as valuable as this book is, it dates to *after* the Islamic period began in India. Is there anything earlier, anything before the Islamic period? Yes.

349

The *Bhavishya Maha Purana,* by Sutta, was written in Sanskrit in 115 CE, and describes a meeting between King Shalewahin and Jesus that took place at Wien (in India) in 78 CE. They met as King Shalewahin was leaving Kashmir to go to the Deccan (a plateau area in south-central India). Thus we know that Jesus would have died after this date. Further, if Pravarasena was Jesus, and he presided over the Fourth Buddhist Council from 79 to 80-81 CE, then his death had to take place after 81 CE. Several sources have mentioned the date of the tomb of Jesus as 112 CE, but they don't list the actual earliest sources used for establishing this date.

The Tomb of Jesus

The tomb in Kashmir, known as the tomb of Jesus, is a Hebrew tomb. It may also have been a Christian place of worship for generations, but all traces of either religion are being hidden. Its official name is 'Rouza Bal.' This translates to 'Holy Prophet Tomb' or 'Holy Place.' A simple house-like structure covers the tomb for protection against the weather. The present stone structure was built over a more ancient stone sepulcher in typical first century Jewish style. The original door had intricately carved wooden panels depicting scenes from the life of the deceased. The original blue and white paint, the specific blue color we mentioned earlier that was commanded in the Old Testament has been replaced with Islamic green in recent times. The original carved wooden 'cage' that surrounded the casket has been taken away. Also missing is the large copper shield that once hung over the door.

There was also an ancient sign that proclaimed the name of the man buried within was Yuz Asaf, or simply, 'son of Joseph.' The casket has been opened and through the years people have removed, hidden, or sold off its artifacts and scrolls at different times. One can imagine the wealth it once contained, perhaps even copies of the alluded to 'Q' Gospel. It was inside this casket that the rod of Moses was originally placed for safe keeping, probably by the apostle John.

The study of the tomb of Roza Bal now becomes not only a religious quest, but a historical and a political one. Shortly after the arrival of Islam in Kashmir, the tomb and the casket were opened and the rod was removed. We will never really know the extent of the items taken from the tomb. After being passed around to several mosques, the rod finally remained at Aish Muquam; this is the former location of the Hebrew tomb that Jesus built. The rod, the tomb, and the mosque quickly came under the control of various waqf ever since, as a way to generate income for the local Imams.

It is unknown how the scroll that contained the genealogy of Jesus came into the possession of a local family many generations ago. They claim, based upon this scroll, that it proves they were descendents of Yuz Asaf. Also missing, as K.N. Ahmad (*Jesus in Heaven on Earth*) stated, is an ancient sign affixed to the tomb specifically naming this the tomb of Jesus. For 'unknown reasons' which he says 'can readily be guessed' the original sign is now gone. So are the original scrolls.

The tomb has been extensively 'altered' in recent times, in what is called 'modernization.' It really amounts to wholesale destruction of antiquities under the Wahabi influence among some of the current Directors. This is why the older books about Roza Bal are so valuable. They document the rapid changes and the rapid losses and destruction of the original structure. By their accounts we can determine each year what has changed and what has gone missing.

In addition to the missing rod, scrolls, and manuscripts, there were other artifacts in the tomb. There was a wooden sword, a carved candlestick, a stone 'alter' as a place for candles and incense, and another carved stone showing the crucifixion wounds on the feet.

The wooden sword becomes another vital clue. Kalhana mentioned that Pravarasena had a jeweled sword that was very sentimental to him. The wooden piece left at Roza Bal is obviously not a cross, as some describe it, but a sword. This is evident from the handle, which appears in older photos of the tomb and in books by Fida Hassnain and Aziz Kashmiri. It appears that whatever jewels or decorations once covered the sword, these have been picked off through the years. Nevertheless, it would still be a priceless relic to examine and properly date before assigning it to a safe museum location.

Thinking the old rock slab in the tomb was just a place to set down candles, Professor Hassnain intended to clean off the thick old layer of wax that had covered it for centuries. But when he removed years of thick candle wax he found that the rock was carved with the impressions of a man's feet. They bore large irregular scars, the crucifixion wounds. The pictures of this rock appear in this book, and in most books about the tomb.

The wooden sarcophagus contained ancient scrolls and artifacts but it never contained a corpse. Underneath the main floor is a chamber, a cellar that could once be reached by stairs (now sealed off). In the ground below are *two* graves. One stone marker is aligned east-west for a Hebrew. The other stone is aligned north-south for a Muslim. These could not be Buddhist or Hindu because they have always cremated their dead. But why *two* graves? Especially why would one be Jewish and another Muslim in the same space? We'll answer this shortly.

The second grave was added in the 12th century C.E. when a lowly chowkidar (a poor man who cleaned the grave- yards once or twice a month) was buried there. Why wasn't he buried in the graveyard next to the tomb? This soon becomes evident. It is because this is a way to 'take over' a site and then prevent others access to it on religious grounds. This has happened at numerous religious sites of other faiths as Islam spread.

 The first sign of serious struggles for control of Roza Bal (and the money it was generating) appears in 1776. There was a legal battle over rights of ownership and the impressive donations that were left for the tomb of Jesus. Earlier we discussed the formation of Waqfi, or trusts to take over these lucrative religious places for personal income and gain. An article in wikipedia.com ('waqf' March 2007) explains the driving force behind waqf this way:

Powerful families began to direct the empire's affairs…they controlled significant individual wealth, including tax farms that had been bought in auctions from the state as well as "illegal seizures of state lands."

…Waqf gained negative state attention as a vessel of hereditary money laundering by which the revenues were set aside in name for a foundation but actually passed to the next generation in a family. In this way, vizier and pasha families solidified themselves at the top of a hierarchical chain, one which in principle included the meritocracy created by the devshirme system of recruiting western Christian children to become soldiers (janissaries) and even bureaucratic leaders.

The defining feature of waqfs' righteousness ironically allowed for their corruption. Because of the traditional and well-guarded (by the ulama) standing of Islamic Law in the Ottoman Empire, pious foundations were protected from confiscation. "Thus, they offered a revenue source that was secure…derived not from the state but from individuals (who) in the seventeenth century gained financial autonomy with their corruption of waqfs by endowing un-seizable property and establishing hereditary wealth. Increasingly, as pious foundations slipped from the fist of the sultanate, the ulama and independent viziers gained 'religious' legitimacy.

Now we fully understand the background behind seizing holy places like the Temple Mount and Roza Bal. Regarding Roza Bal we even have the unique opportunity to see the actually court document produced when it was seized for a waqfi. It is located in the Department of Historical Records in Srinagar, dated 1194 A.H. (A.H. is the Islamic *lunar* calendar, not the Gregorian or Julian *solar* calendar; A.H., A.D. or CE difference is plus 622 years, plus allowance for eleven days less in the lunar calendar than Gregorian calendar; thus 1194 A.H. is approximately 1776 CE.)

Excerpts from the complete court document appear here (note: This was an Islamic court that made its decisions with an Islamic view because they had invaded and occupied Kashmir at the time)

> *Rehman Khan, son of Amir Khan, submits that kings, nobles, ministers, and multitudes come from all directions of the kingdom to pay their homage and offerings in cash and kind at the lofty and holy shrine of Yuz-Asaph the Prophet. May God bless him....*

> *Now this court, after obtaining evidence, concludes that during the reign of Raja Gopadatta (Gondopharnes) who got built many temples and got repaired the Throne of Solomon on the hill of Solomon; Yuz Asaph (son of Joseph) came to the valley. Prince by descent, he was pious and saintly and had given up earthly pursuits. He spent his time in prayers and meditation. He proclaimed oneness of God till he passed away. His shrine is known as Roza Bal....*

> *The shrine is visited by devotees, kings, and common men, both high and common, and since the applicant is the hereditary custodian of the shrine, it is ordered that he be entitled to receive the offerings made at the shrine and no one else shall have any rights....*

The first glaring question is "who was the *other* party in this litigation?" He is never mentioned by name. Was he Christian? A Hindu, Pandit, or Buddhist? The second problem is a 'hereditary custodian.' There is no such thing as a 'hereditary custodian' in either Islamic or India law. It simply doesn't exist anywhere, or in any law books. Was this hereditary because he was related to Yuz Asaf? Why does he have the Muslim name 'Khan' if the tomb is not Muslim? That name did not exist in Kashmir until after the arrival of Islam. Was it hereditary because this family lived closest to the tomb and was there to greet all these foreign pilgrims of high and low birth, and accept their donations? That seems the obvious conclusion here. The court decree tells us that even in 1776, this tomb was recognized as the tomb of Yuz Asaf, and even kings from many foreign countries were visiting here and making large donations. It appears to have been a choice candidate to seize for the assets and for the world-wide fame and substantial income it generated. If the former caretakers or custodians or the actual descendents of Yuz Asaf were *not* Muslim, this would represent a classic example of an illegal seizure for the purpose of establishing a personal trust account, a waqf.

Did the courts suggest that Khan was hereditary custodian through his bloodline? Would this be the bloodline of the chowkidar? Or of Yuz Asaf? Certainly no one can be converted posthumously, and clearly this had always been a Hebrew-Christian grave, so we can rule out claims that this was a sacred Muslim site.

A hereditary bloodline would have been an integral part of any court document if in fact the claimant, Rehman Khan, *had* any bloodline connections with the tomb. He would clearly have stated this was a family tomb.

If challenged in a modern court of law, this decision would be overturned immediately. The tomb would then be managed under a newly-formed and preferably inter-faith Board of Directors. This has always been Hebrew-Christian and should at least be placed under inter-faith trust for its future protection.

There have been numerous comments made to me from visitors who were too frightened to discuss any religion while at the tomb, so aggressive were those who surrounded and antagonized them. This is the display of cultural and religious intolerance that has brought the world to its present state of conflicts and tensions. The respect that Islam demands for itself is not reciprocated by them to other faiths.

Downtown Srinagar 2003; a daily site, soldiers with guns dealing with constant militancy and daily disruption of normal life. All sides claim victim status.

Photo from 'The Greater Kashmir Times.'

Why would intervention be necessary now in the case of Roza Bal? Why not simply let the present system continue? It is necessary to take action and produce immediate changes because of the rapid and deliberate destruction of the tomb's true historicity. Just recall the fate of the tomb of the Patriarch Joseph. There are now two negative factors clouding the future of the tomb; first the illegal waqf that seized it for its assets; second, the Wahabi-Taliban fundamentalism that would destroy all art, all tombs and most all artifacts around the world regardless how ancient, how beautiful, and how historically or culturally significant. This is based on their interpretation of the Qur'an and the belief that Mohammed abhorred music and art in any form, especially the form of anything living. This also leads to seizing historical assets for sale or for destruction. This situation exists now and was already escalating when I was in Srinagar. Flaming the fires were the previously mentioned actions such as destruction of the Bamiyan Buddha, desecration of the Church of the Nativity, and complete destruction of Joseph's tomb at Nablus.

Imagine someone standing before one of the world's great monuments: the Bamiyan Buddha (now gone) the 'Pieta' by Michelangelo; the Eiffel Tower; the Statue of Liberty; 'David'; Angkor Watt in Cambodia; the Sphinx; the Pyramids; the Hagia Sophia in Istanbul; Petra in Jordan; Machu Pichu in Peru: or even Mecca: now imagine that person *demands* the right to destroy one monument after another, backed by intimidating wealth and oil-based power **(82).** According to one of several recent surveys (source: Interfax, 01 November 2005) Islam is *not* the fastest growing, but the fastest dwindling religion on the planet. With every act of terrorism and religious intolerance people leave Islam in large numbers. In Russia alone over two million have left Islam within the past two years.

At what point should there be intervention? Before the hand pushes the dynamite plunger, or after?

In Saudi Arabia, where such fundamentalism is nurtured, a Saudi architect, Mr. Sami Angawi, an acknowledged specialist on the region's Islamic culture, told the newspaper '*The Independent*" that the final farewell to Mecca is imminent. He said fewer than 20 structures remain that date back to the lifetime of the Prophet Mohammed. Historic buildings associated with the Prophet since 1,400 years ago could be bulldozed at any time. The Saudis are building modern lucrative hotels and office buildings over these sites. "This is the end of the history of Mecca and Medina and the end of their future." Mecca is the most visited place of pilgrimage in the world and Medina holds the Prophet's tomb. And yet the Wahabbi powers of Saudi Arabia would have them bulldozed. If they can show so little regard for the historic value of sites related to their own Prophet, how much less for the prophet of another faith?

It is not yet proven that Roza Bal is the tomb of Jesus. But we cannot know that with certainty until the tomb is thoroughly examined by archaeologists. If there is one chance in a million or even one chance in a *billion* that this is the tomb of Jesus, that is a very significant discovery and all religions of the world have the right to know this truth. It is not about guess work; it is about using science as the absolute proof. When I lived and worked in India and Pakistan, I came to know and respect people of all faiths who are deeply committed to defending the antiquity, the history of their home ground.

Kashmiris, whether Hindu, Muslim, Sikh, Pandit, or Christian, have a huge stake in the outcome of saving Roza Bal and all its artifacts. These are a wonderful people with an incredible and rich history that is worth defending, worth knowing. Kashmir is beautiful and the world should be free to visit and explore in safety. To destroy its history is to rob from everyone who has their roots here. To rescue the truth about Roza Bal will help an entire nation-state to recover as well.

The problem lies with a very few, not with the many. But it only takes a few to do the damage that will last an eternity. When you see the hand is on the dynamite, but that hand is attached to your father, your brother, or a local respected religious leader or businessman, *then* what should you do? Solutions do not come easily. Immediate solutions require bravery and fortitude. 'Political correctness' could not save the Bamiyan Buddha and will not save Roza Bal. Only direct and firm intervention can save these sites now.

The present building of bricks and mortar was raised over an ancient stone sepulcher. This was known as the tomb of the king of kings, the king to whom all others came for advice. The ancient stones had a decorative motif, but recently they have been plastered over with cement so the pictures and scenes can probably never be recovered. They could have revealed a lot about the age and identity of the tomb. There were decorated stones in the cellar, now also destroyed. The casket is removed, the rod of Moses is removed, the scrolls are removed, the sword is removed, the small stone alter is removed, the brass shield and the heavily carved wooden doors are all missing. The sacred Hebrew blue is gone, and now it looks like a modern storefront instead of an ancient and sacred place of pilgrimage and history. Of course this pleases the Wahabis very much, for they want no visitors there who intend to make a pilgrimage. This is forbidden in their interpretation of the Qur'an.

The Rod of Moses

The original sarcophagus was just over eight feet in length. This was not because the deceased was a giant, but because the rod that was once hidden inside the sarcophagus is just over eight feet long (8' 2"). There is a historical manuscript that describes the rod. It was translated into the Sharda language. It is called *The Rishi Nama* or 'history of the rod'. Rishis were a group of ancient patriarchs of India who kept historical records, not unlike the Sarman Brotherhood that we met earlier. Professor Fida Hassnain provided the translation of the *Rishi Nama* from the ancient Sharda language. He said the rod was known as the rod of Jesse (father of King David) then the rod of Moses, then the rod of Issa (Jesus).

No one has yet mentioned if there are any inscriptions on the rod because this too has been hidden away from the general public and from archaeologists and scientists. It appears in a photograph in two books, *Jesus in Heaven on Earth,* by Khwaja Nazir Ahmed and *The Crumbling of the Cross* by Mumtaz Ahmed Faruqui. Although the same photo has been reprinted in books since then, these was the last known photograph taken of the rod. Khwaja Nazir Ahmad said he personally took the photo (after much difficulty) in July, 1947. After passing through several hands, the filial at the top was broken off, probably as a souvenir or good luck charm. It would have been of brass or gold and richly decorated with symbols to identify its owner. A large metal nail or knife or sword tip was stuck in its place for no apparent reason.

After the rod was removed from the tomb of Yuz Asaf, it got passed around to several private individuals. Now it is currently at a mosque called 'Aish Muquam,' 47 miles outside

Srinagar on the Pahalgam Road. I have made the journey there several times, in preparation for obtaining updated photos and examining the rod for any marks or symbols. I was always under heavy armed security because of militancy in the area. The Army and police, sometimes twenty in number of India's finest, these handsome, intelligent, and brave men would surround me, a lone, foreign little old lady. They were dressed in their bullet-proof vests and heavy helmets and fully armed with rifles and hand grenades and all the accruements of a well prepared soldier. They walked with me past the village shops and up the long steep hill to the mosque. We must have been an oddly remarkable parade! I felt like an easy target right in the middle of them and clearly circled and identified. I had already been witness to bombings and deaths. At times the beautiful valley of Kashmir looked and felt more like the war-torn Warsaw ghetto than paradise. Under these circumstances I felt too uncomfortable to make the return trips necessary to photograph the rod. However the good-natured, jovial and considerate Kashmiris, whether Hindu, Sikh, or Muslim, have always left wonderful memories on my heart. In spite of difficult and often dangerous circumstances for us there was always a sense of congeniality and warmth.

This mosque was built on a high peak overlooking the valley. There is a long burial cave that follows the general layout of similar tombs in Jerusalem. It's beautiful for the large shell-shaped design carved into its stone walls for the entire length of the cave. There are wide stone shelves that run down each side and a smaller chamber in the rear, off to the left side.

Hebrews would have laid the deceased out on the shelf along one side until the bodies were sufficiently desiccated. Then they would get placed in an ossuary or large jar, sealed up, and moved to the shelf on the other side of the cave. The cave had always been known as 'Aishi Wader' (lofty place of Jesus) after the king called Ashosh (Isha-Issa-Jesus) it became 'Ashosh Muquam' then 'Aish Muqam,' the name it carries today. At the base of the hill is Pahalgam, or Shepherd's village, also named for Jesus because he lived here for several years.

Who Owns Roza Bal and the Artifacts?

One of the most basic issues affecting cultural heritage preservation is the question of ownership. Who "owns" this cave? Who "owns" Roza Bal? The private family who are his descendents, and who are of many faiths? Surely they have rights and a duty to protect the graves of their loved ones, and they are the true inheritors of the relics. Or because of the ancient historical value, is the state or the country accountable to protect this heritage? How and when should they intervene to protect such sites? Like the Pyramids of Egypt or the Eiffel Tower, governments *are* responsible to preserve their history. What does religion owe to such sites? Do they have any responsibility? The Vatican in Rome, and Churches in general, for all the abuse hurled at them, have preserved their historical relics. Buddhists and Hindus routinely move among temples and shrines that are thousands of years old and still in use. In Ethiopia I was mesmerized when the priests allowed me to look at ancient manuscripts that may have been thousands of years old by their accounts, and once in the hands of great kings and queens. People do care about their past. They care very much.

DNA of God?

Any private individual or group of people can partition the courts to intervene on behalf of Roza Bal. Anyone presuming to be a relative also has the right to request DNA, through the courts if necessary, to determine the validity of ancient records and scrolls. In America recently a black family partitioned the courts for the DNA of past U.S. President Thomas Jefferson. He was exhumed, and his DNA proved that they were linked genetically to males in the Jefferson family. Although there are many examples, some examples of recovery of ancient DNA include the following;

** DNA obtained by Dr. Zahi Hawass from several Egyptian mummies 3,000 years old

** 49,000 year old Neanderthal found in a cave in Germany

** the 5,000 year old Italian frozen man known as Otzi

** Several Native American remains that date from 23,000 BC to 500 BC.

** the 2,000 year old remains of Saint Luke, from his bone relics in Padua, Italy

** The Tocharian Mummies of 2,000 B.C. (over 30 mummies have already been sampled

** the 'Cheddar Man', a 9,000 year old corpse found in a cave in England

** the 'Lost Tomb of Jesus' in Jerusalem known as the Tiaplot tomb yielded several 2,000 year old DNA samples; two were labeled as 'potential' Jesus and Magdalene DNA. Of course these conclusions are unverifiable and highly disputed

** Egyptian Mummies have been in museums around the world for a long time, and now many of them have yielded DNA in near perfect condition. Molecular biologist Scott Woodward of Brigham Young University has been a pioneer in the study of Egyptian mummy DNA, especially the 18th dynasty pharaohs.

** I was granted permission to obtain DNA samples from both Roza Bal and the alleged grave of Mother Mary, in order to establish if a mother-son relationship existed between these two sites. The second purpose was to compare DNA with those who claim to be descended from Yuz Asaf. Some of these families are in America, and some have remained in Kashmir. It is presumed that the project will continue again in the near future. I have continued to support those Kashmiris who are still actively trying to save the tomb and the recover the artifacts and relics that belong with the tomb.

Who Else Can Help Roza Bal?

Sadly, Kashmir has yet to produce a leader who will protect and champion the history of Kashmir the way Dr. Zahi Hawass champions Egypt's treasured relics and mummies. At any time, the Government of India can intervene and take control of the tomb and artifacts and declare them National Treasures that belong to all of India. Then it can house them in special museums, similar to the Cairo Museum that holds the treasures of Tutankhamen and the pharaohs or the Louvre in Paris. Such a historical museum in Srinagar would attract millions of visitors from around the world and benefit all Kashmiris. Alternately, application can be made to designate the site as 'World Heritage' and worthy of international protection. What does current international law allow for?

World Symposium on Cultural Terrorism in Asia Article

Cultural heritage preservation has become a much-debated topic in recent decades. As colonial-era concepts of cultural property ownership are frequently contested and world monuments are increasingly held hostage to political and ideological aims, the preservation community has been forced to reevaluate current international conventions.

An internationally recognized expert on the history, art, and archaeology of Afghanistan, Nancy Hatch Dupree has dedicated a lifetime to documenting and preserving Afghanistan's cultural heritage. Mrs. Dupree is also involved with the Society for the Preservation of Afghanistan's Cultural Heritage (SPACH). She has had to confront problems in Pakistan and Afghanistan quite similar to that of Roza Bal. In an interview (published March 2007) with the Cultural Heritage Preservation in Asia Society, she said,

> "I think that a country is entitled to keep its heritage. But, at the same time, in keeping their heritage they have the responsibility to protect it...We would not pay the astronomical prices the dealers were asking (for looted goods from heritage sites and museums), be-

cause we did not believe it was proper to reward looters... You cannot have 1,500 people wandering around
doing their own thing when you're trying to establish a
national strategy...Afghanistan is not the only place
where this has happened; look at Cambodia... I asked
the director (of the Kabul Museum during war with the
Taliban) "Would you consider having an exhibition?"
That would have been one way to take (relics and an-
tiques) out (of Afghanistan) without the critics being
able to say they (artifacts) had been sold for personal
benefit. This way, they would not only be on display,
but they would be gathering income. Look at what happened with the Tutankhamen exhibit: long, long lines
all over the world.... Local people often don't see there
is anything unique in some of the things they work with
daily. You have to raise their awareness of this, because for a long, long time the government will not be
able to take care of everything itself, nor should it. It
should be the community acting out of a sense of responsibility for their past... the education sector must
become involved, and this includes aggressive lobby-
ing... lobby aggressively... But that doesn't do all that
is necessary. You have to produce reading materials,
posters, and other awareness-raising materials. And
even that is not enough. Unless you have a good dis-
tribution system, this will all be concentrated in the cities. You need to get the information out to everyone,
so civil society can be intelligently informed about its
heritage and how to protect it."

"A country is entitled to keep its heritage. But, at the same
time, in keeping their heritage they have the responsibility to
protect it..."

Visiting the Grave

To visit the grave of Yuz Asaf at this time in its history is a troubling and difficult experience. There are sand bunkers in the middle of streets where soldiers have machine guns pointed at all who pass by. Violent encounters are a daily occurrence. Sewage and dirty drain water splash along sides of the tomb walls. Local youths have been known to form mobs to behead young girls, or throw acid in their faces for not wearing a veil. They harass and threaten tomb visitors. Acts of militancy and terrorism are destroying Kashmir every day. The doors to the tomb (the original have been removed because they contained six carved wooden panels that may have had clues to the deceased identity) now remain permanently locked. The tomb is stripped bare. I cannot give you a more optimistic description at the time of this writing.

I used to visit the tomb regularly. I would sweep and clean inside and remove fallen branches from the graves outside. I personally spent an entire Christmas day unnoticed and alone inside the tomb. I can say with certainty that it is rarely visited, even by locals. No one goes there on Christmas. Who was left to visit on Christmas? Certainly no one in the world or in Kashmir had been there for Christmas (or Easter, or any Christian holiday) in many years, and probably not for many centuries. This was also the Christmas right after 9-11, a deeply troubling time for the world and a time of deep intro-spection for me personally. For several years I had little contact with the events and the attitudes and mood of the outside world beyond Nepal, Tibet, Afghanistan, Kashmir and Pakistan. I witnessed 9-11 from their perspective, on the streets and in the villages that the terrorists themselves called home.

Within the narrow confines of this world I developed a deep and lasting compassion for the importance and fate of this tomb, a place I came to be intimately associated with on a daily basis.

One cannot help but realize just how much is at stake here. Ignoring this tomb, or not making the effort to protect and preserve it is like condemning Jesus to death twice; first on the cross, then to an even worse death by apathy and neglect. Jesus can now be sold off in unidentifiable little pieces as relics on E-Bay, or bombed or crushed by bulldozers driven by Wahabbi fundamentalists.

It was precisely because of the world situation that the Christmas I had inside the tomb of Jesus was such a profound and moving experience for me, the experience that led me to writing this book for you now. It would be a profound experience for many if they could be there, I'm sure. I hope I have been able to provide enough evidence to interest you in investigating this tomb more thoroughly. Regardless who is buried in Roza Bal tomb, he and his mother in nearby Murree deserve better than this. They don't deserve to be cheap bids on the internet, or worse, targets for bombs, terrorists, religiously intolerant fanatics, and lies.

From *The Rod of an Almond Tree in God's Master Plan* by Peter A. Michas, Robert Vander Maten and Christie Michas;

> 'According to rabbinical commentary and stories passed from generations, the rod transferred from Adam successively down the line to Enoch, Shem, Abraham, Isaac, Jacob, Joseph, Moses and David. According to the Midrash Yehlamdenu:
>
> The staff with which Jacob crossed the Jordan is identical with that which Judah gave to his daughter-in-law, Tamar... [*Genesis* 32:10; 38:18]. It is likewise the holy rod with which Moses worked... [*Exodus* 4:20-1], with which Aaron performed the wonders before Pharaoh [*Exodus* 7:10] and with which, finally, David slew the giant Goliath...' [I *Samuel* 17:40].
>
> Let us not be too quick to discard information based upon legend (stories passed down through the generations)... Perhaps at some future time, a discovery will be made to verify the history of this divine rod.

It seems that the rod was handed down by Adam to Enoch and then to Methuselah. From Methuselah, it would have been transferred to Shem, the son of Noah...Shem was also the head of an academy teaching God's knowledge, and he was Abraham's tutor. According to the Merovingian book, *'Bloodline of the Holy Grail'* by Laurence Gardner, the budding Rod of Jesse designates the royal lineage of David. He said;

> 'From the previously quoted Scripture (II *Sam.* 15:23,24,25,30,31), it is known that Aaron's rod was positioned in front of the Ark in the Holy of Holies...As King David was vested with the responsibility of preserving the rod and the authority to carry the rod. '

Was this rod brought by the magi at Jesus' birth? Was it intended to be the hereditary rod of kingship for him? Is this the relic of Moses that would identify him as the next prophet? Is this the rod Joseph carried with him on the flight to Egypt? Does this rod represent the 'wealth' that Jayendra stole from Sandimatti? Is this the same rod that Judas Iscariot and the Samaritan zealots tried to steal from Mount Gerazim before Pilate intercepted them? Could this rod be the 'magic parasol' of Queen Mother Amri-ta-praba? Is this the same rod that Jesus carried from the Holy Land to Kashmir in the caravan that brought Mother Mary home?

If all these statements are true, then the rod from the tomb of Jesus is one of the most valuable and significant relics in all Christendom, even more valuable to the Church than the controversial Shroud of Turin. Why doesn't anyone investigate these claims further? Because Christians are *not* looking for a survivor of the crucifixion. They do not seek an 'old' Jesus in Kashmir. Christians believe Jesus died on the cross and anything related to his possible survival after that is quickly rejected. If they continue to keep their head in the sand, then Christians become the great losers of their own cultural and religious heritage. They lose the truth. What follows next could be the end of the entire Christian faith, then a domino effect on other religions. Could this be the real, long-term Wahabi objective? Yes. Of course it is. Each religion thinks they are right, or oldest, or best and justify their methods accordingly.

"Thou shalt not follow a multitude to do evil." (Bertrand Russell quoting Exodus 23:2)

The Baptism of Christ by Aert de Gelder (1645-1727) which can be found in the Fitzwilliam Museum; like many early paintings about the life of Christ, this is unusual for depiction of 'heavenly spheres,' or 'flying shields' often in the sky near Jesus. Were the Elohim still visiting earth? These paintings were often done by artists who had access to private files stored within the Vatican. (see 83, 84 for more pictures)

'Desposynoi' The Descendents of Jesus Today

The farthest back anyone can suggest lineage to the family of Jesus in the western world 'might be' a grandson of James or Jude named 'Jacob of Kefar Sikhnin' of about the second century. James Tabor points to two stories preserved in supplements to the *Mishnah* called the *Tosefta Chullin* (2:22-24) that refer to 'Yeshu ben Pantera.' He states that Biblical scholar Richard Bauckham, Professor of New Testament

Studies at the University of St. Andrews, argues in *Jude and the Relatives of Jesus* that Jacob of Kefar Sikhnin might well be James, son (or grandson?) of Jude the brother of Jesus.

In the *western* world there is absolutely *no* verifiable direct link to Jesus through any children he may have had. According to Dr. Ron Moseley, of the American Institute for Holy Land Studies, the first fifteen bishops (presidents) of the Church at Jerusalem were all relatives of Jesus. All were of Hebrew descent. According to Eusebius they were approved 'by those who were able to judge of such matters, and were deemed worthy of the episcopate.' References to the 'Desposynoi' are to members of this entire Church family. According to Julius Africanus, only relatives of Jesus were termed 'desposynoi' or 'the heirs' and appointed to the bishop (president) position. Desposynoi is a term which means 'those who belong to the Master [or sovereign: despotes]. He explains how they were one of those Jewish families who had preserved their geneal-ogy when Herod burned the public genealogical records. He then reports:

> 'From the Jewish villages of Nazareth and Kokhaba they traveled around the rest of the land and inter-preted the genealogy they had [from the family tradi-tions] and from the *Book of Days* [i.e. *Chronicles*] as far as they could trace it.
>
> The meaning is probably that members of the fam-ily of Jesus, traveling around Israel and preaching the gospel to their fellow-Jews, used a family genealogy, like that in *Luke* 3:23-38, as a way of explaining the Christian claim that Jesus was the messianic Son of David. Kokhaba is most likely the Galilean village of that name (modern Kaukab), about ten miles north of Nazareth. It may have been, like Nazareth, a traditional home of members of the family. But the significance of the two villages, as the centers from which the mission of the desposynoi operated, may also lie in their names. They may have been given special messianic significance because each can be related to one of the most popular texts of Davidic messianism. Nazareth could be connected with the messianic Branch (neser)

from the roots of Jesse (Is. 11:1), while Kokhaba, meaning 'star', recalls the prophecy of the messianic Star from Jacob (Nu. 24:17).

This information from Julius Africanus is of great interest. Julius Africanus has to explain what it means, and clearly it is not a term he would himself have used had he not found it in his source. It must be the term by which members of the family of Jesus were known in those Palestinian Jewish Christian circles in which they were revered leaders. It demonstrates that not only 'the brothers of the Lord', but also a wider circle of relatives - 'the Master's people' - played a prominent leadership role.'

Richard Bauckman created a dynastic chart showing that Joseph and Mary had an additional six children, bringing the total, with Jesus, to seven children. He then explains: "The brothers of Jesus were evidently known as 'the brothers of the Lord' in early Christian circles (*Gal.* 1:19; 1 *Cor.* 9:5), but since the term 'brother' by no means necessarily refers to a full blood-brother, the question of their precise relationship to Jesus, along with that of Jesus' sisters, arises. The Epiphanian view, which is the traditional view in the Eastern Orthodox churches, is that they were sons of Joseph by a marriage prior to his marriage to Mary... the family of Jesus then disappears into the obscurity that envelops the subsequent history of Jewish Christianity in Palestine."

After 135 CE and the Bar Kochba revolt the Jews were banished from Jerusalem and the city was renamed 'Aelia Capitolina'. The Jews were forced to leave for 100 years. During this time the Church was turned over into the hands of non-Jews and the quest to rid the Church of all things Jewish began, including Jewish lineages. The first non-Jewish leader of the Church was Mark. This was nearly the middle of the second century. So how can we establish direct children of Jesus?

In 1980 a 2000-year-old cave was discovered in Jerusalem's Talpiot neighborhood. In it were 10 coffins, six of which bore inscriptions, which - translated into English - included the names 'Jesus son of Joseph,' the name 'Maria' twice, and 'Judah son of Jesus.' The second Maria is hypothesized to be Maria Magdalene, while the tomb bearing the name Judah could indicate Jesus had a son. But the senior Israeli archaeologist, Professor Amos Kloner, who thoroughly researched the tombs after their discovery and at the time the inscriptions were deciphered, cast serious doubt on it. Professor Kloner said, "It's a beautiful story but without any proof whatsoever...the names that are found on the tombs are names that are similar to the names of the family of Jesus, but those were the most common names found among Jews in the first centuries BCE and CE." Kloner then dismissed the combination of names found in the cave as a "coincidence." If that is not the cave of Jesus or his family, then all the more reason to examine the Kashmir locations, where we DO have a tradition for the marriage and children of Jesus, and for a tomb of Jesus.

We have already seen that the grave in Kashmir is most probably that of Jesus. Examining the king lists from the *Rajatarangini*, we find the most likely king who was Jesus was Pravarasena, whose mother was Amri-ta-Prabha, the senior Queen, or Queen Mother. From the *'Kings of Kashmir'* lists we know that Pravarasena had two sons who were to rule jointly. There may have been more children, additional sons and daughters who did not leave their mark on history's records. Between these two sons, we can only locate one grandchild, the young man connected with the 'wintry places' of the British Isles. According to British genealogical records, Mary's mother Anna was at least part British (and Greek). If confirmed, Jesus' birth lineage would be Judah-Pharez in his paternal side and Judah-Zarah in the maternal side.

Now where do we go from here? What records exist for this child? What was his name in Britain? Is this the son of Pravarasena-Jesus?

12. Tomb of Jesus

I wish I could wave a flag and shout "Here is a Grail child!" This has become a popular scheme in the west following the release of fictional movies and books about a secret grail child who recently came forth for the purpose of sales, publicity, ego, dreams, visions, or dollars, but with no actual proof of any kind. Meanwhile, in Kashmir several 'grail' children go quietly about their lives waiting for more solid proof of their history. The genealogy scrolls were often photographed and examined, and, unfortunately, are now temporarily "missing." We can continue to search for more clues from the casket and from within Kashmir. An old Persian book, *Negaris-Tan-i-Kashmi*, (from the Farsi Library in Islamabad) tells how Jesus became a husband and father but no English translations of these records have yet been found.

Bashrat Saleem (Shaheen, now deceased) whose family once had the ancient genealogy scrolls of Jesus. His family has consented to DNA comparisons with Yuz Asaph if these are ever made available. Photo courtesy of Ken Lee at eleven shadows website

Sahibzada Basharat Saleem (Shaheen), a retired restaurant owner from Kashmir, and a highly respected intellectual in the local community, claimed that his family once had possession of the original genealogy scrolls. He was often photographed with them and begged for someone to take an interest in their historical merit, but no one took further interest in the subject and now, since his death, the original scrolls seem to have disappeared. Hopefully this is just a temporary situation.

Jesus is explicitly mentioned as 'Shahzada Nabi Hazrat Yura Asaf.,' (the holy prophet and Prince Yuz Asaf *son of Joseph'*). His wife, children, and grandchildren are also listed on this scroll. "According to the family history and genealogical tables (written in Persian) the name clearly and explicitly mentions Yuz Asaf. From him, we believe that the lineage comes down to my father and to me."

Bashrat Saleem passed away in 2001, just two weeks before we were scheduled to meet and discuss the scrolls, and now his family scroll has disappeared. This scroll represents the critical missing link that may resolve the questions about European ancestry by revealing the missing names in the records. Even one name can be the link the world needs to piece the rest of the puzzle together.

Meanwhile, Professor Fida Hassnain believes he has located several duplicates of the scrolls that were in the possession of other family members, and he is working on establishing the genealogy for publication in the near future. Until then, Mr. Shaheen's claims, and those of his children, cannot be proven. When DNA is recovered from the graves, it can then be compared with his family DNA and that of others around the world. Meanwhile, there is little anyone can do until the scrolls surface again, or until Professor Hassnain's research is successful in the near future. And of course the efforts to obtain the DNA from the two men now interred in Roza Bal can succeed at any moment in the future. Permission granted twice before assures there are no barriers for success in the future.

Dr. Hassnain was born in Srinagar, the city that houses the tomb of Jesus, in the year 1924. In 1954 he became the Director of the Kashmir State Archives, of Archaeological Research and Museums, and retired from that position in the year 1983. He has been an active researcher and advocate for the preservation of Roza Bal tomb and is the Kashmir counterpart to Dr. Awaass of Egypt.

It is not for some fond attachment to the royal bloodlines of Europe, or for ego trips on the world's stage that there is interest from the probable descendents of Yuz Asaph. It is about the desecration of his grave, the theft of his artifacts, and respect for the memory of a loved one who is simply admired and respected as someone's beloved ancient grand-father.

I had the great privilege to be given permission to obtain the DNA from both Roza Bal and from the grave of Mother Mary. It was in Pakistan that the idea first began among a small group of interested people who lived near the grave of Mother Mary. They were sincerely devoted to her memory and interested in making this project available to the scientific world. Regardless that considerable effort was repeatedly made, the outside world seemed reluctant to come forward with assistance. This complete lack of interest was appalling, especially when so much is known about these graves.

While I was in Kashmir and discussed the project with local historians, soon the idea was born to recover DNA from Roza Bal so possible mother-son could be compared. It was the great hope of the locals that such work would bring much needed tourism and pilgrims to Kashmir, which meant jobs and a better life for local residents. Kashmir could finally capture the attention of the world in a positive way. For a few months it looked like the project would be successful and everyone involved supported it wholeheartedly.

As tensions mounted after 9-11, especially during the Afghan and Iraq wars, this heightened the awareness of 'cultural identities.' Different religions will have very different hopes and expectations about the outcome of the project. However, personal agendas quickly created obstacles for everyone. At the eleventh hour the research was brought to a crashing halt because someone leaked unfavorable news to the press out of jealousy and his apparent lack of sufficient baksheesh. The hopes and aspirations of hundreds of people in several countries were dashed and years of effort and planning were sadly put aside until some future date. For now, we can only reflect on the possible discoveries yet to be made in the future, and I know there will be many more. When this happens, the fate of Kashmir will surely turn around and be one of peace and prosperity as tourists and pilgrims flood in to pay homage to the richness and significance of Kashmir's people and history.

The Final Death of Jesus

Testament of Abraham:

> 'Abraham lived all his years in quietness, gentleness, and righteousness, and was exceedingly hospitable. He received everyone both rich and poor, kings and rulers, the maimed and the helpless, friends and strangers, neighbors and travelers. God summoned his arch-angel Michael and said: 'Go down to Abraham and speak to him concerning his death, that he may set his affairs in order, for I have blessed him as the stars of heaven and the sands of the shores, and he is in abundance of long life and many possessions and is exceedingly rich.
>
> Beyond all men, moreover, he has been righteous, hospitable, and loving to the end of his life. Go to Abraham and announce to him his death and assure him thus: Thou shalt at this time depart from this world and shalt quit thy body and go to thy Lord. So Abraham finished seeing to the needs of the living and beloved. His family tended to his body with divine ointments until the third day after his death, and buried him in the land of promise, near the oak tree of Mamre. And Isaac buried his father beside his mother Sarah, glorifying and praising God.'

The Rajatarangini describes the final days of Pravarasena (Jesus). He was very old (most accounts agree he was between100-120 years old) when, as with Abraham and Moses before him, he received a message telling him to prepare for his final journey.

379

'In you our father is exceedingly pleased. You have done his work well. There is nothing left for you to do here. Make your preparations to come home. Your father is waiting for you.' (Rajatarangini)

Jesus sent for his beloved old friend Ba'Bar. In other accounts it was Anjuna that he sent for. In fact, they were probably both the same man.

As we discussed earlier, some scholars suggest that Babar was Thomas. However, this would be impossible. Thomas was killed in 72 CE, and Jesus was present at the Fourth Buddhist Council in 79 CE. The only man among the apostles who was still alive was John, whom the Buddhists knew as the monk Anjuna who stayed a long time at Taxila, where he was known as a teacher to the teachers. 'Baba' and 'Babar' also mean wise old teacher, guru, or friend. Jesus had given John the name Boanerges and it could be that from Persian, Greek, or Aramaic to Sanskrit, this became interpreted as Bahab, Baba (as in Sai Baba, a common title still in use in modern India), or Babar.

John's brother, James, was the first of the apostles to die, where John, on the other hand, was the last. All of the other original apostles met a violent death. John, however, died peacefully in Ephesus at an advanced age around the year 102 CE. The Basilica of Ephesus is the reputed site of his grave. However the Church of Rome transported his bones to Cantebury Cathedral in 656 CE. Thus John was the only apostle who could possibly have been alive at the time of Jesus' death. Kalhana left the record of the death of Jesus, plus local legends and gypsy songs provide us this overall description of his last days in Kashmir.

Like Abraham and Moses before him, Jesus distributed his property and said his last farewells to loved ones, making certain that arrangements for everyone were completed. Then, early one morning John and Jesus put on the robes of the High Priests of the White Brotherhood and silently slipped away in the dark. Carrying the Rod of Moses with them they walked in the moonlight to the gardens on Hari Parbat Hill. At a small ancient shrine on the side of the hill they rested and waited for dawn. Then they faced east to greet the rising sun and say their last prayers together. And what are prayers? I like to think of prayer as a form of telepathic communications with those in another place, another dimension, another realm. Perhaps it is communicating with those light forms that exist right beside us or millions of miles across our galaxy. Whatever the underlying explanation for such phenomenon, prayers can be powerful. Prayers can be mastered by us all. Prayers can be answered.

At some time during the morning they arrived at the meadow. Pravarasena handed the rod to John and stretched out on the grass in the traditional Hebrew east to west burial position. His last moments on earth were a loyal tribute to his Jewish heritage. He took one last look at the world around.

381

This world had been his home for a hundred years. He bore no grudges and he had no regrets. He cursed no one and carried no ill will against those who had brought him so much suffering. He felt gratitude, love, and joy for the time he had spent here on earth, and for the extraordinary people he knew and loved and shared this time with.

Then in anticipation of the next great adventure he smiled contentedly and closed his eyes. As his body lay still on the meadow, in a state somewhere between life and death, the angels came in their vimanas and greeted him.

For the last time his spirit rose from his body and he greeted them and went with them in the direction of Mount Kailasa. This is how his death was described by Kalhana. It was quite simply like the death of Abraham and the death of Moses, a peaceful death in his old age, yet still with a touch of the mysterious, the magic and unexplained, just as had ushered in his birth. The Elohim, those visitors from the heavens who ushered in the Old Testament then departed with Jesus in the New Testament, they were never heard from again. The New Testament brings to a close the genealogy of the gods and of the prophets who walked and talked with them.

When Kalhana stood on that very place to recount this story for us, he said the marks from the vimanas were still visible in his day. The sign left for us at Roza Bal tomb said simply, 'Yuz Asaf; This is the tomb of the prince, son of Joseph.' He died a peaceful death in advanced old age and yet he lives on in the hearts of millions of his followers today.

Could the implications in this story about the spirit of Jesus rising be similar to the rabbinical views of the death of Moses? Recall that according to Rabbi Israel Chait, Moses was referred to as a 'Sachel Nifrad'... 'a separated intelligence.' This means to say that Moses reached the highest level of any human; he operated completely through his intelligence and in complete control of his instincts. The Rabbinical conclusion is that God must have *orchestrated* the event of his death in order that there would be no possibility that Moses become deified.

12. Tomb of Jesus

As we recall the death of Abraham, we see the similarities: "Go to Abraham and announce to him his death and assure him thus: Thou shalt at this time depart from this world and shalt quit thy body and go to thy Lord."

This 'separation of intelligence' from the body. It's one of the great mysteries that are instinctively understood and sought after, that lies at the very heart and core of every religion on earth. For Christians, if it is proven that Jesus survived the crucifixion and died a peaceful death in his old age very similar with that of Abraham and Moses, this would require a dramatic shift in how one approaches the meaning of his life and death. It represents regeneration, a renewal of the entire religion but this is certainly possible.

Jesus was a remarkable man and an incredible survivor. Through his survival the example of his life and teachings has influenced every religion and society on earth. He didn't die for our sins. He almost died *because* of our sins. Without uttering words of anger, hate, or revenge, he saw our potential and he kept faith in us.

How long does it take God to make a soul? A lifetime, however short or long that lifetime has been. And what a life Jesus had! Jesus once said:

> 'Truly I tell you - there will be no rest in Paradise unless we meet this thing in the face. I come to do only what I am sent to do, I have no plans, for all plans are of my Father, I wrought no wisdom of my own for I have no such, all Wisdom is by my Mother. I serve with dispassion and know not the purpose of my Father in heaven. My task is made easy for I am told what to do at every turn. Let us not run from the face of God; Come with me and walk through the purifying fire...' (*The Eastern Bible: Acts of Yesu the Savior*, 46)

Today, scientists search for life in the universe, expecting to find it soon. Almost everyone on this planet now believes that we are *not* alone, and that the universe is teeming with life. Some of that life may prove to be the 'gods' of the Bible who took our prophets on their fantastic voyages of ascensions, gods who married the beautiful women of earth, produced exotic and unusual children who would become the great men of old, and showed us the future awaiting mankind in great societies among the stars. Is this the message from Adam to Jesus that we must learn?

The Bible is their story. It may not always be told to perfection. Man slipped in a few curses, rituals, and blunders of his own making in all those sacred scriptures he wrote. There is no perfection in sacred scriptures because man is not yet perfected enough to write wisely about the gods and about our future. We write and interpret like children because we are still children among the stars. But we're growing up fast.

The Biblical prophets experienced ascensions in fiery chariots, and the miraculous births of strange but beautiful children. They experienced miracles and failures. They walked and talked with God.

We have come to the end this saga about the Hebrews of Kashmir. We understand who the gods were, and the God that Jesus knew as intelligent, benevolent and loving light is a life form that science now acknowledges is probable. We have discovered what race we can expect Jesus to be, a race with a long history in the Himalayas. We have realized that all existing religions in the world today have been influenced by these messengers from the gods.

This was a place of remembrance and origins for them, a place they were drawn back to time and again. We have discovered the ancient Hebrew connections to Kashmir may include secret chambers under old temples. Like the baris and arks of old, Noah's Ark and the Ark of Testimonies, the tomb can now be thought of as 'the ark of the tomb,' a place to store ancient and secret relics.

We have found out why Jesus was crucified with the title 'King.' We have realized the Buddhist family connections to Jesus and Magdalene, and the multitude of 'miraculous births' that help to vindicate the dubious immaculate conception of Mother Mary. We have discovered the Rod of Moses and the tomb of Jesus. Now we know that scrolls really do exist about the probable family of Jesus and Magdalene.

And we have managed to prove that mankind doesn't need more Buddhism, or Hebrew-ism, no more of Hinduism, or Islam or Christianity. Mankind needs the truth.

Bullfinches Mythology, Chapter Six, (excerpts) say of our Hebrew teachers:

'The vital conviction which, during thousands of years, at all times pressed home upon the Israelites, was that they were a "chosen people," selected out of all the multitude of the earth, to perpetuate the great truth that there was but one God--an illimitable, omnipotent, paternal spirit, ...This sublime monotheism could only have been the outgrowth of a high civilization, for man's first religion is necessarily a worship of "sticks and stones," and history teaches us that the gods decrease in number as man increases in intelligence. (Reginald S. Poole)... "In the early days the Egyptians worshipped one only God, the maker of all things, without beginning and without end. To the last the priests preserved this doctrine and taught it privately to a select few..."The Jews took up this great truth where the Egyptians dropped it, and over the beads and over the ruins of Egypt, Chaldea, Phœnicia, Greece, Rome, and India this handful of poor shepherds--ignorant, debased, and despised--have carried down to our own times a conception which could only have originated in the highest possible state of human society....

How many nations have perished, how many languages have ceased to exist, how many splendid civilizations have crumbled into ruin, bow many temples and towers and towns have gone down to dust since the sublime frenzy of monotheism first seized this extraordinary people! All their kindred nomadic tribes are gone; their land of promise and their holiest sites are in the hands of strangers...If the Spirit of which the universe is but an expression--of whose frame the stars are the infinite molecules--can be supposed ever to interfere with the laws of matter and reach down into the doings of men, would it not be to save from the wreck and waste of time the most sublime fruits of civilization...?'

This little family of Jews that we have followed for thousands of years have had a huge impact on shaping the destiny of all races, all religions, and all mankind. They have taken us from the Ice Age to the Space Age with little more than a rod, a staff, true grit, and determination to see their responsibilities through. They were chosen as messengers for the gods, and often they were reluctant messengers. The rewards for being chosen were great, but the price for being chosen could also be very high. Few men and women were up to it. They wavered and stumbled, suffered, cursed, and lamented, but ultimately they did not fail. For however far into the future we may survive, however far our journey takes us to new stars and new galaxies, we are here because of them and we will be there because they led the way. They compelled us to look to the skies and wonder. There can be no future without some kind of past and theirs has been an incredible one. One day we too will meet their gods directly. Based on the information they passed down to us, we can only wonder and eagerly anticipate what the future holds.

The Book of Kolbrin, rescued from the Glastonbury fire in 1184, says:

> 'Greetings unborn ones now asleep in the dark womb of our future. Greetings from we who were once like you are now and like whom you will be one day. Were you choosing a gift from the past to the future, what would it be? If it be worldly wealth and fame, then we are disappointed in you, for our labors have been in vain. What good these things a thousand years into your futures? You are our children, of our past, heirs to those who have lived and died before you. Dear unborn friends, we trust you have no cause to reproach those who once held stewardship over your estate. But whatever you think of that heritage, you cannot put it aside.

12. Tomb of Jesus

This we give you. The Hidden Books containing the accumulated wisdom and truth from generations past to you, in our futures. May this knowledge serve you well.'

They *have* served us well, but truth, like the valuable tombs and relics of old, has also become a victim, and if we lose the truth, we are going to loose our way home.

We don't need more religion, not yours or mine; we need the truth, and we'll find it in Kashmir, among the relics and DNA from the tomb of Roza Bal, if we get there on time.

And the message of the cross is...?

'If they remain silent, the very stones would cry out.'

Luke 19:3

Bibliography

1▪ Ahmad, Khwaja Nazir,

   Jesus in Heaven on Earth-Ahmadiyya, Lahore (1998)

2▪ Allen, Charles

   The Search for Shangri-La-Abacus Press, London (1999)

3▪ Armstrong, Karen

   A History of God- Mandarin Paperbacks, London (1994)

4▪ Aronson, Martin

   Jesus and Lao Tzu, The Parallel Sayings-Ulysses Press (2002)

5▪ Baigent, Michael

   The Jesus Papers- Harper, San Francisco (2006)

6▪ Baldwin, John D.

   Pre Historic Nations-Adamant Media Publishers (2005)

7▪ Bargeman, Lisa Ann

   Egyptian Origins of Christianity-Blue Dolphin Publishing (2005)

8▪ Beveridge, H.

   Akbar Nama of Abu-L-Fazl-D.K. Publishers, Delhi (1996

Bibliography

9▪ Borg, Marcus

        Jesus and Buddha, The Parallel Sayings-Ulysses Press (2004)

10▪ Boyce, Mary

        Zoroastrians-Routledge, Abingdon, U.K. (2001)

11▪ Bulfinch, Thomas

        Bulfinch's Mythology, Gramercy, USA (1988)

12▪ Cotterell, Arthur

        Encyclopedia of World Mythology- Parragon, London (1999)

13▪ Dani, Ahmad Hasan, PhD

        Taxila- Sang.E.Meel Publications, Lahore (1986).

14▪ Das, Lama Suraya

        Awakening the Buddha Within-Doubleday (1997)

15▪ Donnelly, Ignatius

        Atlantis, The Antediluvian World-Echo Library (2006)

16▪ Dutt, Chunder

        Rajatarangini, Kings of Kashmir-D.K. Pub. Delhi (1997)

17• Elder, Isabel Hill

    (1) Buddha the Israelite-Cambrian Episcopal Church of the Grail (2004)

    (2) Celtic, Druid, and Culdee-Covenant Publ. London (1986)

18• Eisenman, Robert

    James, Brother of Jesus- Penguin (1998)

19• Ellis, Ralph

    (1) *K-12, Quest of the Gods*- Adventures Unlimited (2002)

    (2) *Jesus, The Last Pharaoh,* Adventures Unlimited (2002)

20• Elst, Koenraad

    Aryan Invasion Debate- Aditya Prakshan, New Delhi

21• Faruqui, Mumtaz A.

    Crumbling of the Cross- Ahmadiyya Lahore, 1997

22• Forstater, Mark

    Spiritual Teachings of Seneca-Hodder&Stoughton (2001)

23• Fuller, R.Buckmaster

    Glimpses of World Religions-commentary Shah Publishers (1997)

24 Gardner, Laurence

Bloodline of the Holy Grail- London: Bantam Press. (1997)

Genesis of the Grail Kings- London: Bantam Press. (1999)

25 Gupta, Chitrarekha

Brahmins of India- Delhi: Sundeep Prakashan (1983)

26 Hancock, Graham

Sign and the Seal- London: Random House (1997)

27 Hassnain, Fida

The Fifth Gospel- Kashmir: Dastgir Publications. (1988& reprint Blue Dolphin Publishers, 2006)

28 Haug, Martin

Sacred Language, Writing, and Religion of the Parsis- University Press (2002)

29 Hesse, Hermann

Siddhartha- Shambhala Classics, Boston (2000)

30 Hope Trust, The

*The Kolbrin-*Hope Trust, New Zealand (1994)

31 Horne, Charles F.

Sacred Books and Early Literature of the East- New York, Austin, & Lipscomb (online edition) (1917)

32• Hyerdahl, Thor

The Search for Odin Project

33• Jaspers, Karl

Socrates, Buddha, Confucius, and Jesus-Harcourt-Brace Translation (1962)

34• Jumsai, Sumet

Naga, Cultural Origins in Siam and the West Pacific- Chalermnit Press (1997)

35• Kak, Ram Chadra

Ancient Monuments of Kashmir- Aryan Books Intl. Delhi (2000)

36• Kashmiri, Aziz

Christ in Kashmir- Srinagar: Kashmir, Roshni Publications. (1988)

37• Kersten, Holger

Jesus Lived in India- London: Element Books (1981)

38• Kimball, Glenn

Hidden Politics of the Crucifixion- Ancient Manuscripts Publishing, Utah (1998)

39▪ Khokhar, Zaman

The Nine-Yard Graves of the Beloved of God in Pakistan (Private Publication) (2000)

Kolbrin, The: *see Hope Trust*

40▪ Leonowens, Anna

Anna and the King of Siam- London: Tor Books (1999)

41▪ Mair, Victor H.

Genes, Geography, and Glottochronology, The Tarim Basin During Late Prehistory- Proceedings of the Sixth Annual UCLA Indo-European Conference, Institute for the Study of Man, L.A. (2004)

42▪ Marshall, Sir John

Buddhist Art of Gandhara-Oriental Books, Delhi (1960)

43▪ Martin, Ed

Jesus, King of the Travelers-Jonah Publ. (1999)

44▪ Matlock, Gene D.

(1.) *Jesus and Moses are Buried in Kashmir*-Author Choice Publications (2000)

(2) *From Khyber Pass*- Author's Choice (2002)

(3) *Super Religions*; iUniverse Press (2002)

44B▪ Michas, Peter et al

The Rod of the Almond Tree in God's Master Plan

Wine PR Publishers (1997)

45▪ Ninan, M.M.

History of Early Christianity in India- (e-book) acns.co

Emergence of Hinduism from Christianity (2006) Global

46▪ Okada, Amina

Ajanta- New Delhi; Brijbasi. Photographs by Jean Louis Nou (1996)

47▪ Osman, Ahmed

Moses and Akhentaen- Bear & Company (2002)

48▪ Osman, Ahmed

*Jesus in the House of the Pharaohs-*Bear & Company, U.S.A. (2004)

49▪ Palmer, Martin

*The Jesus Sutras-*Wellspring/Ballantine U.S.A. (2001)

50▪ Pandit, K.N.

Chronicle of Medieval Kashmir- (web) kashmir-information.com

51▪ Pandit, R.S.

Rajatarangini, Saga of the Kings of Kashmir- Lahore: Vanguard Books Ltd. (1991)

52▪ Parpola, Asko

Deciphering the Indus Script- New Delhi: Replika Press. (2000)

53▪ Radhakrishna, S.Dr.

*Glimpses of World Religions-*Jaico Publishing, Mumbai (2001)

54▪ Rahul, Ram

Central Asia, A Textbook History- New Delhi: Munshiram Press. (2000)

55▪ Rahula, Dr W.

What the Buddha Taught- Bangkok: Thailand (2002)

56▪ Rajaram, Navaratna S.

Vedic Aryans and the Origins of Civilization- New Delhi (1997)

57▪ Ray, Suriel Chandra

Vitasta Religion and Philosophy and the Early History of Kashmir-

(web) koausa.org/vitsatsa

58▪ Ryan, William & Pitman, Walter

Noah's Flood, the New Scientific Discoveries about the Event that Changed   History Simon & Schuster (1999)

59. Russell, Bertrand

(1)The Conquest of Happiness- Liveright (1996)

(2)Why I am Not a Christian- Routeledge (2004)

60▪ Shali, S.L.

Kashmir History and Archaeology through the Ages- Delhi: Indus Publishing (1993)

61▪ Singh, Dharam Vir

Hinduism- Travel Wheels Publication, Jaipur: (1995)

62▪ Singh, N.K.

Buddhism in Kashmir- Srinagar: Gulshan Publishing (2000)

63▪ Sitchen, Zachariah

The Earth Chronicles- Avon Books (1978)

64▪ Stein, Auriel

Selected readings from private library of Fida Hassnain

65▪ Sykes, Bryan

Seven Daughters of Eve- W.W. Norton Company; New York (2002)

66- Tabor, James

    The Jesus Dynasty-Simon & Schuster U.S.A. (2006)

67- Thapar, Romila

    Asoka and the Decline of the Maurayas- New Delhi: Oxford (2000)

68- Tilak, Bal Gangahar

    Arctic Home of the Vedas, Tilak Brothers, New Delhi (1971)

69- Voorst, Van, Robert E.

    Jesus Outside the New Testament-Wm. B. Beardsman Press, U.K. (2000)

70- Ward, Paul Von

    Gods, Genes, and Consciousness Hampton Roads Press(2004)

71- Wadell, Austin

    Buddhism and Lamaism of Tibet- New Delhi: Guarav Pub. (1998)

72- West, E.W.

    Sacred Books of the East,-Oxford University Press. (1897)

73- Witzel, Michael

(1.)   *On Indian Historical Writing, The Role of the Vancavalis-* Journal of Japanese   Association for South East Asian Studies. (1990)

(2.)   *Electronic Journal of Vedic Studies-* Vol. 7 (2001)

74- Yogananda, Paramhansa

Autobiography of a Yogi- Jaico Publishing, Mumbai (1997)

75- Young, John M.L.

By Foot to China- Tokyo Radio Press. (web)aina.org/byfoot.html (1984)

Additional Internet Resources

76 (web) webapps.uni-koeln.de** Sanskrit, Tamil, and Pahlavi Dictionaries

(with special thanks for their personalized help)

77 (web) .zencomp.com/greatwisdom/ebud/mahavamsa/gene.html: This website has published the entire genealogy of Siddhartha Buddha, *The Mahavamsa.*

78 (web) Kashmir-information.com** destruction of Kashmir temples

79 (web) rafonda.com** Ronald Alan Fonda:

80 (web) salagram.net** the history of the Kabba and its roots in Sanskrit and Hinduism.

81 (web) panix.com** Half of Asia, for a Thousand Years, by Joe Bernstein

82 (web) debate.org.uk** Historical errors in the Quran

83 (web) homepage.ntlworld.com**UFOs in religious art

84 (web) marcogee.free.fr**   UFO's in Religious Art

85 (web) reluctantmessenger.com** full canons and manuscripts from Islam, Buddhism, Hinduism, Christianity, Coptic, and more

86 (web) koausa.org. ** Pandavas dynasty and early Kashmir.

87 (web) fordham.edu/halsall/ancient/asbook.html**

88 (web) newadvent.org ** History and profile of India,

89 (web) solomonstemple.com** Hebrew history.

90 (web) livius.org ** Jona Lendering on the magi.

91 (web) crystalinks.com **Sumerian king lists

92 (web) tombofjesus.com **History of the Tomb of Jesus in Kashmir

93 (web) journals.uchicago.edu ** American Society of Human Genetics. Traces races and anthropology.

94 (web) ccbs.ntu.edu. ** Naga, Yaksini, and Buddha: Local Deities and Local Buddhism at Ajanta, by Richard S. Cohen, Vol. 37, May 1998. Pictures painted at Ajanta of the king, Harisena/Pravarasena.

95 (web) fordham.edu **Sumeria temple priestesses at Gipadru in ancient Sumer.

96 (web) mythicalireland.com ** The Hill of Tara in Ireland, linked to Noah's grave mound at Tanda

97 (web) viewzone.com/** Who Was Abraham? By Gene D. Matlock, B.A., M.A.

98 (web) ambedkar.org**History of India Discussions

99 (web)http://lakdiva.org/mahavamsa/genea.html** Buddha genealogies

100 (web) ctlibrary.com** British Forces attack Magadha in Ethiopia

101 (web) wikipedia.com**Torah

102 (web) newadvent.org** Aaron

103 (web) friesian.com** Mahayana Buddhism

104 (web) yadav.com**castes and tribes of India

105 (web) sacred-texts.com** Book of the Bee

106 (web) atributetohinduism.com**Persian-Hindu Connections

107 (web) http://en.wikipedia.org/wiki/Bharata_(emperor) Lunar and Solar Dynasties

108 (web) http://www.vigyanprasar.gov.in/comcom/vimana.htm Flying machines in India circa 4,000 BCE

Bibliography

Index

569047

Made in the USA